Preachin' the Blues

Preachin' the Blues

The Life and Times of Son House

DANIEL BEAUMONT

University of Rochester

New York City

OXFORD
UNIVERSITY PRESS

OXFORD
UNIVERSITY PRESS

Oxford University Press, Inc., publishes works that further
Oxford University's objective of excellence
in research, scholarship, and education.

Oxford   New York
Auckland   Cape Town   Dar es Salaam   Hong Kong   Karachi
Kuala Lumpur   Madrid   Melbourne   Mexico City   Nairobi
New Delhi   Shanghai   Taipei   Toronto

With offices in
Argentina   Austria   Brazil   Chile   Czech Republic   France   Greece
Guatemala   Hungary   Italy   Japan   Poland   Portugal   Singapore
South Korea   Switzerland   Thailand   Turkey   Ukraine   Vietnam

Published by Oxford University Press, Inc.
198 Madison Avenue, New York, New York 10016

www.oup.com

Oxford is a registered trademark of Oxford University Press

Library of Congress Cataloging-in-Publication Data
Beaumont, Daniel E.
Preachin' the blues: the life and times of Son House/Daniel Beaumont.
p.   cm.
Includes bibliographical references.
ISBN: 978-0-19-539557-0
1. House, Son.   2. Blues musicians—United States—Biography.   I. Title.
ML420.H673B43 2011
782.421643092—dc22   2010036390

1 3 5 7 9 8 6 4 2

Printed in the United States of America
on acid-free paper

Son House, Philadelphia, PA, 1964. Courtesy of Dick Waterman.

PREFACE

Son House said many wise things, as befits a preacher—even an ex-preacher. Perhaps my favorite is this: "If you tell a lie, it will be all over the country in a day or two. But if you tell the truth, it will take ten years to get there." Which, come to think of it, sounds more like Mark Twain than a preacher. House had something else in mind at the time, but he could have been speaking about his own music. In fact, it took not ten years, but more than thirty for the music he recorded for Paramount Records in 1930 to "get there," to be heard and appreciated all over the country.

At the time of its humble origins, no one could have foreseen the influence the blues would eventually exert not only on American popular music, but also on American culture generally, and then, through the latter, on global culture as well. And what is true of the blues in this respect is especially true of a species of blues played by Son House and some other musicians in the Mississippi Delta. The names of otherwise obscure people, places, and events mentioned by Delta musicians in their songs are now known far beyond the confines of the African-American community of north Mississippi and are applied to radio shows, Hollywood movies, and a Japanese record label. The meaning of blues idioms and the significance of obscure events mentioned in blues songs form part of a discourse of an international community of writers and listeners. Notable sites in the Mississippi blues history—like Clack's Grocery—are marked by plaques on a "Blues Trail," and these places are visited by "blues tourists" who may, if so inclined, stay in a bed and breakfast located on a plantation where their quarters are "authentic sharecroppers' shacks"—somewhat refurbished, to be sure, with amenities like heat, air conditioning, indoor bathrooms, and Wi-Fi that sharecroppers seldom enjoyed.

But no one could have foreseen these developments in 1902, when blues was an upstart musical form in a marginalized and impoverished community in the American South. To understand Son House's life is to understand in part how this happened, how a curious and somewhat unusual musical form in that small community would, by and by, become recognized the world over.

TABLE OF CONTENTS

Preachin' the Blues

CHAPTER 1

The Second Coming of the Son

THE RETURN OF SON HOUSE

The trip—long, hot, and cramped—had taken the three young men from New York City to Memphis. From that city on the banks of a new-world Nile, their search had led them down into sweltering small towns and plantations of the north Mississippi Delta. In the Delta they had learned of someone in Memphis who might be able to help them in their search. They had found that man lying in a hospital bed, and he had, in turn, given them the name of someone else, someone in Detroit. And now, on June 23, 1964, their quest had led them to the staid upstate city of Rochester, New York. It had been hot that day, in the upper eighties, and it was still quite warm that evening as the three young men in the red Volkswagen cruised slowly through the black neighborhood on Greig Street looking for number 61—and though they probably were not aware of it, there was another sort of heat rising in that neighborhood, as would become apparent in a few weeks time. Greig Street ran from Plymouth Circle south three blocks to Clarissa Street. Clarissa Street was the heart of the black community in Rochester. The address the young men sought was a four-story apartment building at the south end of Greig Street where it joined Clarissa, just before Clarissa crossed over the Genesee River.

They came to Rochester seeking an older black man who had been a blues musician in Mississippi before World War II. Their search had begun with some liner notes on a record album and some mistaken information from another blues musician about the man's whereabouts. But following a trail of tips, they had finally spoken to the man himself by telephone from Memphis two days earlier.

Their search for this musician was a quest peculiar to that time and place evoked by the phrase "the sixties." And, indeed, the year 1964 had already witnessed several events that would become essential pieces of the motley collection of personalities and events now designated by those words. In February, the Beatles had made their first appearance on *The Ed Sullivan Show*—by April their records held the top five places on *Billboard*'s chart. In March, Secretary of Defense Robert McNamara had announced the change in policy that would lead to the rapid escalation of the conflict in Vietnam, and in early May the first significant demonstrations against the Vietnam War had taken place across the nation. With the possible exception of the Beatles' rapid rise to fame in America, most of these events must have seemed to most of the citizens of Rochester, New York in June of 1964 rather remote. Rochester was then a city of more than 300,000 people, whose lives were shaped by the presence of the Eastman Kodak Company, which employed 33,075 of them.[1] In early 1964, the number of US troops in South Vietnam was still only about 21,000, and the civil rights struggle was for white Northerners still only something to do with the South.

The owner of the Volkswagen, Nick Perls, was a skinny twenty-two year old New Yorker, whose wealthy Jewish parents owned a Manhattan art gallery. While Perls was a student at American University in Washington D.C., he added a new passion for blues to his other great passion, smoking hashish and marijuana. Perls had fallen in with a local circle of blues enthusiasts that included such people as Mike Stewart, Dick Spottswood, John Fahey, and Tom Hoskins. These people were part of a larger group who would be dubbed the "blues mafia." They had come to blues through an interest in jazz and begun mostly as record collectors. Most would remain collectors, but some would become musicians, others would become writers on blues, others would start record labels, and still others would work for established labels. They were united by a passion for blues, but the competition of collecting would often make their relations tense and suspect. Perls had begun to frequent a Washington coffeehouse where some of these people gathered to listen to "rediscovered" blues musicians like Mississippi John Hurt and Bukka White perform. Through these associations, Perls had formed a list of singers he was eager to locate in the hopes that they would also perform on the folk music circuit.

---

1. From the Kodak Historical Collection 003, Rush Rhees Library, University of Rochester.

He and another blues enthusiast, Mike Stewart, had also begun making tape recordings of old 78-rpm records owned by various collectors, and by this means they had amassed one of the world's largest collections of blues recordings. In 1968, Perls would start his own record label that would specialize in reissuing prewar blues recordings. He initially called it "Belzona," which was an allusion to the song "High Sheriff Blues" by Charley Patton, the Mississippi Delta musician for whom Perls had developed something bordering on an obsession—an obsession within a passion. But after the label's first five releases, he renamed it "Yazoo" after the river that defined the eastern extent of the Mississippi Delta.

Perls' two companions, Dick Waterman and Phil Spiro, were similarly of Jewish backgrounds, but they were both then living in Cambridge, Massachusetts. Waterman was in his late twenties. After doing cryptography during a stint in the army in the late 1950s, he had pursued a journalism degree from Boston University and worked for a few years as a sportswriter and photographer. In Cambridge, he became involved with a group of young people interested in folk music, and he began writing about musicians from a "folkloric" standpoint. He had also begun to book and promote shows in the Boston area for bluesmen such as Mississippi John Hurt and Bukka White. As a consequence of this trip, Waterman would ultimately end up making a career of managing blues musicians.

Phil Spiro, who was about two years older than Perls, had gotten into the blues through a young musician named Geoff Muldaur, then a student at Boston University. Spiro had begun doing radio programs at Massachusetts Institute of Technology and had also begun producing some concerts in the Cambridge area, but his day job was with a corporation called Itek that made cameras for CIA spy satellites. Spiro developed optical-design programs, and, curiously, almost all of his colleagues at Itek had a Rochester connection in their backgrounds, either through Kodak, or the optics program at the University of Rochester. The search had been scheduled around Spiro's two-week vacation from his Itek job.

Cambridge, where Spiro and Waterman lived, was then a center of what is still sometimes called the "folk revival" or even the "folk movement"—though the latter term implies some structure and organization, both of which this "movement" lacked. In actuality, it was simply a loose-knit group of young people bored and dissatisfied with the stultifying climate of American culture in the Eisenhower phase of the Cold War. Their boredom and dissatisfaction had spurred them to seek out certain cultural expressions from the earlier part of the century that were seemingly uncontaminated by drab middle-class sensibility—by the "culture industry," to put it another way. The influence of the Beats on them was obvious. The result garbed the enthusiasm of a Jack Kerouac in the language of an Alan Lomax.

In practice this meant they were interested in reissues of old 78-rpm recordings made in the 1920s and 1930s by poor Southerners, both black and white (some of whom, however, would subsequently become quite wealthy and famous). And nowadays, few would argue with the proposition that such music is on the whole more interesting than the recordings of such late fifties chart stalwarts as Mantovani, the Bert Kaempfert Orchestra, and Steve Lawrence. However, for most in the folk revival, their tastes entailed a disdain for nearly all contemporary commercial recordings. But such a disdain blinded them to the fact that a number of other artists also making the charts in the late 1950s and early 1960s—musicians like The Everly Brothers, Ike Turner, and Jimmy Reed—were actually the musical progeny of the artists on the old 78s they revered.

The involvement of Spiro and Waterman with folk revival circles would be crucial if and when the time came to find an audience for the musician they sought. And, indeed, the way that musician was received would reflect in some degree the conceptions and misconceptions of the folk revival.

Many of the blind spots and naiveties of the folk revival—which, by and by, both Spiro and Waterman would question—followed from the fact that few of the participants had really thought through what the use of notions like "folklore" and "folk music" really meant in American culture. Since they were oblivious to the origins of the notion of "folklore" in European Romantic thought, they did not really consider whether the communities of poor Southerners, white and black, that spawned the musicians on their reissues were really "folk" in the sense of the German peasantry of the Middle Ages. But without that somewhat dubious premise, there were no "folk." And if there were no "folk," then there was no "folk music." With the growth of the music industry, there were amateur musicians and professional musicians—and various shades and hues between.[2]

2. For more on folklorists and the folk revival, see Benjamin Filene's *Romancing the Folk: Public Memory & American Roots Music* (Chapel Hill, NC: University of North Carolina Press, 2000). The notion of folklore brought with it a vocabulary of terms like "spontaneity," "authenticity," "purity," and "primitive" that had become bywords of the study of folklore, and would become part of the vernacular discussion of popular music, despite their questionable relevance for American popular music (including the blues). For a critique of these notions as applied to popular music, see Simon Frith's essay "The magic that can set you free" in *Popular Music* 1 (1981), pp. 159–68.

Despite the lack of a "folk" in America, folk revivalists had found evidence of their existence in a compilation called *The Anthology of American Folk Music*. This album was compiled and annotated by one Harry Smith, who, although he was many things—an abstract expressionist painter, experimental filmmaker, and magician to name a few—was, nevertheless, not really a folklorist at all. However, his brainchild would exert a decisive influence within the folk movement, and with the *Anthology* as its scripture, the folk movement would be decisive in one way for both the blues revival in general and for the musician the three young men were seeking. "Folk music" would become a genre of commercial recordings. And the market for folk music that grew out of the *Anthology* and the folk movement would become, at least initially, the market for blues reissues, and later, for the old bluesmen themselves. As "folk musicians" the bluesmen could be marketed to young, white, folk music fans. And, make no mistake, an existing market had to be found if the blues were going to be sold to a young, white audience.

It was in this atmosphere—amidst the stirrings of the folk movement and the interest kindled by the reissues of old blues recordings—that the impulse to find and promote prewar blues musicians developed.

Rediscovery

In the case of the blues musician these three young men were seeking, the most important reissue was a record released in 1962 by Origin Jazz Library, a label started in 1960 by Bill Givens and Pete Whelan to reissue blues recordings of the 1920s and 1930s. The label's second album, *Really! The Country Blues 1927–1933* featured, among others, Tommy Johnson, Skip James, Henry Thomas, Garfield Akers, and, the man they were looking for, Son House.[3] House's two tracks were "My Black Mama," Parts 1 and 2.

Another reissue label Folkways stoked the fires the next year, 1963, with an album called *Son House and J. D. Short: Blues From the Mississippi Delta*.[4] The first side contained six bootlegs from House's Library of Congress recordings.

3. This was only the label's second release; earlier that same year OJL had released *The Immortal Charlie Patton*.
4. Short was a Mississippi native, but musically active in St. Louis, but no matter.

As Dick Waterman recalled, almost everyone who bought these records had assumed that the people on them were dead. The "rediscovery" of Mississippi John Hurt in 1963 changed that assumption. Phil Spiro noted the importance of this event:

> Before 1963, the idea that the bluesmen we listened to on old records might still be alive hadn't really occurred to us. That all changed when Tom Hoskins rediscovered Mississippi John Hurt.[5]

Spiro saw Hoskins at Newport that year and asked him how he had found Hurt. Hoskins' modus operandi was disarmingly simple. The last time Hurt had been heard from was in 1928 when he recorded for the race label Okeh. One of the songs he recorded was "Avalon Blues" which had the line in it "Avalon's my hometown, always on my mind." Hoskins found Avalon on an old map of Mississippi and drove there. Thirty-five years later Avalon was still John Hurt's hometown.

This first rediscovery had a comic aspect that set the tone for the others that followed. When Hoskins told Hurt he wanted to take him back to Hoskins' hometown, Washington D.C., Hurt was stunned. As he later said, "I thought he was the F.B.I. When he asked me to come up North, I figured if I told him no, he'd take me anyway, so I said yes."[6]

Hoskins seems not to have given much thought to the ethical issue involved in introducing oneself into the life of a total stranger with the intention of altering his life; an oversight that, it seems, can be written off to two things: youth and the ambience of the times—particularly that of the folk scene. In any event, Hurt and eventually other old bluesmen would profit from their rediscovery, but the process would not be without its bumps and bruises.

In the wake of Hoskins' find, John Fahey and Ed Denson found Bukka White, who had last recorded in 1940, by following Hoskins' simple but successful method with one slight variation. In 1940, White had recorded a song about *his* hometown of Aberdeen, Mississippi, so Fahey and Denson wrote a letter addressed to "Bukka White (Old Blues Singer), c/o General Delivery, Aberdeen, Mississippi." Aberdeen was no longer White's hometown, but the

---

5. Eric Von Schmidt and Jim Rooney, *Baby Let Me Follow You Down* (Amherst: University of Massachusetts, 1979, 1993), p. 190.

6. Jas Obrecht, "Mississippi John Hurt," http://www.mindspring.com/~dennist/mjhjas.htm.

letter found its way to White in Memphis where in 1963 he was working in a tank factory. And the "folk rush" was on.

As Waterman remembered, these events were like resurrections: "It was absolutely astounding that from this album of 'dead people' in a couple of years suddenly four or five of them were back in our midst playing again."[7] The revival of Mississippi John Hurt's career had shown blues enthusiasts that not only was it possible to find a musician who had recorded before the war, but more important, from their standpoint, it might be possible to promote him to the folk music audience.

The next year, 1964, Bukka White played in Boston, and he stayed with Spiro and his roommate Al Wilson—Wilson would form the band Canned Heat the following year and would also play an important role in the revival of Son House's musical career. While White was in Boston, in the midst of a conversation with Wilson and his friend David Evans, then a student at Harvard, he said in response to Evans' mention of Son House that a blues-singing friend, Lillian Glover, had seen Son House in Memphis the previous year.[8] Wilson told Spiro, and they filed the information away—although it turned out that White was mistaken.

Independently, Nick Perls had learned from Bernie Klatzko that Son House and Willie Brown had performed in the Lake Cormorant area in the north Delta in the early 1930s, information that Klatzko had included in the liner notes he wrote for Origin Jazz Library's reissue, *The Immortal Charlie Patton*,[9] released earlier that year, 1964. Klatzko's notes recounted a research trip he made in the Delta with Gayle Wardlow the previous August, but he added that they did not have time to follow up on the Lake Cormorant story. Thus, the young men had two leads. If Mississippi John Hurt had been found simply on the basis of a 1928 recording that mentioned Avalon, the odds might have seemed somewhat better for finding Son House since one of the leads—albeit the mistaken one—was quite recent.

---

7. Dick Waterman, interview with the author, May 5, 2009.

8. But known as "Ma Rainey" due to her talent. Slightly different accounts are found in Von Schmidt and Rooney, *Baby, Let Me Follow You Down*, p. 192, and "How We Found Son House," Spiro's *Broadside* article, Vol. 3, Issue 11, (June 24, 1964). Here I follow Ted Gioia's *Delta Blues* (New York: W.W. Norton 2008), p. 372 which sorts through the discrepancies.

9. Usually spelled "Charley" but sometimes "Charlie."

Perls, who had a car and a tape recorder, got together with Spiro. Spiro's roommate, Al Wilson, was already performing professionally and had gigs scheduled in early June, so he could not make the trip. Waterman was then brought in. Spiro would write years later: "Our notions about what was to be done on the trip were firmly rooted in the field trips of folklorists. We took recording equipment in spite of the difficulty of fitting it and three people into a VW Bug, and when we found performers, we recorded them."[10] Spiro and his two companions saw themselves as carrying on the work of folklorists like Cecil Sharp, John and Alan Lomax, and Sam Charters. As Spiro said, "We sought out performers, we asked questions, and we recorded the music we heard as best we could with the tools of the period." While these activities were incidental to finding Son House, they were important to the three who felt, in Spiro's words, "a certain unspoken obligation to do a good job of it—to live up to role models."

Waterman also saw a potential story from his perspective as a journalist. He was then a freelance writer for *The National Observer*, doing sports and music features for them. He asked his editor if he could have an assignment to go to Mississippi to look for this old bluesman, and the editor told him, "If you find him, you've got a story. If you don't find him, there's no story."[11]

However, the real goal was not simply to locate Eddie "Son" House, but to relaunch his career on the folk music circuit in the same way that the careers of John Hurt and Bukka White had been relaunched. But first they had to find him.

They left New York on June 10 in Perls' red Volkswagen. And it is difficult to imagine such a quixotic enterprise, part Henry Stanley and part Tom Sawyer, an enterprise whose ramifications, in keeping with the spirit of the sixties, could not have been completely clear to any of the participants—it is difficult to imagine such a trip, with all the senses that word would soon acquire, undertaken in any vehicle except a Volkswagen bug.

As it happened, it would take the search party almost two weeks to find out that Bukka White's information was wrong. In the meantime, the three young seekers wandered into the vortex of Mississippi in the summer of 1964.

10. Phil Spiro, personal correspondence with the author, February 27, 2009.
11. Waterman, interview May 5, 2009.

MISSISSIPPI, JUNE 1964

Sam Charters in his notes to the Folkways' reissue of Son House in 1963 (that had helped to stoke the trio's interest) had written of the Delta:

> Northwest Mississippi is one of the most vicious areas of human intolerance and brutality on the face of the earth...A stranger in a town like Avalon or Port Gibson is followed as he goes down the street. If a car is left outside a store a sheriff is leaning against it waiting to ask questions when the driver comes back outside. Someone with a camera will be forced out of a shack area, someone asking questions will be forced to leave the county.[12]

If anything, Mississippi had grown even more dangerous by the next summer. For months, both federal and state officials had expected the summer in Mississippi to be a long, tense and probably violent one. In January, an alliance of civil rights groups announced the "Mississippi Summer Project" to register Mississippi blacks to vote. In April, the Klan burned crosses at sixty-one locations throughout the state, and the next month civil rights groups began holding training sessions in the North to prepare for "Freedom Summer." On June 14—about the same time the three Son House seekers had arrived in the area—three young civil rights activists, Andrew Goodman, Michael Schwerner, and James Chaney, had attended one of these sessions at the Western College for Women in Oxford, Ohio.[13] Three days later, the Klan firebombed the Mt. Zion Church in Neshoba County.

Spiro, Perls, and Waterman were not oblivious to the dangers of whites and blacks traveling together in Mississippi—both Waterman and Spiro had lived in the South—but as Spiro recalled decades later, the three were more aware of those general dangers than they were of the specific dangers arising from "Freedom Summer."[14]

---

12. *Son House and J. D. Short: The Blues of the Mississippi Delta*, Folkways Album FA 2647, 1963. My version is found in Stephen Calt's biography of Skip James, *I'd Rather Be the Devil*, (New York: Da Capo, 1994) p. 239.

13. In 1974, the college became part of Miami University.

14. Phil Spiro, personal correspondence with the author, February 27, 2009. Spiro wrote, "We were much more aware of those ongoing issues than we were of the particular issues of that particular year and month." And, indeed, the next month Nick Perls would return to Mississippi, along with another blues fan Stephen Calt to search for records with the Mississippi collector and researcher Gayle Wardlow.

In Memphis, their first stop, these out-of-season magi did not find Son House, but they did find another former bluesman, Robert Wilkins, yet another rediscovery of the early 1960s. Wilkins was then sixty-eight years old and since 1950 had been the Reverend Robert Wilkins. Wilkins had played in Memphis and north Mississippi in the 1920s and early 1930s, and his recordings of "Rolling Stone" and "That's No Way to Get Along" had been issued in 1928 and 1929.[15] In 1936, Wilkins had quit playing blues altogether as a result of a homicide that occurred at a Hernando house frolic he was serenading. Concluding that playing the blues was too dangerous, he joined the Church of God in Christ. Thereafter he devoted his musical energy to writing and performing spirituals—he would later restyle his 1930s song "That's No Way to Get Along" as "Prodigal Son," transforming a complaint about a lover into the parable from the Gospel of Luke.

Wilkins was born in Hernando, Mississippi, about twenty miles south of Memphis, not far from the last known residence of Son House, Lake Cormorant (but called "Lake Carmen" by the black residents of the Delta). Wilkins had known Son House before the war, and he offered to take the three young men down to Lake Cormorant. Besides Wilkins' generous offer of assistance, the only other piece of good luck in this potentially dangerous undertaking was the fact that the Ku Klux Klan had never been a strong presence in the Delta, having been largely kept out by the dominant regional power, the wealthy white planters whose fortunes depended on their labor force of black sharecroppers. So, off to Mississippi from Memphis went this unlikely quartet in Perls' red Volkswagen—the three young whites and the black reverend, sporting his white shirt and tie and his wire-rim spectacles above the high cheekbones that hinted at the Cherokee part of his heritage. Some years later Waterman would describe the trip this way:

> It was insufferably hot. Spiro and me with our Boston accents, Perls with his New York accent, traveling with a black minister... The daily newspapers were full of reports of people being trained to come in to help with voter registration... We were just not welcome there because of the way we looked and sounded, and when we said what we wanted, they didn't like that either. "What do you want that nigger music for?"[16]

15. "Rolling Stone" is an entirely different song than the Muddy Waters' song with the same title.

16. Von Schmidt and Rooney, *Baby*, p. 193. The rest of Waterman's description of the incident is also from this source.

Days of walking down baking dirt roads and through blazing fields of cotton turned into a week and then two. There were tense conversations with local whites.

Waterman described one incident with two young whites, who were in Waterman's words, "big, heavy, beefy red-faced guys with their hair cut short almost to the skull, with big, beefy arms." Reverend Wilkins had gotten out of Perls' Volkswagen. Leaning on the roof of the car, he asked the two white men for directions to a certain farm. For a long time the two said nothing as Wilkins waited patiently. The two men stared at Wilkins, their looks, as Waterman recalled, full of "loathing and hatred." One finally spat in contempt and told the quartet it was the third farm down. As the two men walked away, the reverend thanked them.

Although the search party did not find Son House, they did assemble an assortment of black musicians as they traveled around the north Delta. They found Fiddlin' Joe Martin who had played with Son House in Delta juke joints in the late 1930s and early 1940s, and who recorded with him in 1941 on the first of Alan Lomax's Library of Congress sessions. Martin, a thin man of about fifty years who had burned his hands and switched to playing drums, fell in with them.[17] And one night, true to their folkloric mission, they used Perls' equipment and set up a recording session with Martin on drums, a Woodrow Adams on guitar and a piano player called Piano Red.[18]

Martin also put them in touch with a man named Benjamin Brown Sr. whose son had once been married to Son House's stepdaughter. They found Brown in a hospital bed in Memphis, and he told them that he thought House was living in Rochester, New York, but there was no listing in Rochester for an Eddie House. So Brown's son then put them in touch with his ex-wife's current mother-in-law, a woman named Virginia Strong, and she gave them her son's telephone number in Detroit. Her son had an address for Son House in Rochester, and they sent a telegram asking House to call them collect. But there was no return call. Finally they were

17. Martin also played with a young Muddy Waters. But his connection with Son House would have been unknown to the three prior to meeting him since the Lomax recordings from 1941 had not yet been issued, only some of the 1942 recordings, but those only featured House.

18. There were many "Piano Reds" and at least two who made recordings, one an Alabama musician who moved to Chicago, the other a Georgia musician whose "Mr. Moonlight" was covered by the Beatles, but the Delta Piano Red was apparently a third.

put in touch with a friend of Son House in Rochester named James Knox who drove to House's apartment and had him call the trio in Memphis on June 21. Waterman would write that House told them he was "in good health and wanted to play again."[19]

Part of that statement was not entirely accurate. No matter. Spiro, Perls, and Waterman had gotten lucky. They had found the man whose Paramount recordings had already become legend, the musician who was a primary influence on Robert Johnson and Muddy Waters.

They also were lucky in an entirely different way. They had survived Mississippi. Sunday, June 21, the day they reached Son House by telephone, was the same day the other trio of young men, the civil rights activists Michael Schwerner, Andrew Goodman, and James Chaney, were murdered in Philadelphia, Mississippi by Klansmen and their auxiliaries in the Neshoba County Sheriff's Department. By coincidence, Perls knew Goodman, having attended the same private school with him in Manhattan.

The three seekers left Memphis, but they did not head straight to Rochester. Having also received a tip from a neighbor of Piano Red about the whereabouts of another lost legend, the bluesman Skip James, and having, as they saw it, been lucky with Son House, they instead drove to Poplar Bluff, Missouri, some 240 miles north of Memphis to see if lightning might strike twice. But no one there had ever heard of Skip James. And as Spiro put it, working on "the bird-in-hand principle," they left for Rochester after only a day in Poplar Bluff.[20]

It was early in the evening of June 23, 1964, when the three young men approached a lean, older black man sitting on the front steps of his apartment building at 61 Greig Street in an African-American neighborhood of Rochester, New York.

"Can you tell us which apartment Son House lives in?" Perls asked.

"This is him," the man said, rising. He smiled and extended his hand. When they mentioned Bukka White's claim that he had been seen in Memphis the year before, House told them that he had not been in Memphis for at least fifteen years.[21]

19. Richard (Dick) Waterman, "Finding Son House," *The National Observer* (July 1964): p. 16. Much of the preceding account is also based on this article.

20. The same day, June 23, the three met House in person, Skip James was found in a Tunica County hospital by John Fahey, Bill Barth and Henry Vestine.

21. Waterman, "Finding Son House," p. 16. More likely, it was twelve years; see chapter 7.

Waterman, Perls, and Spiro would spend three days in Rochester with House. The second day they brought a guitar and listened to him play. In Waterman's own words, "He was nervous at first, and confessed that he hadn't played regularly for about four years." If "regularly" meant what is usually does, it was probably many years more than that. Nevertheless, after some coaxing and practice, they recorded House singing and playing a few blues. Even after his long musical layoff—more likely seventeen or eighteen years at least—one piece, "Trouble Blues," was good enough to end up on an album released in 1971. They also succeeded in convincing him that there was an audience that would be eager to hear him perform again.

On the third day of their visit, June 25, House's wife Evie took a photo of her husband and his three young admirers. The photograph shows Nick Perls, Dick Waterman, Son House, and Phil Spiro sitting in front of the Greig Street apartment. House has his arms draped around the shoulders of Waterman and Spiro, while Perls beams with delight. House wears a standard necktie rather than the antique string tie he would often sport later when he was playing coffeehouses and colleges. With their cheerful

Nick Perls, Dick Waterman, Son House, and Phil Spiro, June, 1964. Courtesy of Dick Waterman.

pre-Beatles looks and House's weathered features and shrewd expression, they make an even odder foursome than they must have made with the Reverend Wilkins. Songs of innocence, songs of experience.

As soon as Waterman got back to Cambridge, he contacted the booking agent for the Newport Folk Festival, Ralph Rinzler, and asked him if he would be able "on short notice" to include Son House in the program that summer. He rushed the recordings of House they had made in Rochester to Rinzler in Newport. The Newport Folk Festival was then the biggest popular musical event in the country, and among the blues and gospel performers scheduled to perform that summer were Mississippi John Hurt, Skip James, Sleepy John Estes, Fred McDowell, and the Reverend Robert Wilkins. Rinzler listened to the recordings and agreed to book Son House for the festival.

Newsweek cover, July 13, 1964. Courtesy of Shel Hershorn.

The rediscovery of Son House made a minor splash in the national press. Waterman would write an article for the *National Observer* called "Finding Son House." And in July, *Newsweek* (whose music critic was Waterman's brother-in-law) also ran a story about it.[22]

As it happened, *Newsweek*'s cover story for that issue concerned other events in Mississippi. The photograph on the cover of the July 13, 1964 edition was shot in Philadelphia, Mississippi and featured a deputy sheriff and an older white man in civilian clothes. The older man on the left in a white short-sleeved shirt, under what must be a dyed straw hat, has a soft, toad-like appearance. His dull, waxy flesh seems to melt in the Mississippi heat and run towards his paunch. The younger man, the deputy, is hard. His short-sleeved shirt bears the emblem of the Sheriff's Department of Madison County. He wears a light blue helmet, and beneath it he grimaces, his features pinched, compressed. A police-issue Remington 870 twelve-gauge is propped on his hip and menaces the heavens. The deputy's features are somewhat flattened—he looks a little like a monitor lizard with a shotgun. The two men squint into the heat and haze, as though looking for something to kill. The caption reads simply, "Mississippi, Summer 1964."

The three-page lead article spoke of the concerns of President Johnson, Attorney General Bobby Kennedy and other federal offficials after "a week of bombings, burnings, and worst of all, the presumed murder of three young civil rights workers." It would not be until August 4 that the FBI would find the bodies of Chaney, Schwerner, and Goodman buried in the earthen dam at the Old Jolly Farm, six miles southwest of Philadelphia.

The reference to Mississippi in the article about the rediscovery of Son House was, on the other hand, in the most neutral of tones: "Dick Waterman and Phil Spiro of Cambridge and Nick Perls from New York combed the Mississippi Delta towns for sixteen days..." The two Mississippi's in the articles seem to be two entirely different places that simply share the same name. As the second *Newsweek* article had tidied up Mississippi, it also tidied up what Spiro, Perls, and Waterman had discovered in Rochester:

> They came back with a guitar the next day, but he could not make his fingers behave. A little wine eased the strain. First he began to recall snatches of songs, and then phrases and finally whole songs with

22. The story also covered the "rediscovery" of Skip James.

their complicated harmonies. "You sure they want to hear this old music?" he asked his marveling audience. The next day they taped his blues. By the end of the week record companies were actively competing for him and this month's Newport Folk Festival had happily altered its plan to make way for the return of Son House.[23]

It was a lost and found story with a happy ending.

The encounter that warm June evening on Greig Street was in its way a very American sort of event; an encounter between two parties who, though nominally citizens of the same country, lived for all intents and purposes in separate worlds. What the three young seekers knew of the man who greeted them that evening in 1964 was scant: a handful of songs and the association of his name with other names that were, at that time, similarly opaque.[24] On the basis of that knowledge and their acquaintance with some other old bluesmen, they had no doubt formed some rough image of the man, but of the "actually existing" Son House sitting on the steps of 61 Greig Street and his life story, they did not know anything and could not have known anything. Compounding this was something else: the three were faced with a man who may have been an enigma even to himself.

For his part, the man they found, Eddie "Son" House, was in June of 1964 unaware that any of his prewar recordings had been reissued, and certainly oblivious to the social currents that had lead to his own rediscovery, and that were about to transform him into a "folk blues singer." We can only hazard a guess at how surprised and perplexed House must have been by his young white visitors and their proposals concerning a part of his life—the blues—that he had regarded for some years as closed. His reaction is mentioned in the article Spiro wrote for *Broadside* on the heels of their trip, when he noted, "Son seemed to be a bit puzzled as to why we had been looking for him and how we knew of his music; nobody else had shown any interest in the last twenty odd years."[25]

What had appeared dead and buried, House's musical career, was now about to be resurrected. House told his three new friends that he was willing to perform again, and, for the time being, that was all that was necessary. His three new promoters were young and well intentioned, if necessarily still somewhat naïve about the difficulties ahead. If they had

23. *Newsweek* (July 13, 1964): p. 82.

24. Son House would be the most important source of information that would, in some degree, dispel those enigmas.

25. Phil Spiro, "How We Found Son House."

any reservations in June, they put them aside and forged ahead with their project of remounting House's musical career in the context of the folk blues revival.

According to Spiro, he and Waterman were "very familiar with the folk music scene of the day, with a fair to good general understanding of what it would be like for a rediscovered bluesman to play that circuit and deal with that world."[26] But they were soon to discover that House would present special difficulties if they wished to revive his musical career, difficulties that eluded a "good general understanding" of the task ahead for the very reason that the difficulties belonged to the man himself and not the folk music scene.

"YOU CAN ALWAYS COME BACK, BUT YOU CAN'T COME BACK ALL THE WAY"[27]

In July, Spiro and Waterman brought Son House to Cambridge, where he played a couple of coffeehouse gigs with mixed results at best. After Spiro's roommate Al Wilson got a look at Son House in person, he wrote in a letter to his friend David Evans, "Son arrived in Cambridge with an old age tremor making guitar playing impossible unless he was drunk."[28] Wilson also complained about House subjecting the coffeehouse audiences to incoherent, rambling sermons about the Bible, about God and the Devil, about heaven and hell—House had also been a Baptist preacher, but certain of his pastimes had pulled the plug on that career.[29]

No matter, at this stage the initial difficulties in the Cambridge gigs could not dampen the youthful enthusiasm that had been kindled among his rediscoverers. The enthusiasm can be detected in the articles Spiro and Waterman quickly published, Spiro's "We Found Son House" in the journal *The Broadside*, which had been started to document the activities of the folk scene, and Waterman's article "Finding Son House," in the July issue of *The National Observer*. Waterman's article elided some salient details. No mention was made of the hostility the search party had encountered from whites in Mississippi—such details would have undermined the upbeat tenor of the

---

26. Spiro, personal correspondence, February 27, 2009.

27. Bob Dylan, *Love and Theft*, "Mississippi," Columbia Records 2001.

28. Rebecca Davis, "Child is Father to the Man: How Al Wilson Taught Son House How to Play Son House" *Blues Access* (Fall, 1998): p. 42.

29. It should be said that what Wilson took at that point for incoherent, rambling sermons would later become more or less fixed pieces in House's performances.

piece which was written so as to prepare the way for reviving House's career. Waterman wrote, "By the time we left, Son House was playing as well as he had over 30 years ago."[30] Thirty-four years later, Waterman would write, "When we found Son, he was a major-league alcoholic. He had no motivation to play. If he had a guitar, he would pawn it. He could still sing though. He could always sing and he could play slow blues things."[31]

Both Waterman and Spiro had already produced and promoted shows, and when they set out looking for Son House they had him in mind as another act they would promote, on the assumption that he would be happy to have his musical career revived and would be pleased to reap the rewards of it. Yet, the evidence suggests that in this early stage they underestimated the problems of the man they had found. The two bluesmen who had played Cambridge in the previous year, Mississippi John Hurt and Bukka White, had possibly led them to believe that it was simply a matter of finding these old gentlemen and pointing the way to the stage and *voilà*—"Ladies and Gentlemen, Son House!" But Hurt and White had never ceased playing—or at least not for as long as House had—and they had taken better care of themselves than Son House had. Among the statements Spiro and Waterman made at that time, one senses a well-intentioned, probably unconscious and certainly unspoken consensus to "accentuate the positive." And this too was also very much in keeping with the times. The tenor and mood of the folk revival scene encouraged the sort of youthful bravado that was already manifest in their undertaking. So, despite the problems with House's Cambridge appearances, his new "management" forged ahead and attempted to have him perform at Newport. But that was not to happen, and indeed it was the failure at Newport that would begin to reveal the dismaying dimensions of their project to resuscitate the musical career of Son House.

In the third week of July, Perls and Waterman drove House to Newport in the red Volkswagen, and they arrived on the festival grounds on Thursday afternoon. But the triumphal return of the preeminent Delta bluesman was soon aborted.

By Thursday evening House was in the emergency room of a local hospital complaining of pain in his lower abdomen. He was scheduled to perform on both Saturday and Sunday afternoons, but from the emergency room he was admitted to the hospital, and he lay in a hospital bed

---

30. Waterman, "Finding Son House," p. 16.

31. Davis, "Child," p. 42. We will, however, hear a different view from a young Joe Beard, himself a blues musician: Beard became House's neighbor in the spring of 1964.

throughout the entire weekend of the folk festival. The pain was possibly from a hernia, for when Stephen Calt visited him in the hospital he grimaced and pointed to his groin.[32] On the other hand, Phil Spiro would recall years later, "Son only had about a third of his stomach left, according to the doctors, and he would get seriously plastered on only a drink and a half. And some admirer was always sure to offer him another drink. Waterman, Perls, and I were too new to the situation to know how to manage it, or if the situation was even manageable at all."[33]

Al Wilson, writing to David Evans after the Newport fiasco, said, "Unfortunately, on Thursday night he was in the emergency room of a Newport with a) truss b) appendix c) hernia. I'm not sure exactly which."[34]

In Wilson's letter to Evans, one senses clearly his growing consternation at all the complications and difficulties attached to what, after all, had a short time before been only a name on some rare old 78s. After cataloguing House's infirmities and incapacities, Wilson concluded, "Death is an obsession, at least when he drinks." But the genie was out of the bottle, so to speak.

Truth arises from misrecognition. And it was in the last weekend of July in a hospital bed in Newport, Rhode Island that something resembling the truth would emerge. If it had not already done so, House's condition at that point would compel his new young promoters to take a second look at the man they had found and to recognize the name linked to some old recordings as a complicated and contradictory man with myriad problems and a shadowy history. A man, whom, it would soon become clear, was both proud of and tormented by what they viewed as his greatest achievement, his music.

The shock of recognition was also apparent in another encounter at the Newport hospital festival, in a conversation between Phil Spiro and Tom Hoskins, John Hurt's "rediscoverer." Hoskins, in Spiro's words, thought of himself as something of a "Virginia gentleman," and when he heard of their problems with House, Hoskins took them aside and carefully outlined their dilemma. The trouble, Hoskins said according to Spiro, wasn't simply that Son wasn't sober. "Gentlemen," he earnestly explained, "you have a problem. You have a *nigger* on your hands." As Spiro recalled, House's rediscoverers stood stock still, "flabbergasted."[35]

---

32. Stephen Calt, personal correspondence, March 4, 2009.
33. Spiro, personal correspondence, February 27, 2009.
34. Davis, "Child," p. 42.
35. Spiro, personal correspondence with the author.

Hoskins' remarks did not strike Spiro as ironic, but it seems possible that Hoskins meant them ironically. Hoskins may have been both reminding these Jewish Northerners of his Southern background and warning them of the complications and difficulties that would surely attend managing a man whom society at large viewed as a "nigger."

Whatever Hoskins meant, House's finders were undeterred and forged on. But unlike the cases of Mississippi John Hurt and Bukka White, resurrecting House's musical career proved to be a major salvage operation. Dick Waterman and Al Wilson directed it, and except for their efforts, there would have been no second coming of Son House. Not so much by design, but because of their different abilities and interests, they occupied themselves with different aspects of the complicated conundrum called Son House. In effect they divided the man—or his world—into two spheres, one off stage and one on stage. Waterman oversaw everything off stage that was necessary to get House ready to go on stage. Waterman acted as his booking agent and his accountant, helping him to manage his new income; and while he was performing, he managed his star's alcohol intake: a critical task—his finder had become his "minder."

Al Wilson, on the other hand, became involved in everything Son House would do once he got on stage. After the Newport fiasco, Waterman and Wilson took him back to Cambridge, and Wilson played guitar with House everyday as he worked through his prewar repertoire. Wilson would have been especially helpful since his own approach to the old blues was to learn the songs note for note. For Wilson the songs were, like scripture, not to be tampered with. Many years later Waterman would give credit to Wilson this way: "Al Wilson taught Son House how to play Son House. I can tell you flatly that without Al invigorating and revitalizing Son, there would have been no Son House rediscovery. All of Son's successful concert appearances, recordings and him being remembered as having a great second career—all that was because of Al..."[36]

While Wilson played an important role in resurrecting House's career, to say he "taught Son House how to play Son House" seems to be something of an overstatement. Son House's recorded prewar repertoire was not large: eight sides and a "test" record made in the 1930 Grafton sessions for Paramount Records, and the fifteen songs recorded by Alan Lomax for the Fisk University-Library of Congress project in 1941 and 1942.[37] And a

---

36. Davis, "Child," p. 43.

37. The last two Paramount sides, "Mississippi County Farm Blues" and "Clarksdale Moan," still missing in 1964, would—amazingly enough—be found in 2005.

few of the latter songs are reworked versions of the earlier Paramount sides. By the time of his rediscovery, four Paramount sides had been re-released, "My Black Mama" Parts 1 and 2, and "Preachin' the Blues" Parts 1 and 2. In addition, six of the Library of Congress recordings had been released, "Special Rider Blues," "Walking Blues," "Low Down Dirty Dog Blues," "Depot Blues," "American Defense," and "Am I Right or Wrong?"[38]

It seems unlikely that House would have forgotten his signature piece "My Black Mama" (by now called "Death Letter Blues"). But Wilson did know all of the other re-releases and could have prompted House to remember bits and pieces of songs, acting something like a human phonograph. On the other hand, staples of House's post-1964 repertoire such as "Pony Blues" and "Jinx Blues" had not yet been re-released, so Wilson could not have known them, and thus could not have "taught" them to him. Probably it was as much Wilson's interest and enthusiasm that played a vital role in motivating House to recover his old repertoire—something House might well have done on his own had he realized there was now a new market for his music and had he an interest in performing it again.

Spiro too would later say, "What really happened was that Al sat down with Son in our apartment, playing records and hearing Son's reactions. He played Son his old recordings and also played for him on the guitar. He was reminding Son of what he had done in the past, *not* teaching him how to play."[39]

After Wilson had helped and motivated House to recover his own repertoire, he would sometimes perform with the old bluesman, backing him up on second guitar or sometimes harp, and he would also record with him. But the most critical part of his contribution to the Son House salvage operation was over. Waterman's work would continue—and indeed continues even to this day.

From the vantage point of hindsight, Phil Spiro would later say of the rediscovery process: "I'm half inclined today to say that if I had to do it all over again, I wouldn't do it...To be sure, many of the ones who were found got their rocks off in their old age, at a time when there was no reasonable expectation of anything more exciting than a Social Security check. But what was the price we asked of them?"[40]

---

38. These titles are now standard for the Library of Congress, the titles on 1963 release *Blues From The Mississippi Delta* differ.

39. As quoted in Ted Gioia, *Delta Blues*, p. 374.

40. Von Schmidt and Rooney, *Baby*, p. 198.

When Spiro wrote in his *Broadside* article about Son House being "a bit puzzled..." perhaps some presentiment of the difficulties ahead occurred to Spiro himself.

Whether or not Spiro had presentiments then, the ambivalence in his later statements is clear. The ambivalence grew out of a contradiction inherent in the folk revival. On the one hand, there was the belief that "spontaneous" and noncommercial music existed and could be found if one searched diligently. On the other hand, to present the musicians who it was thought played such music, it was necessary to take into account how to market them. And for the producers and managers involved in the folk scene, this often involved instructing the performers on how to sound "spontaneous" and "noncommercial" so as to meet the expectations of the folk music audience. As Spiro wrote, "We also consciously or unconsciously tried to shape the music on stage. The same statement could be made for the guys running Paramount during the thirties, but at least their motive was simple profit, which motive the artist shared."[41] Put simply, the attitude of those in the folk revival was all too often to regard the musicians as relics. It was one thing to misapprehend the music and life of someone like Charley Patton who died in 1934, but to treat the living as though they were museum pieces was a misapprehension of another sort. Again, Spiro recognized this: "Worst of all, aside from a couple of people like Chris Strachwitz and Dick Waterman, the rediscoverers all too often didn't see the old guys as real, breathing, feeling, intelligent people."[42]

Later still, Spiro would edge back toward a more positive appraisal: "The Hobart Smiths and Son Houses—the old guys in the aggregate—generally had a good time during their day in the sun and a few even made money from it. In the end, the blues rediscoveries ended up being an overall positive thing for the old guys."[43]

The ambiguities of the rediscovery of old bluesmen would also manifest themselves in the tense relations that soon developed between various parties in the folk scene. Dick Spottswood battled Ed Denson and John Fahey over Skip James.[44] Tom Hoskins and Waterman contended over

41. Ibid., p. 198.

42. Ibid., p. 198.

43. Much later Spiro would say, "My comments in *Baby, Let Me Follow You Down* mostly still hold, but they reflect a much longer, more experienced, and more downright cynical view of rediscoveries than anyone could have had in 1964, and to repeat, were *not* about Son, and should not be presented as though they were." Personal correspondence with the author.

44. Calt, *I'd Rather Be the Devil*, pp. 277–78, 286–87.

Mississippi John Hurt.[45] Despite these conflicts, some people in that scene clung to the illusion that they were engaged in some enterprise more altruistic than the music business.

The guiding principle was that the musicians should sound as much like they had on the recordings from more than thirty years earlier. This applied to both the songs they played and the instruments they played. As Spiro said, "For the ones who had recorded before, like Son and Skip and Booker [Bukka] we kept comparing them to their younger selves, and they knew it."[46] In 1965 when Al Wilson accompanied Son House on his Columbia album *Father of the Folk Blues*, some in the folk movement looked askance. David Evans, who earned a Ph.D. from UCLA in folklore and is now a professor at the University of Memphis, stated, "I felt that Al really went a little too far in performing with these artists in public... That's not how I was trained as a folklore graduate student—not to contaminate the music."[47]

But the original, uncontaminated experience sought by the folkies of Cambridge and the Village was an illusion. When the blues rediscoveries were put back on stage, to ask them to reproduce their recorded or live performances of thirty years before, simply given the totally different cultural context in which they were now performing, was to ask an impossibility of them. This was especially true in the case of Son House. In that respect, there was nothing to "contaminate." Son House could still play blues, but he had not spent the last thirty-five years of his life carefully rehearsing, note for note, his 1930s repertoire. So, without the mediation of Al Wilson and Dick Waterman, Son House probably would not have been motivated enough to reassemble a repertoire to record and to perform that conformed closely enough to the expectations of his audience to make him a viable performer. His audience did not want to hear him perform "Don't Your Peaches Look Mellow Hanging on the Tree." They wanted to hear "Preachin' the Blues." And shortly they would hear it. But it was not the "Preachin' the Blues" of 1930. On stage at the Gaslight Café in Greenwich Village, Son House would not and could not recreate Grafton, 1930. He would create MacDougal Street, 1964.

45. See Elijah Wald's *Escaping the Delta: Robert Johnson and the Invention of the Blues* (New York: Amistad, 2004). The chapter "The Blues Cult" especially pp. 236–45 is a well-informed and sometimes funny account of the ironies of the "blues revival." See also the chapter "The Blues Revival" in Gioia's *Delta Blues*.

46. Von Schmidt and Rooney, *Baby*, p. 198.

47. Davis, "Child," p. 43.

CHAPTER **2**

Ramblified

THE EARLY YEARS OF EDDIE "SON" HOUSE

As a child and as a young man, Son House displayed the same restless and relentless energy that would later find expression in his music. Eddie "Son" House Jr. was born to Eddie and Maggie House in Lyon, Mississippi, a Delta hamlet just north of Clarksdale, on March 21, 1902.[1] Beyond these biographical certainties, things get murkier. As the British writer John Cowley lamented in his obituary of the blues musician, "anomalies plague House's biography."[2]

His father's name, Eddie James House, is found in World War I draft records from the year 1918, the date of his father's birth being given as December 27, 1877. His mother's maiden name is unknown and, likewise, her date of birth. House's father is also mentioned in the 1920 and 1930 censuses. In the 1920 census, House (James Jr.) is listed as living with his father, his father's second wife Mabelle, and a half brother Newt who was four and a half years old—House said his parents separated when he was young. The 1930 census lists his father as being fifty years old, which is consistent enough, certainly given the time and place, with the draft records, but House is not listed (he may have been in prison). His father seems to have taken a third wife; a Rowena is also listed in the 1930 census, and her age is given as twenty-eight, which is how old House himself was then.

1. Although March 21, 1902 is the date found on all of Son House's legal documents, doubts arose about its accuracy due to statements House made to Dick Waterman when he was his manager. But the evidence is clear. Son House was born in 1902. In some accounts his birthplace is said to have been Riverton, a hamlet just south of Clarksdale. Clarksdale has since absorbed both Riverton and Lyon, so in present-day terms the question is whether he was born on the north side or the south side of a town now of slightly more than 20,000 people. In an interview in May of 1965, House clearly stated that Lyon was his birthplace, and that would seem to settle the matter.

2. John Cowley, "Son House: 1902–1988, An Historical Appreciation." *Blues & Rhythm* no. 41 (Dec. 1988), p. 8.

Eddie Jr. was the middle child, having an older brother Rathel and a younger brother Lee Jackson known as L.J. who died young, in the late 1930s according to House's stepchild, Beatrice Powell. Of Rathel, nothing more is known. Mention of another possible brother—but more likely a cousin—Frank, is also found.[3] The 1920 census lists two other households headed by a Robert and another Frank, both probably uncles. The assertion that the younger Frank was a brother was probably based on a strong family resemblance. In 1969, Willie Moore, a musician who knew the family, would say of Frank simply, "He was killed."

House was born into a musical family and recalled of his youth, "I always sung. I was brought up singing church music and most of my family were 'songsters.'"[4] He said his father Eddie Sr. had seven—or sometimes nine or eleven—brothers "and they had a little band that played music all the time for the Saturday night balls."[5] His father played "bass horn"—tuba, that is—and House said of his father, "I only knew him to do three things. Blow his bass horn with his brothers. And he'd play guitar a little bit when he wasn't with his brothers. And blacksmith. Those three things. And drink corn liquor. That made four. That's it."[6]

His father had been a member of a church, Allen Chapel in Marks, about fourteen miles east of Clarksdale, but his habits imply he left the church for a period of time. Ultimately, however, House recalled that "...he laid it all down, quit drinking, and became a deacon. He went pretty straight from then on."[7] His father, that is, experienced the same conflict between religion and secular music that his son would experience, but the outcome for his son would be quite different.

3. Sheldon Harris, *Blues Who's Who: A Biographical Dictionary of Blues Singers* (New Rochelle, NY: Arlington House, 1979), p. 247 states that he was "one of at least three children." This is supported by evidence from the U.S. Census of 1930. However, elsewhere it was asserted he was one of seventeen brothers, but this along with other "facts" like spending his whole youth in New Orleans and having been married "five times" must be rejected. There is mention of House playing music with another younger brother James as well as L.J., but that is the only reference to a fourth son.

4. Lawrence Cohn, "Son House: Delta Bluesman," *Saturday Review* 51, No. 39 (September 28, 1968), p. 69. This is actually a reprint of an article Cohn first published in a small journal *Sounds and Fury* in 1965.

5. Julius Lester, "My Own Songs," *Sing Out!* (1965), p. 39. The information about Allen Chapel is found in the first newspaper article written about him after his rediscovery in Rochester's *Times-Union* article of July 6, 1964, written by Betsy Bues. House would also vary the number of his father's brothers; sometimes it was ten or twelve.

6. On a tape recording by Harry Oster on April 24, 1965. Now part of the collection of The American Folklife Center in the Library of Congress.

7. Lester, "My Own Songs," p. 39.

The first piece of music Eddie Jr. ever listened to "wasn't church music and it wasn't blues."[8] It was music made by his father and his uncles. He remembered the occasion this way:

> ...it was a piece they used to dance by an old country ball, my auntie, she used to sell whiskey...and she would sell it on Saturday nights, and her brothers, which was my daddy and his brothers—there was twelve brothers—and they had a little old band between them. They called them a brass band in those days, and they'd play music...She'd sell this whiskey and sell sandwiches and stuff like that, fried fish, and my daddy would take me along with him...and the first time, I hated all music...and the first piece they was playing was "Tear the Rag," "Tear the Rag."[9]

House said he was never tempted to try playing one of the horns his father and his uncles played. But his father owned a guitar also: "When he wasn't with his brothers, and they wasn't together and he was at home and they was some other place, he'd sit down and play the guitar." And House recalled that his father did play some blues, one song being called "Four O'Clock Blues"—though whether this song has any relation to later well-known songs of the same title is unclear.

Many years later when House would hear Mississippi John Hurt perform, he suggested that his father played some of the same sorts of pieces, songs like "Fix Me a Pallet on the Floor" or what House termed "all that old time stuff."[10] That is, songs that were already old when House was still a child.

This accounts for most of what House had to say about his father and the sorts of music his father and family played. The brevity of his memories is likely due to the fact that his mother and father separated when he was still quite young.

After his parents separated, his mother took him to Louisiana:

> We moved to a place called Tallulah, Louisiana. That's up in the north part of Louisiana, across the river from Vicksburg. My mother and my father, they separated. I started working. One while, I was gathering moss down in Algiers, Louisiana. That was in 1916, '17 and up to about '20. I wasn't big enough to occupy a heavy job. I was

8. The interview by John Fahey on May 7, 1965, is now in the Southern Folklife Collection at the University of North Carolina at Chapel Hill. Barry Hansen and Mark LeVine were also listed as interviewers, but Fahey asked all the questions. Only occasionally can Hansen or LeVine be heard saying something in the background. Hereafter: Fahey, "Interview."

9. Ibid.

10. Ibid.

gathering that grey moss out of trees. Did it near like they do cotton. Bale it up and ship it away and they would make mattresses and things out of it. I was quite young then—twenty, twenty-one—along in that category.[11]

This imprecision is characteristic of the interviews House gave in the 1960s. Mention of moving when he was probably seven or eight years old to north Louisiana (Tallulah is just across the Mississippi River from Vicksburg), is followed by a move to New Orleans-Algiers when he was in his early teenage years. He speaks of being twenty or twenty-one years old while in Algiers, but he also spoke of being in north Louisiana when he was nineteen. So there must have been at least two periods of residence in Louisiana, and probably there were three.

A statement House made in 1969 hints at one of the problems behind the contradictory statements he made to various people about his early years. In a *Rolling Stone* article that year, House recalled that at one point he had stopped playing blues entirely: "Six, seven years ago I quit playin' the blues. I did. I quit and went right and joined the church in the city where I live now…After I heard that most of all my old boys had died, I got scared and quit playing the blues…"[12] The latter is an unmistakable reference to the death of his close friend Willie Brown. But Willie Brown had died *seventeen* years earlier, in December of 1952. "Six or seven years"—if not simply an error in transcription—would instead fix the date when he quit music just shortly before Perls, Spiro, and Waterman showed up on his doorstep in 1964. With specific dates, House could be highly accurate. For example, thirty years after the fact he correctly placed the year of Charley Patton's death in the same year that he married Evie Goff—1934. But how much of his youth was actually straight in Son House's own mind by 1965 is a stubborn question. By the 1960s, House had *only* his own memory to consult for events in his life up until 1934 when he married Evie Goff. Apart from his wife, there were no older siblings or relatives or childhood friends left to aid his recollections or to correct them. He was, for all intents and purposes, alone, the sole survivor of a world that had largely vanished.

When House's mother took him to Louisiana with her, she probably also took his younger brother L.J. House was silent about it, but L.J. cropped up in accounts of his life into the 1930s. L.J. was also said to be musically inclined.

---

11. Lester, "My Own Songs," p. 38.

12. Goodwin, "Son House: 'You Can't Fool God,'" *Rolling Stone* (December 27, 1969,): p. 16. It is possible the transcription erred, replacing "sixteen or seventeen" with "six or seven."

Stephen Calt indicated that House often played with L.J., also known as "Pump," and another younger guitarist named Son Emmett.[13] But in another account L.J. is said to have died suddenly of pneumonia when he was twenty-three.[14] However his other brother, Rathel apparently did not follow his mother, since at this point he vanishes from House's stories. Probably the older boy stayed behind with his father to work. If he was in his teens, Rathel would have been considered a regular member of the labor force.

House always emphasized the importance of Sunday school and the church when recalling his childhood. Quite often he mentioned the church and his detestation of bluesmen in the same breath: "Brought up in church and didn't believe in anything else but church, and it always made me mad to see a man with a guitar and singing those blues and things. Brought up to sing in choirs. That's all I believed in then."[15] In an interview a few years later, House described his involvement in the church when he was young in similar words: "Because when I was a kid, a youngster—a young teenager and up like that, I was more churchified. Then that's mostly all I could see into. 'Cause they'd had us go—we'd had to go to the Sabbath School. Every Sunday we didn't miss going to no Sabbath School."[16]

House stated that at some point his father gave up music and alcohol and went back to the church, but that was probably after his parents separated, and House's detestation of blues seems to have coincided with that part of his youth when he lived solely with his mother. Of his attitude toward the blues at this time, House recalled, "I said it's too wrong, it's no good, no use of that. I was so churchy."[17]

Throughout his youth and early adulthood, he recalled religious revivals as important semi-annual events: "We'd be into that and then in this church there some of the ones a little larger than me and like that, and it come time of year for 'em to run a revival meeting, some pastor come to open up the revival meeting, oh, for a week or more. Well, we'd all be going to the thing they call the mourners' bench. Getting on your knees, you know, and letting the old folks pray for you."[18]

---

13. Calt, album notes for *The Real Delta Blues* (Blue Goose 1974). Hereafter, Calt, 1974.

14. David Evans, notes to CD "Son House: Delta Blues and Spirituals," (1995) album notes, p. 18.

15. Lester, "My Own Songs," p. 38.

16. Jeff Titon, "Son House," *Living Blues* (March-April 1977), p. 15. This and the 1965 Lester article provide the best general accounts of Son House's life. Most other interviews were more focused on music and musicians.

17. Ibid., 16.

18. Ibid., p. 15. The "mourners' bench" was a bench where the newly repentant lodged themselves in what was tantamount to public confession and a request that others pray for them.

When he was in his early teens, his mother took him—and presumably L.J.—to Algiers, Louisiana, then a suburb of New Orleans on the other side of the river. Since House began preaching at fifteen, he was probably in Algiers when he first presented himself to a congregation.

While preaching and gathering moss in Algiers, House had yet another occupation: shining shoes. And among the shoes he remembered shining were those of Louis Armstrong: "I used to shine his shoes every morning."[19] Armstrong was, as House put it, "already a big man."[20] In his memories of his time in Algiers and New Orleans, House also dwelled on the musical differences between New Orleans and the Mississippi Delta: "The singers were a little different in New Orleans. They sang mostly ballads and not blues."[21]

In his recollections of his "churchified" youth, Son House would skip quickly from preaching while in his teens to becoming a full-fledged pastor: "I was Baptist. I pastored a Baptist church a good while, in the Baptist church. And then I turned a few years later on after that, then I got to be a pastor of a C.M.E. church, which is Colored Methodist Episcopal church...That was pastoring. Pastor the people, yeah. And the people paid—yeah."[22]

However, a critical experience must have intervened between his youthful preaching and his becoming a pastor. Simply being "churchified"—that is, merely observing the visible forms of religion by going to Sunday school, singing in the choir, and kneeling on the mourner's bench—was not, he soon realized, enough. Something else was lacking. Despite his religious faith, somehow House did not have "religion." He needed to "get religion."

To "get religion," meant in this community an intense personal experience that showed that one was now "saved." In House's memories of Sabbath school and revival meetings, the very mystery of the experience clearly helped to stoke his powerful desire to "get it"—it is a little like the mystery of sex for a youth who has not yet experienced it. One knows that

19. Bob West, "Son House Interview," *Blues & Rhythm*, 207 (March 2006), p. 4. This is a reprint of a 1968 interview. Ed Komara and Bob Groom have both suggested that the Louis Armstrong episode is probably apocryphal. As Ed Komara said, House may simply have been giving an interviewer some "local color."

20. Cohn, "Son House: Delta Bluesman," p. 19. Al Wilson also asserted in an article about House published in 1965 that much of his early life had been spent in New Orleans, "Son House, Pt. 8," *Broadside* 10 (July 7, 1965): p. 4. Cohn—perhaps simply following Wilson—likewise mentioned New Orleans, but he placed House's time there in House's early childhood: "At the age of three or four his family moved to New Orleans, Louisiana, where he remained for about twenty years," p. 19. But any claim that House spent most of his youth in New Orleans is inconsistent with all other accounts of his youth.

21. Cohn, "Delta Bluesman," p. 19.

22. Titon, "Son House," p. 21. C.M.E. has now become "Christian Methodist Episcopal" church.

it is something momentous, but—what else? At the revival meetings he must have been bewildered by witnessing people shout, "I've got it!" But whatever "it" was, what a young Son House had seen and heard seemed to indicate that "it" could be "got" only by praying and praying. And as fervently as House also wanted to "get religion," it would be a little while before he could claim that experience.

Carrie Martin

By the time he was nineteen, House was back in the Delta in the Clarksdale area, for it was there he took up with a churchgoer—although he was probably not a pastor yet in any proper sense of the word. On several occasions House spoke of having been married five times, but it is likely that most of these were simply "jump the broom" affairs, occasions when he and a woman set up housekeeping together. However, one of these relationships prior to 1934 seems to have had some formal basis, his marriage to Carrie Martin.

House was speaking of Carrie Martin when he said, "Got married. Married a girl out of New Orleans. She was a woman. She was thirty-two and I was nineteen."[23] House was fairly reticent about his relations with women, but his relationship with Martin was an exception. House said they were married in a church, but his family refused to attend their wedding and for a time would have nothing to do with them. Then he, his bride and his cousin Frank moved to her hometown, Centerville, which is in south central Louisiana, about sixty miles north of Lafayette. The marriage seems to have foundered when House came to suspect that his wife's real motive for being with him was to furnish her aging father with a farmhand. As he put it, "I left her hangin' on the gatepost, with her father tellin' me to come back so we could plough some more."[24] Unlike his 1934 marriage, there was no certificate for this union, and it was probably the fact that the ceremony was performed by a preacher that made this union a real marriage in House's eyes.[25]

He would tell one writer of Carrie Martin, "she wasn't nothin' but one of them New Orleans whores."[26] Martin may have been a one-time prostitute

23. Fahey, "Interview."
24. Calt, 1974.
25. Letter from Stephen Calt to the author, February 17, 2009.
26. Calt, 1974.

who had taken to attending church services to better her situation. Likely, she latched onto House because he was a younger man whom she thought she could manipulate—and, for a while at least, she succeeded. In any case, something about their romance and marriage left House with a long-lasting antipathy still apparent in his recollections forty years after the fact.[27]

How long the marriage endured is uncertain, but given House's restless itinerary in the 1920s, it cannot have lasted more than a year or two at most. In other words, House probably left Martin "hanging on the gatepost" about the same time his mother Maggie died which was said to be 1922.

According to John Cowley's obituary, House moved back to the Delta "in the 1920s on the death of his mother."[28] But taking into account his marriage to Carrie Martin, he was probably not living with his mother when she died. It is also known that at some point in his late teens or early twenties he was living with his father once more in the Clarksdale area, since he recalled running off for two weeks to Memphis because he was fed up with plowing on his father's farm.[29]

House described the restless mobility of young black men like himself at that time, young men for whom sharecropping was a last resort, when he remarked:

> If they get far as St. Louis, oh Jesus! They thought that was way somewhere. I did it myself! I had a friend who was up there working in the Commonwealth Steel Plant in St. Louis. He came back and told me about it, and the first thing you know, I'd sneaked out and gone to St. Louis. We were getting a dollar an hour along then. That was big money, you know. That was along in 1922 or '23...I stayed up there about eight months and got the hotfoot again and came on

27. House's union with Carrie Martin is probably the one described by Robert Palmer in *Deep Blues*. There he says the woman was a member of House's congregation, and says that it was this union that put an end to one stint as a pastor, and that sent him to Louisiana:

"His downfall was a woman in her early thirties. After a sizzling affair they ran off to her home territory, northern Louisiana, where they farmed for a while. But House had had his fill of hard manual labor before he began preaching, and by 1926 he was back in the vicinity of Lyon, alone. There he drank, rambled, half-heartedly attempted to resume his preaching career." *Deep Blues* (New York: Penguin, 1981), p. 79. But Palmer's sources were unavailable to the author.

28. John Cowley, "Son House, 1902–1988: An Historical Appreciation," *Blues and Rhythm, the Gospel Truth*, (Dec. 1988), p. 8. David Evans places her death "around 1922," album notes 1995, p. 12.

29. Calt, 1974.

back down to Mississippi. I wasn't contented anywhere long. I was
young and just loved to ramble. I was just ramblified, you know.[30]

In his own rambles, House held a variety of jobs, besides sharecropping.
He worked for brief periods as a deckhand on a riverboat, on a trolley in
Memphis, on a train line in Kentucky, and yet again in north Louisiana,
this time on a ranch where he helped raise horses.[31] In this same period,
House also worked on levee gangs—he recalled toting sandbags to shore
up the levees during the catastrophic Mississippi flood of 1927. And of
course, he worked in the steel plant in East St. Louis. The job on the
Louisiana horse ranch was, unusually, work he rather enjoyed, seen in the
fact that he would continue to wear the cowboy hat he wore on that job
("brown with a white band") once he began to perform.

Apart from the ranch job, it is clear from his recollections that he found
nothing uplifting or self-improving in all of this grueling, hard work.
Years later, when asked about his friend Charley Patton's attitude toward
work, he chuckled and said, "Charley hated work like God hates sin. He
just natural-born hated it. It didn't look right to him."[32] Being of a more
religious cast than Patton, House may not have considered work "sinful,"
but beyond that there was not much to recommend it.

His and his friend Patton's attitudes were understandable. The sharecropping system was little more than legalized slavery, and a sharecropper
was lucky to make any money at all. Sharecropping was usually done on
the "halves"; the planter furnished everything the tenant needed to make
the crop and then they split the profits. However, the sharecropper usually had to borrow to get through the winter, and the planters often loaned
money at 33–40 percent interest.[33] *The Southern Tenant Farmers Union
News* published an anecdote in which a teacher asked a student, "If the

30. Lester, "My Own Songs," p. 39. That House lived in New Orleans from the time when he was
sixteen until he was twenty or twenty-one is highly unlikely, since that leaves out the Carrie Martin
episode that took place in the Delta and central Louisiana. Likewise, Waterman wrote in his obituary
that, "House once told an acquaintance of living in East St. Louis during World War I and being con-
siderably older than his mid-teens in the 1917–18 period." Waterman, Obituary, pp. 48–49. But his
time in East St. Louis was more likely after his last sojourns in New Orleans and north Louisiana.

31. Some writers equate this work with his work on the farm of Carrie Martin's father, but
this seems unlikely both because of the chronology and because House recalled the ranching job
as a pleasant memory. But nothing associated in his memory with Carrie Martin was pleasant.

32. Stephen Calt and Gayle Wardlow, *The King of the Delta Blues: The Life and Music of Charlie
Patton*. (Newton, New Jersey: Rock Chapel Press, 1988), p. 110. Note again how work and religion
are mentioned together.

33. Donald Grubbs. *Cry From Cotton* (Chapel Hill: University of North Carolina Press, 1971, p. 9.

landlord lends you twenty dollars, and you pay him back five dollars a month, how much will you owe him after three months?" "Twenty dollars," was the student's answer. "You don't understand arithmetic," the teacher scolded. "You don't understand our landlord," the student replied.[34]

House recalled the work conditions in those years in this way: "At that time, there was mostly farm work, and sometimes it got pretty critical. Low wages and—well, people kind of suffered a little during some of those years. Suffered right smart." House remarked that if people cleared forty or fifty dollars for the year once they had paid off their debts to the plantation owner, they were "satisfied." The system was devised in such a way that sharecroppers knew they would always have food and housing even if they had no money—as in the days of slavery. "So," House said, "they didn't complain and worry too much about it."[35]

But his own dissatisfaction with the dreary treadmill of sharecropping was apparent: "Old folks were always bossin' you: the biggest they all wanted you to do was plough..." he said dismissively.[36] In this context, "biggest" clearly carries a negative connotation—the "biggest" was still paltry in House's mind. Years later, House consistently represented himself as an ambitious young man, who was frustrated with the menial tasks his elders tried to impose on him—the sort of work Carrie Martin's father tried to get him to perform that finally drove him away from her.

Getting religion

A temporary respite from such toil could be found in church. From Sabbath school to the choir, from revival meetings to "getting religion" in a cotton field, one thing was constant: religion was relief from backbreaking work that barely paid, if at all. And it was a socially sanctioned form of relief. But while he might find a temporary relief in a revival meeting, or steal time by praying in a cotton field, the culmination for House of this opposition between religion and hard physical labor was becoming a preacher. For the black preacher was the only man in the world of young Son House who stood some chance of escaping the brutal conditions of rural labor in the South. As House himself emphasized, "That was pastoring. Pastor the people, yeah. *And the people paid—yeah.*"

34. Ibid., p. 10.
35. Lester, "My Own Songs," p. 39.
36. Calt, 1974.

House recalled that he "got religion" in his early twenties. He said the experience occurred about six or eight months after a revival meeting. He was working in an alfalfa field when he got down on his knees to pray and—it happened: "Dew was falling. And man I prayed and I prayed and I prayed and—for wait a while, I hollered out. Found out then: I said, 'Yes, it is something to be got, too, 'cause I got it now!' "[37]

He went back to his home and bragged to a cousin Robert, and even woke up a white overseer to tell him what had happened. The circular logic of House's affirmation is noteworthy: It is something to have because *I* have it.

It was probably shortly after that experience in the vicinity of Clarksdale that House took his first position as a pastor. While he had preached since he was fifteen, he could scarcely have become a pastor without that credential. "Getting religion" was one of three essential qualifications for becoming a preacher in the vast majority of rural churches, where the preachers had no formal seminary training. The first, of course, was being literate and having read the Bible. The second was "getting religion." A third qualification was having a strong voice—as Willie Moore, a Delta musician himself and a friend of House, observed dryly, "It takes a big-mouthed man to be a preacher."[38] Once House "got religion," he had all three. His youthful hostility to the blues, while not a qualification, was certainly part of the job. Religious devotion, hard labor, and antipathy to the blues: the three formed, as it were, a trinity which defined House's life before 1927.

Unfortunately, preaching was a straight and narrow path, and House soon found it difficult to stay on it. Sometime before he took up music, House had begun drinking. As he recalled, there "...got to be a rumor among my members, you know. And I began to wonder how can I stand up there in the pulpit and preach to them, tell them how to live, and quick as I dismissed the congregation, I'm doing the same thing..."[39] The rumor was true. At a concert in 1964 he introduced "Preachin' the Blues" by saying: "Well, I got in a little bad company one time, and they said, 'Aw, c'mon, take a little nip with us.' I says, 'Naw.' 'Aw, c'mon!' So I took a little nip. None of the members were around, so I took a little nip. And that one

---

37. Titon, "Son House," p. 15. House would clearly place this experience in his twenties in this interview, but he also connects it with revival meetings in his teens in the same interview.

38. Calt and Wardlow, *King*, p. 29.

39. Mark Humphrey, "Prodigal Sons," in *Saints and Sinners; Religion, Blues and (D)evil in African-American Music and Literature*, ed. Robert Sacré.

little nip called for another big nip."[40] It might have been little solace to House, but he was hardly alone among preachers in taking nips, big or little. In 1931, Reverend W.M. Moseley recorded a sermon that chastised "jack-leg" preachers: "You drunken preachers, you ungodly preachers . . . stay out of widows' houses."[41]

Women were probably also a problem for the Reverend House. While apart from Carrie Martin there are no other names from the twenties, it is clear that in the thirties he had multiple romantic liaisons, at times simultaneously. He explained the end of one affair in the early thirties by saying, "I had so many back up there around Lake Carmen and places, I couldn't bring 'em back with me, but I'd talk trash and make like I's so crazy 'bout 'em and everything . . ."[42] And later, when he was married to Evie Goff, he attributed his move to Rochester to a conflict among a former girlfriend, his present girlfriend, and his wife. It seems unlikely that such behavior only began when he was thirty years old—especially if he was already cutting corners on other matters of ethical concern to the church.

Trying to estimate how long he stayed in the church, House said, "Oh Jesus, I stayed in church near about—whew—way over a half grown; I was up in my 20-somethings, then, between 26 and 7 years old. I'd got married."[43] So House fixed the date of his leaving the church sometime after the Martin marriage. But "leaving the church" in this context must be understood as meaning fully committed to it, since House would be in and out of the pulpit well into the 1930s.

So what had promised to be a way of escaping hard labor proved to be incompatible with House's new tastes for corn liquor and women, and by 1927, his experiences with both religion and hard work must have left him disgruntled and dissatisfied. Yet he was an intelligent man who was unable and unwilling to simply resign himself to backbreaking work that was, at best, a break-even proposition—if it did not actually leave one deeper in debt. In short, by 1927, Eddie "Son" House was a man ready for a change.

40. As quoted in Luigi Monge, "Preachin' the Blues: a Textual Linguistic Analysis of Son House's "Dry Spell Blues" in *Ramblin' On My Mind*, University of Illinois, Champagne-Urbana, 2008, p. 228.

41. Paul Oliver, *Songsters and Saints* (Cambridge UK and New York: Cambridge University Press, 1984), p. 201.

42. Perls, "Son House Interview," p. 60.

43. Titon, "Son House," p. 16.

CHAPTER 3

The Blues Blowed My Spirit Away

APOSTASY AT A FROLIC

One Saturday evening in 1927 in Mattson, just a few miles south of Clarksdale, Eddie "Son" House went for a stroll, unaware that he had set out on his own road to Damascus.[1] According to House, that evening he happened past a "frolic" or house party where a small crowd was gathered around a bluesman playing guitar with a bottleneck. Years before, House had once briefly heard the sound of bottleneck guitar, but he was still "churchified" then. He now recalled that instance years earlier, but this time the effect was quite different. This time he didn't "kick against" the man with the guitar. This time he didn't say, "It's too wrong, it's no good. No use of that." He stopped to listen, and this time the strange wailing sound of glass on steel transfixed him. What he heard would change the course of his life forever.

House would give several versions of this fateful encounter that set him on the path of his musical career.

In a 1965 interview with Julius Lester, House described the episode this way, "I started playing guitar in 1928, but I got the idea around about 1927. I saw a guy named Willie Wilson and another one named Reuben Lacy. All before then, I just hated to see a guy with a guitar. I was so churchy! I came along to a little place they call Mattson, a little below Clarksdale."[2]

Although it was the crowd that drew him at first, it was the strange and unfamiliar sound of glass moving against steel, the bottleneck sliding up and down the strings of the guitar, that captivated him:

---

1. Or possibly 1926, that is the year House would give Alan Lomax in 1941.

2. Lester, "My Own Songs," p. 40. Mattson is still the name of an area about five and a half miles southeast of Clarksdale on present-day Highway 49. Old Highway 49 runs parallel to the new highway about a quarter of a mile to the west.

Well, I stopped, because the people were all crowded around. This boy, Willie Wilson, had a thing on his finger like a small medicine bottle, and he was zinging it, you know. I said, "Jesus! Wonder what's that he's playing?" I knew that guitars hadn't usually been sounding like that. So I eases up close enough to look and I see what he has on his finger. "Sounds good!" I said. "Jesus! I like that!" And from there, I got the idea and said, "I believe I want to play one of them things."[3]

House had certainly heard people playing blues on the guitar before 1927, his own father for one, but this time the effect of the bottleneck sliding on the strings made the difference. Musicians from Texas and Georgia and elsewhere played bottleneck guitar, but the style was an especially prominent part of the Delta blues. The eerie and peculiar sound that Saturday night seems to have been the siren song that lured House onto an entirely different and unexpected path in life.

Within a matter of days, House bought a guitar from a man named Frank Hopkins for $1.50. It had five strings, and a hole in the back. So he took the injured instrument to the same musician he had heard playing at the "frolic" on Saturday night, Willie Wilson, and told him that he wanted to learn to play in that same style. Wilson looked at House's purchase and said, "Well, you'll never learn this way. You need another string. Takes six strings. It's all busted in the back, too. Tell you what I'll do. I'll see if I can fix it up for you."[4]

Wilson got "some tape and stuff" and somehow patched the instrument up to the point where it could be played. He also tuned it for his apprentice to a "Spanish," or an open G tuning, which meant House did not need to learn any fingerings to form simple major chords. House made his own bottleneck—and cut his finger a few times in the process—but, soon, as he put it, "...I started to zinging, too." And, as with most other blues musicians, he now put the musical learning he had acquired in church in his youth in the service of "the Devil's music": "I used to be a leader in the choir and they were singing the old vocal music at that time, you know, like the do-re-mi's, so I got the idea to make the guitar go like that, and in a couple of weeks time, I was able to play a little tune. It was a little tune I'd heard Willie Wilson play called, 'Hold Up, Sally, Take Your Big Legs Offa Mine.'"[5]

"Take Your Big Leg Offa Mine," is a piece that Mississippi John Hurt would record in 1928 as "Big Leg Blues," but it was known as early as

3. Ibid., p. 40.
4. Ibid. p. 40.
5. Ibid., p. 40.

1900.[6] Elsewhere House mentioned that his mentor Willie Wilson did standards like "Salty Dog" (yet another song in Hurt's repertoire). House compared Wilson to another musician who influenced him, Rube Lacy: "Ruben Lacy had him beat a little, but he was good, too."[7] Wilson, House said, was also known as "Lemon," because of the number of Blind Lemon Jefferson songs he performed.[8]

The essential parts of this account are confirmed by another account. However, in the second account some of the names and details change.

In House's other version of the story, it is a different but likewise hazy figure who exerts a decisive influence, a musician named James McCoy. In his interview with John Fahey in May of 1965, House stated that the first musician he saw playing a guitar in an open tuning with a bottleneck was McCoy: "A guy by the name of James McCoy...And the first guy that I paid attention to get my mind on trying to learn to play guitar was a guy by the name Ruben Lacy. And he was the first guy, him and this other guy I just mentioned, was the first I see play with this slide. Now they used medicine bottles."[9]

Like Willie Wilson and Frank Hopkins, McCoy is, except for his contact with Son House and his influence on him, a total obscurity. According to House, McCoy taught him what would become his two most important pieces, "My Black Mama" and "Preachin' the Blues." The former was originally a simple vocal song with instrumental accompaniment whose structural anomalies may show the traces of a work song.[10] The latter House also claimed to have learned from McCoy, although Bessie Smith had recorded a song called "Preachin' the Blues" in 1927. Her influence cannot be ruled out as an additional factor, since House said that he saw Smith perform in Memphis in the 1920s, and he expressed admiration for her style of singing. In any case, House transposed these two songs to a Spanish tuning and began reworking them. Especially with respect to McCoy's influence, House's music bears out the adage, "Mediocre artists borrow. Great artists

6. Vance Randolph, *Roll Me in Your Arms: Unprintable Ozark Folksongs and Folklore*, Vol. 1 (Fayetteville: University of Arkansas 1992), p. 130. Randolph's informant told him first heard the song performed in a medicine show in Fayetteville, Arkansas, in 1900. Hurt recorded the song for OKeh, December 21, 1928. See *Encyclopedia of the Blues*, ed. Edward Komara, (New York: Routledge 2006), Vol. 1, p. 484.

7. Calt, 1974. Lacy's name is sometimes also spelled Lacey.

8. House would tell Lomax that a musician Willie Williams was also known as "Lemon," but from other details it is clear he must have been speaking about Willie Wilson.

9. Fahey, "Interview."

10. See Edward Komara's, *The Road to Robert Johnson* (Milwaukee: Hal Leonard, 2007), p. 25.

steal." The two songs House learned from McCoy became his two finest pieces. His versions of "Preachin' the Blues" and "My Black Mama"—later to be retitled "Death Letter Blues"—are both classics that can stand with the very best songs created by blues musicians.

The Wilson and McCoy stories can be reconciled to some degree by information found in yet a third source, the article Al Wilson published in 1965 in *Broadside of Boston*. Willie Wilson hailed from Leland, about forty-five miles south of Clarksdale on Highway 61. House thought he was about ten to twelve years older than himself, in his mid to late thirties, that is. But Wilson sometimes played in the Clarksdale area. Moreover, he and McCoy apparently knew each other. McCoy, like House, was also from Lyon, and apparently House met both men around the same time in Lyon. House thought McCoy was probably a few years older than Wilson.[11] As Al Wilson put it, "...all three men became good acquaintances and would often appear for general revelry where either Wilson or McCoy might be playing."[12] These meetings "for general revelry," according to Al Wilson, began shortly before House actually took up the guitar. In other words, House undoubtedly first met Willie Wilson and James McCoy as drinking buddies. Al Wilson states that McCoy never used a bottleneck, but that contradicts what House told Fahey. No matter, given the circumstances of "general revelry," nearly forty years after the fact, House certainly might have had difficulty recalling whether it was Wilson or McCoy playing the bottleneck that night in Mattson.

All the accounts of Willie Wilson and James McCoy also agree in mentioning Rube Lacy, and House told Stephen Calt that it was after seeing Lacy perform on Roy Flowers' plantation near Mattson in 1927 that he adopted Lacy's bottleneck technique.[13] Compared to the dim figures of Frank Hopkins, Willie Wilson, and James McCoy, Rube Lacy is a celebrity. He made a record with Paramount in 1928, "Mississippi Jail House Groan"/"Ham Hound Crave" (which admittedly flopped), and he would be interviewed about his career years later.[14] By 1928, Lacy, who was about a year older than House, had been eking out a living as an itinerant musician for some years. He hailed from the Jackson area and had played with

11. Bob Groom, "An Interview with Son House," *Blues World*, 18 (January, 1968), p. 6.

12. Al Wilson, "Son House: an analysis of his music and a biography," *Blues Unlimited*, Collectors Classics 14, Reprints Vol. 3 (October 1966), p. 2. This is a reprint of the *Broadside* serialized articles of the year before.

13. On another issue, if one accepts this date, then this might also decide the date of House's "conversion" experience to 1926.

14. Lacy also recorded four sides with Columbia in 1927, but these were unreleased. In the 1930s he would abandon blues for preaching.

musicians like Tommy Johnson, Charlie McCoy, and the Chatmon family.[15] On his 1928 side for Paramount, "Mississippi Jail House Groan," Lacy can be heard stomping his feet like Patton and House. Lacy, like House also, had a preaching background, and his moaning on "Mississippi Jail House Groan" may anticipate the moving use that House would make of moans in his own vocal style. And indeed, such House titles as "Mississippi County Farm Blues" and "Levee Camp Moan" from both the Grafton and the Library of Congress sessions may speak of Lacy's persisting influence. Of Lacy's versatility and skill with a guitar, House would say, "Yeah, he played Spanish, cross and natural. He was good with them all."[16]

However, of these three early musical influences, House seemed to consider McCoy the best. House compared his singing to Skip James: McCoy, he said had "a high, fine voice like Skip's."[17] Wilson's voice House thought was merely "average," whereas he found Lacy's "strange."

Despite the discrepancies among the three accounts, the important points are common to all of them: the suddenness of House's change of heart; his dedication to his new profession; and his awareness that, whatever the future would bring, he had taken a momentous step that would change his life. House's sudden transformation from a man of the church scornful of the blues to a performing bluesman is remarkable. After years of heaping scorn on blues musicians, House picks up the guitar, embraces what he had bitterly rejected, and within two weeks is himself an apprentice bluesman performing at local house parties. Taking up the blues promised to complicate his sense of himself as a religious man, but as we have seen, there was already evidence that women and alcohol had compromised that. It also seems that House's motives for preaching were already at some level, perhaps an unconscious one, conflicted—"And the people paid!" Blues as an additional source of income had much to recommend itself, and taking up the blues might have suddenly appeared to him as the next—and logical—step along a path he knew in his heart he had already begun to follow. The situation in which he now found himself must have been as strange and as novel to him as the sound of the bottleneck guitar he heard that evening in Mattson.

House's startling change is remarkably similar to a religious conversion—except that in this case it is closer to losing one's religion:

15. Robert Santelli, *Big Book of the Blues* (New York: Penguin, 1993), "Rubin Lacy," p. 245.
16. Fahey, "Interview."
17. Wilson, p. 11.

apostasy. His abrupt change of heart must have sprung from a sense of deadlock in his life. What he did next is also, ironically, common in religious conversions. Like many another new convert House fashioned a narrative to explain what he had done. That text is "Preachin' the Blues," which he would record and then perform for more than four decades. In his later years, this text was never performed without a homily of sorts from House commenting on its significance. And that angry and unrepentant song is probably as close to the truth of the matter as we will ever come.

Once House took up the guitar what happened next is also surprising—the rapidity with which his new career progressed. Within a matter of weeks, he was performing at house parties on his own. Although his account of his musical beginnings focused on acquiring a guitar and learning how to play it, House's rapid progress was no doubt made possible by his talent as a singer, which in turn grew out of his experience as a preacher. The observation of his acquaintance Willie Moore, about needing "a whole lotta mouth" to be a preacher, was even more the case for a bluesman. A strong voice was necessary to be heard over the raucous and rowdy din of house parties and juke joints, and House had a powerful voice—his smoking never seemed to affect it. What is more, a repertoire of three or four songs might suffice to launch one as a part-time musician. In "frolics" and juke joints where the blues was dance music, we hear of musicians in such venues "stretching out" by playing the same song for ten or even twenty minutes, jamming, so that three or four songs might suffice for a "set," or at least for "spelling" a more experienced musician with a larger repertoire—as he seems to have done in his first public performances.

As far as House's first performance, it was Willie Wilson who figured again. House recalled, "So the next time he came by, I showed him I could play it. He said, 'Come on and play with me tonight.' It was Saturday night. I said, 'I ain't good enough for that.' He said, 'Oh, yes, you is. You just play that. I'll back you up.' So I started with him just like that."[18]

That was the last mention of Willie Wilson, who apparently moved on shortly after he helped House get started. But as House said, "I kept on playing and got better and better." House threw himself into his new profession, not simply learning to play the guitar, but more importantly crafting his own songs: "I'd set up and concentrate on songs, and then

18. Lester, "My Own Songs," p. 40.

went to concentrating on me rhyming words, rhyming my own words. 'I can make my own songs,' I said."[19]

Remarkably, during his early musical career House had no interaction with any of the notable musicians in the Delta until 1930 with the sole exception of Rube Lacy. This is especially remarkable given how good House would sound when he recorded in 1930, and given the fact that his musical career was interrupted before recording. For his first year and a half or so as a musician, House performed in total obscurity: the only testimony about his musical beginnings comes from himself. Apart from his mention of Wilson, McCoy and Lacy, House tells us only that at some point he played in a medicine show called Doctor McFadden's. "He sold medicine all over Mississippi, especially 'round Drew. I used to get on a small stage and play just as loud as I could to attract the attention of the people. Boy, we sure sold lots of medicine."[20] And no doubt, House treated himself with such "medicine" too.

Drew would have brought House near to Patton's musical base on Dockery's plantation, and House certainly had heard of Patton already, but he did not meet him at this point. Their meeting was yet to come.

Even after recasting himself as a blues man, House tried to continue preaching—an ambitious but exceedingly tricky combination of careers. Besides playing the Devil's music, his taste for alcohol and women, too— not unusual for a blues man—posed almost insurmountable public relations problems for a Baptist preacher, and at some point the contradictions between the two professions would become too much for him. It would, however, take a few more years for him to reach that point of no return. In the meantime, he tried to straddle two diametrically opposed careers, no doubt at the cost of some psychological tension.

Such is what we know of House's reincarnation as a bluesman until one evening, probably in 1928, when his burgeoning musical career was interrupted by the sort of violence that contributed to the blues' dubious reputation.[21]

The killing of Leroy Lee

At a boisterous frolic in 1928, House shot and killed a man. In a song he would record in 1930, he gives the name of his victim as Leroy Lee—but that recording would not be discovered for seventy-five years. When John

19. Lester, "My Own Songs," p. 40.
20. Cohn, "Delta Bluesman," p. 69.
21. Possibly early 1929. House would give Stephen Calt that year as the date, but 1928 fits the chronology better.

Fahey interviewed House in 1965 (forty years before that old 78 record would be found) he questioned him about the song "Mississippi County Farm Blues" and asked him why he had been on the prison farm.[22] House's response, rather more measured than usual, was: "Well, the first time I had to get in trouble—now of course I was in the right in a way—this guy was named Leroy, Leroy Lee." House then quotes the song lyrics that referred to the incident:

> They put me in jail, wouldn't let me be
> They say for the murder of Leroy Lee[23]

Fahey did not probe the killing any further—he was primarily intent on understanding the song, especially the references to his prison experience. But House revealed more details to Stephen Calt. House told Calt that he was at a Saturday night house party in Lyon with a girlfriend named Cornelius, when a fight broke out between two men. One of the men, Sam Allen, was a friend of House. The other man was Leroy Lee, then unknown to House. When the shooting started, House was outdoors with an uncle who got hit by a stray bullet that broke his ankle. Hearing the shots, House, who was armed with a .32 automatic, crawled indoors through a broken window, getting cut on the neck in the process. Once he was inside, House shot Lee, in defense of his friend Sam Allen he claimed. Allen however left the scene. House then took his uncle to a doctor in Jonestown.

The next morning, the sheriff stopped House's girlfriend Cornelius who was wandering along the railroad tracks leading out of Lyon wearing some of House's clothes, and she gave him an unsolicited account of the killing. House was arrested, tried in Clarksdale, probably for manslaughter, and sentenced to five years on Parchman Prison Farm—the "notorious" Parchman Farm, as it is usually called.

House's later explanation for his girlfriend's action was that the shooting had so rattled her that she had a "breakdown." But as Calt commented, this seemed dubious.[24] It is also curious that House took his wounded uncle to a doctor in Jonestown about eight miles away when they were immediately outside Clarksdale. House was quick to criticize blues musicians who threw together miscellaneous lyrics and called the haphazard result "a blues," and

22. Fahey knew of the earlier Paramount song, but had only heard House's 1942 Library of Congress version "County Farm Blues" which had been re-released in 1963.

23. Fahey, "Interview."

24. Calt, conversation, February, 2009.

in this different context one is tempted to call House on the carpet for the same error, throwing together some unrelated "facts" in hopes of coming up with some sort of story that would justify his action to the authorities. But his account failed in that respect. At his trial House claimed self-defense, but apparently the testimony of his girlfriend, Cornelius, decided the case. House was convicted of killing Lee and sentenced to time at Parchman Farm. Presumably this marked the end of his romance with Cornelius.

A few other pieces of circumstantial evidence may be added to the account. House told Calt that he never mentioned either his conviction or his prison time to his friend Charley Patton—who on the evidence of his songs and those who knew him never did time for anything more serious than public intoxication. And House gave the Paramount song the title "Mississippi County Farm Blues," but House did time for the killing on Parchman Prison Farm, which was the *state* prison farm. House definitely knew the difference—he also did a short stint years later on the Tunica County Prison Farm for an automobile traffic infraction. Finally, the year of 1929 that House gave Calt for the killing also poses the same kind of chronological problems we have seen surrounding House's early life. Most accounts of his incarceration speak of him spending a year or a year and a half on Parchman. It is certain that House was freed and living in Lula by early spring of 1930 at the latest. Some accounts put his incarceration in 1929 others put it earlier, but whatever the calculation, House was definitely free in early 1930. The haziness of the dates, taken together with the other anomalies in his account of the killing, suggest that almost four decades later House may still have been reluctant to furnish all the details about the episode.[25]

However, House was much less reticent about his experiences at Parchman than he was about his reasons for being at Parchman, and in the interview with John Fahey he talked at some length about that experience. As he said, "I thought about that, the time I put up under them 'captains.' They work til it's night. I couldn't forget it."

Fahey was particularly interested in the man mentioned as "Captain Jack" in the 1942 version "County Farm Blues." There House described

25. This author's search of the court docket in Coahoma County turned up no record at all in the years 1926–1929. A subsequent FOIA search for a death certificate for a "Leroy Lee" in the late 1920s did not produce anything. Nor were any records found in the archives of the Mississippi Department of Corrections. At present, one can only infer that if any records ever existed, they have since been lost—which would not be remarkable for an episode of black-on-black violence in Mississippi at that time. The dockets for a much broader range of years were searched, but the killing could only have taken place after 1926 and before 1930.

Captain Jack in some of the more evocative and harrowing lyrics he ever composed:

> Put you down in a ditch with a very long spade (3x)
> Wish to God you hadn't ever been made
> Put you down under a man called Captain Jack (3x)
> He'll sure write his name up and down your back

House told Fahey that Captain Jack was a "prison driver"—the overseer of the work gang of convicts. He said that, in fact, Captain Jack was the driver on the Tunica County Farm, but he went on to talk about things quite clearly related to his time on Parchman. As he put it, "But this is some of the words that went with the same things at Parchman and this place out from Tunica and—it's the same thing."

It appears that at Parchman Farm there were actually two captains, who the inmates called "Little Captain" and "Big Captain" on account of their physical size. But House stressed it was always necessary to address either of them as Captain: "And when you come out in the morning, when you're going out with them big stripes on to work. As they march out like that, and the other one he's standing over there with the rifle like that off from you, to load you on the truck . . . as you walk out, you bow your head and you say, 'Good morning, Captain, please.' 'Good morning, Captain, please.' That's what you had to do."[26]

When Fahey asked about the lyric, "He'll sure write his name up and down your back," House was unequivocal: "That means beat you."

Beatings, in both places, were daily occurrences according to House. The Tunica driver known as Captain Jack turned that task over to a black man, "a great big fat guy" in House's words who "who didn't have to work as hard as the other guys—just call him the 'whup man.'" If Captain Jack decided a prisoner was not working hard enough, he called on his fat assistant whose name was Paul and ordered him to beat the prisoner— whom he would only identify by his number. Paul had a strop about two feet long with a wooden handle on one end which he used to deliver the beating. The prisoners called the strop "Black Annie."[27] House described

---

26. House then says, "That was out at Tunica." But Tunica County Farm is where about ten years later he spent a week or so for a traffic violation. Parchman is south of Clarksdale in Sunflower County.

27. Fahey, "Interview."

the blows, "Pow! Sound like a cannon!" When Fahey remarked that such a blow could knock a "hole in your back," House replied, "Man, they didn't care. Sometimes some of them would die from it. That's the way they whup you."

Fahey asked House if he was ever beaten in that way, and House said he was not, and this was due to the intercession of the planter for whom his father and his uncles worked:

> The man I was working for, he was a big shot. He stood good with the people, and they went by what he said. And he told them to be light on me ... If you stand all right and amount to something, the judge and everybody going to do just like you [the planter, that is] say ... My people, all of them or most of them, was raised up and worked for his daddy for a long time ... my daddy was always a blacksmith for him. That's why he knew him too and he thought very much of the family. So that's why he made it light on me.

House summed up his prison time with the wistful remark, "I'm so well acquainted with Captain Jack, it's a pity."

House languished in such company on Parchman Prison Farm for a year–give or take a few months—until some time in late 1929 or early 1930, when some of his relatives, probably with the assistance of the influential planter House mentioned to Fahey, prevailed on a Clarksdale judge to reconsider his case. The judge released House, but strongly advised him to leave Clarksdale and not come back. As House recalled, "I told him I could cover as much territory as a red fox if he turned me loose."[28] House walked to Jonestown, and from there caught a train to Lula, a backwater town about sixteen miles north of Clarksdale where, improbably enough, his musical destiny awaited him.

Lula

Lula, Mississippi was then a town of perhaps four or five hundred people—Son House said it was "nothin' but a little flagstop—wasn't nothin' to it." When House got off the train in Lula he was in need of money, and so he did what any blues musician would do in such circumstances. He set up at the railway station and began to play for tips. Unbeknownst to House, on

---

28. Calt and Wardlow, *King*, p. 210.

the fringe of the crowd another musician—Charley Patton—had caught sight of him and was listening to him. By a most auspicious coincidence—as far as House's fortunes were concerned—shortly before House was released from prison, some time in late 1929 or early 1930, Patton had made Lula his home—or perhaps his base of operations, would be more accurate—since Patton was as "ramblified" as Son House. The Dockery plantation was as much of a home as he had, but Patton moved around the Delta a good deal, leaving Dockery's sometimes to live near a girlfriend or sometimes because he had been temporarily banned from Dockery's for having caused a problem regarding someone's wife or girlfriend.

Patton, now thirty-nine—eleven years older than House—was born around 1891 near Edwards which is west of Jackson. His family moved to the Delta when he was a child—he is listed in the 1900 census as a resident of Dockery's plantation. He took up the guitar in his early teens, learning from two men, Earl Harris and Henry Sloan, about whom very little is known except that they were his mentors. By 1915 he was well known around the Delta, making his living solely from playing music at house parties, Delta juke joints, and barrelhouses—an income he supplemented by mooching off obliging women.[29] Patton had pioneered the style of blues that House had taken up, the style that would by and by come to be known as "Delta Blues." Of late, he had also become a national recording star.

The previous year, 1929, while House was keeping company with Captain Jack on Parchman Prison Farm, Patton was networking and furthering his musical career. Patton had contacted a general store owner in Jackson, H. C. Speir, who was a talent scout for record companies. Patton made a "test" record for Speir, and the result earned him a recording contract with one of the leading race labels, Paramount Records. His first recording session in June yielded some of Paramount's best sellers that year, among them "Pony Blues," which has been called "the most

---

29. A "juke joint" was a bar in which music was performed. They were usually located on the private land of plantations whose owners tolerated them to provide some form of entertainment for their labor force away from white residents to not bother them with noise and activity, and also so as not to be an open affront to the law. Mississippi was legally "dry" until 1966. A "barrelhouse" by way of contrast was "an all-purpose tavern, gambling den, dance hall, and often, brothel, located (if not in a city) near the railroad depot of a small town, or in a sawmill or levee camp. These white-owned enterprises probably arose in the late 1800s; because their main attraction was bonded liquor, they were decimated by Prohibition. There is no truth to the frequent dictionary supposition, perpetuated by jazz writers, that the term barrelhouse arose from the presence of whiskey barrels on the walls of such places. Rather, the term stems from the outmoded use of barrel to mean liquor, which survived into the 19th century and produced the term barrel fever (Partridge)." From Stephen Calt's *Barrelhouse Words: A Blues Dialect Dictionary*, (University of Illinois Press: Champagne-Urbana, 2010).

complicated and subtle dance blues ever devised."[30] Its opening verses would echo through the Mississippi Delta for decades:

> Hitch up my pony, saddle up my black mare (2X)
> Gonna find a rider, baby, in this world somewhere

On the heels of that success, in the fall, Paramount brought Patton back to the studio. That session produced another hit, "Highwater Everywhere," which memorialized the devastating 1927 flood of the Mississippi. The song is generally regarded as Patton's masterpiece, its frenetic guitar recreating in sound the chaos, devastation, and frantic attempts to escape the deluge:

> Levee broke, rose most everywhere
> The water at Greenville and Leland, Lord, it done rose everywhere
> (Spoken: Boy, you can't never stay here)
> I would go down to Rosedale but, they tell me there's water there

In between those recording sessions, Patton had been banished for the last time from Dockery's plantation for making off with one of the tenants' wives, Katie Williams—which event, he also promptly made the subject of a song, "34 Blues."[31] After the second recording session for Paramount Records in October, Patton skipped around between a plantation near Cleveland and the towns of Pace and Skene, also working for a while with a minstrel show. Then he moved north to Lula.

Lula was a place in which Patton had sojourned from time to time previously, and he seems to have moved there to be with a woman named Bertha Lee Jones. David "Honeyboy" Edwards said of her, "We called her 'Bert.' She was nice lookin,' too: he had every nice lookin' woman."[32] Bertha Lee worked as a cook for a white planter on a plantation between Lula and Dundee, and, in addition to her charming appearance, her job as cook in a planter's household seems to have endeared her to Patton. "That's the way he ate, out of the white folks' kitchen," House would recall years later.[33] A pattern, it should be noted, that House himself would adopt.

---

30. Stephen Calt, liner notes to "Charlie Patton: Founder of the Delta Blues," Yazoo 2010. The spelling "Charlie" is also used.

31. Although he would still visit the plantation from time to time, Calt and Wardlow, p. 188. The account of House's meeting Patton is based mostly on Calt and Wardlow's account, supplemented by the Fahey interview.

32. Calt and Wardlow, *King*, p. 208.

33. Ibid., p. 209.

For Patton's purposes, Lula was also strategically situated. It was sixteen miles north of Clarksdale, and only eight miles from the blues hub of Helena, Arkansas.[34] What is more, there were several nearby plantations with juke joints where Patton had performed in years past. Yet, as Patton's biographers Calt and Wardlow point out, the area despite its location was, in the context of the musically rich Delta, temporarily impoverished. As Patton's biographers Stephen Calt and Gayle Wardlow wrote: "The town's only previous blues guitarist of memory, a man named Rennis Glisson, had left Lula in shackles in 1917. 'He had a wife named Doug,' his one-time playing partner Willie Moore said, 'an' he cut her head off and they sent him to Parchman for life.'"[35]

Perhaps Son House had met Glisson while on Parchman Farm and learned from him of the Lula opening. In any event, his luck was about to change.

That day in early 1930 when House got off the train in the Lula depot, Patton observed him play, but did not approach him. Patton seems to have kept his distance for the moment, perhaps not wanting to contribute a tip—according to House, Patton was rather tight with his money. Patton was probably also being circumspect since another blues man could as easily end up a competitor as a collaborator. However, a woman named Sara Knights also heard House playing, and she invited him to play in front of her café. House liked this idea, especially when he learned that Knights was also a bootlegger. Knights no doubt wanted House to drum up customers for her whiskey business—House had already worked in a medicine show. Four score years before B.B. King would advertise a device on national television to measure blood sugar, blues singers were "doing ads." House's enthusiasm for his new connection with Sara Knights was still evident in his recollection more than three decades later. "I found out she wasn't married. Oh man, I was really happy."[36] House soon struck up a romance with Knights: "I was really in love with her: 'I'll play all night for you, honey.' She sold whiskey too, you know. And I made her like that."[37]

It was while House was performing at Sara Knights' establishment that Patton took notice of the crowd that he had attracted, and as House said, "He come over, and that's what got us teamed up."[38]

---

34. Although Helena was not a venue for Patton; his biographer Stephen Calt suggests that Patton's style may have been somewhat dated for Helena by 1930.
35. Calt and Wardlow, *King*, p. 210.
36. Fahey, "Interview."
37. Ibid.
38. Calt and Wardlow, *King*, p. 210.

Charley Patton, 1929.
Courtesy of Shanachie
Entertainment.

The two men quickly became friends. They shared a number of interests besides blues: if nothing else, corn liquor and women provided a solid basis for a friendship. That House learned quickly about Patton's ways with women can be seen in his own comment on his success with Knights, "Oh oh, here I go, catch up with Charley now!" Patton was then living with Bertha Lee on the other side of the railroad tracks from Knights and House, and House needled Patton, "Okay Charley, you ain't got nothing on me. My woman's got more than yours because she's got a café, a barber shop, and she sells whiskey too!'" House laughed, recalling years later, "He cussed me out."[39]

But Patton had in mind another venue where he wanted to play with House, an establishment operated by a woman known as "Big Sis."[40]

Big Sis was big. "She weighed about three something," House recalled. She operated a juke joint about three miles northwest of Lula near the river at place called Powell.[41] Soon enough, House and his new friend Patton were playing at Big Sis' also.

How much Patton and House actually played together in juke joints like Sara Knights' and Big Sis' in the Lula area is debatable. Some, like Calt and Wardlow, argue that House's 1930 recordings show that it was unlikely

39. Fahey, 1965.
40. Calt and Wardlow, *King*, 210.
41. Ibid., p. 212.

that House and Patton ever teamed up at a Lula juke joint.[42] It is true that in 1930 House was certainly not as versatile a guitar player as Patton. And among some writers there has been a tendency to downplay House's ability on the guitar, especially given the company he kept over the next decade— Charley Patton, Willie Brown, and Robert Johnson—but House was a powerful player within the context of his own music. What is more, relatively complex recorded pieces were not always an indication of the whole repertoire a musician played for audiences who mostly wanted to dance. And from other sources we know that Patton liked to spread out the work at juke joints with other musicians. House's own words on the topic are few, but do suggest that the two men did play together, even if only on occasion. In an interview with Bob West in 1968, when asked if he played often with Patton, House replied, "Well, not too often. We would play at the same places but not together too much."[43] Given their different capabilities, when they played together it was likely with the more musically experienced Patton accompanying or "comping" along on House's songs.

House and Patton certainly spent a lot of time together and together or individually—one man doing a set and then the other "spelling" him— they played juke joints on the nearby Jeffries and Kirby plantations for some months. The power of House's music undoubtedly impressed Patton. He had seen how House could draw a crowd at Sara Knights' place with his powerful voice and his energetic bottleneck style—a style quite distinct from Patton's bottleneck style. As Elijah Wald writes, House "...certainly admired Patton, and played some Patton pieces, but the slide style for which he is most famous, and which was what both Robert Johnson and Muddy Waters were most struck by in his playing, bears virtually no stamp of Patton's influence."[44] The differences in their styles made them complementary when they played in the same juke joints whose patrons were hearing a "double billing" of two of the greatest blues singers ever.

Doubtless, Patton also must have made an immediate impression on Son House—even if some of his guitar technique, particularly in standard tuning, was beyond House's reach at this point. House's new friend, in all other respects—as a composer, as a vocalist, and as a performer—was already one of the most accomplished blues musicians who ever lived, a man who had already left his mark in recordings and in popular memory.

42. Ibid., p. 211.
43. Bob West, *Blues & Rhythm*, No. 207, p. 5 (reprint of a 1968 interview).
44. Elijah Wald, *Escaping the Delta: Robert Johnson and the Invention of the Blues* (New York: Amistad, 2004), p. 158.

And in all of these other areas, House must have greatly benefited from the time spent together. Playing blues must have given House significant leisure time, since it enabled him, like Patton, to avoid the onerous and unprofitable labor of sharecropping. That was time he could employ to absorb musical lessons from Patton. But it may not have been all one way—both men would compose songs on the topic of the drought that afflicted the Delta, House's "Dry Spell Blues" and Patton's "Dry Well Blues," which must have been collaborative efforts.[45]

There were certainly differences in their temperaments. Patton, eleven years older than House, was a blithe character, though whiskey could make him argumentative and somewhat "forward" as House would recall years later.[46] House was in general more serious. But for all his reputation as a man haunted by demons, House clearly also had a humorous side to his personality, which would also come out in his performances and interviews years later. The most significant differences were not between their personalities, but between their attitudes toward their music. As House would say of Patton in the 1960s, "Charley, he'd try to make a record out of anything, you know, 'cause he'd love to clown…He'd name the record anything…you know, to get away with it."[47] House also was somewhat critical of the older songs in Patton's repertoire, "He'd take all them old foolish songs and things…some of them would sound allright…some of them had a meaning to them…some didn't. That's the way he played. He'd just say anything, the first thing he can think of…"[48]

When asked if he and Willie Brown ever tried to "correct" Patton's ways, House replied that they did, but Patton was unswayed by such criticism. House said, "Oh yeah, we often do that [i.e. talk to him about being unserious] and tell him too, say 'Charley, you oughta stop so much of that ol' foolish messin' around.' [then imitating Patton:] 'Oh Man, all I want to do is get paid for it. What's the difference?' I'd say, 'Yeah, but it just sounds so foolish and a lot of junk to it.' [Patton:]'What's the difference, man?' I'd say, 'OK, that's your little red wagon.'"[49]

By the time Son House met him, Patton had recorded about three dozen songs, and was, no doubt, fairly confident about his ability to improvise material as needed in the studio. He must have also realized after the success

45. Cf. the Rube Lacy titles mentioned above with similar ones composed by House.
46. A trait that proved a problem for the rather diminutive Patton who got his throat cut some time after this (and was possibly also shot in the leg).
47. Nick Perls, "Son House Interview. Part One," *78 Quarterly*, Vol. 1, 1967, p. 60.
48. Ibid.
49. Ibid., pp. 60–61.

of his first session in June that the record producers had confidence in his material and—given the difficulties of picking "hits"—were unlikely to reject anything outright. This probably also emboldened him to improvise.

House's remarks nevertheless provide evidence of his own attitude toward the music he made. For House, the blues was not "foolishness and a lot of junk to it." His blues drew upon and gave expression to certain profound conflicts that simmered in the darker recesses of his mind. That was one of the reasons for him taking up music. It is also likely that House's extensive experience as a preacher influenced his conception of what constituted good blues. His comments on the topic—and especially his criticisms of Patton in this respect—make it clear that House thought that, just as a good sermon ought to have a central theme, a blues song should have thematic coherence. And House's compositions—even with allowances for "floating verses"—do possess more coherence in this respect than many blues songs.

Son House found in Lula in 1930 a kind of liberation—and not only on account of his recent release from prison—but a psychological one also. He found it in the crowds in the juke joints on the Jeffries and Kirby plantations, he found it in the recognition accorded him by Charley Patton, and he found it in the music he was making with growing confidence. It is also seen in the fact that, whatever the uncertainties and gaps in the period of Son House's life after 1927, they are nothing compared with those in the period before 1927. And surely there is a comic irony in this, that everything in his life prior to the year 1927 is seen through a glass darkly; that, while in the clutches of the church and clean living (relatively), the details and chronology of his life are almost hopelessly muddled, and it is only when he embraces a musical abomination called the blues—and its close companions whiskey and women—that all the anomalies and inconsistencies begin to blend into something more like a coherent narrative.

By the time he settled in the Lula area, the impasse in which Son House had found himself in 1927 had—somehow—been transcended. Which is not to say that the demons that dwelt in the shadows in his mind were now exorcised. Clearly they were not. But they were now at least given a means of expression and were thus transformed in some way—by means of a sort of musical alchemy. House had lost religion. Now he "got" art. The strange sound of the bottleneck guitar that captivated him was the sound of a door opening—but it was also the sound of a door that was closing behind him. A certain accommodation with life was never going to be open to him again.

CHAPTER 4

My Black Mama

SON HOUSE'S PARAMOUNT SESSION AT GRAFTON, 1930

Some time in the late spring of 1930, the southbound train stopped in the depot in Lula, Mississippi, and a rather unlikely visitor stepped onto the platform, one Arthur Laibley. Laibley wore a suit and tie, and he looked exactly like what he was—a thirty-six year old, prosperous, white businessman from the Midwest who was beginning to go bald. Given Laibley's appearance, what happened next was even more unlikely. A small black man, whose wavy, reddish hair nevertheless gave away his mixed parentage, crossed the street and greeted him. And from the way he greeted him, it was clear that Laibley, the respectable white man, knew the raffish black man, one Charley Patton.

Since 1925, when he succeeded Maurice Supper, Laibley had been the recording director for Paramount Records. Paramount—unrelated to the contemporary entertainment giant—was a subsidiary of the Wisconsin Chair Company. It was Laibley's predecessor, Supper, who had gotten Paramount into the race record market in 1922 in order to save the label from bankruptcy, and now it fell to Laibley to deal with riffraff musicians like Patton.

Laibley was on his way to Texas, and his visit to Lula would only last a few minutes. He traveled to Texas frequently following the great success of Blind Lemon Jefferson in 1926, hoping to find other talent. With the death of Jefferson the previous December, Laibley no doubt felt it even more urgent to find someone to replace his deceased Texas star.[1] H. C. Speir's

---

1. Alex van der Tuuk, *Paramount's Rise and Fall: A History of the Wisconsin Chair Company and its Recording Activities*, (Denver: Mainspring Press, 2003), p. 166. H.C. Speir speaks of the pressure on Laibley to produce "hits."

most recent finds for Paramount, Blind Joe Reynolds, Ishmon Bracey, and Tommy Johnson, had not sold well.[2] In the two weeks Johnson had spent in Grafton, he was mostly drunk and only able to record about a half dozen songs—about eighteen minutes of music, and none of them turned out to be hits.[3] By the end of the year, Patton was the label's only big seller.

When his talent scout in Mississippi, H. C. Speir, was unable to travel to Lula to contact Patton, Laibley got a message to Patton to let him know he would stop in Mississippi while on his way to Texas to arrange another recording session for Patton.[4]

After the impressive sales of Patton's initial hit, "Pony Blues," recorded in June of 1929, Laibley had Patton back in the studio in October for what was then a huge session. Patton cut twenty-four tracks, among them yet another big hit, "Highwater Everywhere." Due to these successes—and Jefferson's demise—Laibley and Paramount had apparently given Patton carte blanche. And now Patton's good fortune was House's good fortune as well.

In all its fundamentals, the record business changed little from its inception until recent years—until the advent of the Internet. Then, as now, anyone with enough money could book studio time and make a recording. However, pressing copies and, much more importantly, promoting and distributing said copies were the preserve of the record companies.[5] Yet, despite their dominance of the market in those ways, record companies had found no way to predict what the market might buy. Record company executives like Laibley had already learned what would continue to be the case in the industry up to the present: hits were rare and unpredictable accidents. The mass of recordings were flops. This was a fundamental reality of the music business—and this was not due to the ignorance of Laibley and other music business executives about the music they were trying to sell. In fact, Laibley frankly admitted he had no idea what made a hit record. As H. C. Speir, his Mississippi talent scout put it, "They always figure they got one hit out of ten. They'd take that much to pay off."[6] And according to Speir, the

2. Tommy Johnson had previously recorded for Victor. He recorded for Paramount probably in December of 1929.

3. Calt and Wardlow, *King*, p. 214. Compare Patton's productiveness in his first recording session when he recorded 14 sides in three different tunings in *one* day.

4. Ibid, p. 212–13.

5. Only recently has the Internet threatened the record companies' dominance. Pressing is unnecessary, and promotion and distribution are almost free.

6. David Evans, "An Interview with H. C. Speir," *JEMF Quarterly* 27 (Autumn 1972) cited in van der Tuuk, *Paramount's Rise and Fall*, p. 166.

pressure on Laibley to produce hits under unpredictable conditions was also the reason why Laibley was constantly searching for new talent. You cast your seeds widely hoping that a few would sprout.

Son House, who had accompanied Patton to the depot, observed Laibley's short conversation with Patton from across the street. House saw Laibley hand something to Patton, then climb back on the train and depart. Then House recalled: "After he left, Charlie come on 'cross there [i.e., the main street of the town] and told me what he said." This news involved another recording session for Patton, House learned. "...Charlie told him about me...so he told Charlie that he wanted me to come with him. I said: 'What?' He say: 'Yeah, he want you to come with me.' I say; 'Yeah, sho' I go, man.'"[7] House also learned that Laibley had given Patton $100 to cover the costs of the trip, a sizeable sum of money at the time.

The precise dates of the Grafton sessions are uncertain. According to Stephen Calt and Gayle Wardlow, House and the other musicians likely left Mississippi five or six days after Laibley stopped in Lula. If they drove straight through, they might have arrived about a week after Laibley's brief Lula visit. This would have been time enough for Laibley to go to Texas and return to Grafton—especially if he conducted his business in Texas with the same alacrity that he did in Mississippi. In any case, some allowance for Laibley's trip and return must be factored in since he was in Grafton when the musicians arrived. House stated, "So it was about three days after then 'fore we lit out on our way to Grafton"—three days after the Laibley whistle stop, he meant.[8] Other writers place it months later, possibly in August, which makes sense given that two songs House and Patton recorded were about the severe drought that did not really make itself felt in the Delta until mid-summer.[9]

Whether they made the trip in late spring or summer, a day or two prior to leaving for Grafton, Patton went up to the Frank Harbart plantation near Robinsonville to gather another musician whom he had known for about fifteen years. When Patton returned to Lula he had in tow a small and

7. Calt and Wardlow, *King*, pp. 212–13.

8. Perls, "Son House Interview," p. 61.

9. Calt and Wardlow, *King*, p. 215. But see also Edward Komara's discussion of the question of the date in "Blues in the Round," *Black Music Review Journal*, 1997, p. 8, notes 8 and 9. House would also make a statement to Al Wilson that suggested an August date. But as we have seen, House's recollections often produced such contradictions. If August, then Laibley's trip must be moved as well, since it seems inconceivable he would have given Patton $100 three months in advance of the session. But whether they left Lula in late spring or August, House probably underestimated the number of days that passed between Laibley's Lula visit and the musicians' departure.

somewhat stout man thirty years of age, a black whose reddish-tinged hair and freckles suggested he, like Patton, also had a not-too-distant white ancestor. Patton introduced the man to House as Willie Brown, and then as House recalled, "We set up all night, drinking and practicing, you know; playing together."[10]

Willie Brown is now known mostly for the lyric in Robert Johnson's "Cross Road Blues" that mentions him, "You can run, you can run, tell my friend poor Willie Brown. I'm standing at the crossroads, I believe I'm sinking down." But years before Johnson would make his acquaintance, Brown had already established himself as an accomplished Delta guitar player. Brown was born in 1900 near Cleveland, Mississippi. He had learned to play guitar from Patton while he was in his teens living close to Dockery's plantation. At sixteen, he had moved north to the Tunica-Robinsonville area where his usual musical partner had been a musician-gambler named Willie Moore, who said they shared vocal duties. Later, Memphis Minnie played with him and Moore, and Moore recalled that the trio often played for white audiences, whom Brown serenaded with pop hits like "You Great Big Beautiful Doll" and "Let Me Call You Sweetheart."[11] But Brown appears to have preferred to accompany, or "second" in the local blues vernacular. Brown was only two years older than House, and that night in Lula when the three men played and drank together marked the beginning of the longest and closest friendship of House's life. From that night until 1943 when House left Mississippi for Rochester, New York, the two would be inseparable friends and musical companions, performing in juke joints in the north Delta where they dominated the local musical scene.

Patton contacted a singer in a local gospel quartet named Wheeler Ford. It must have been some indication of Patton's status as a celebrity that the stern moral code of a singer in a local gospel quartet would be flexible enough to allow Ford to befriend a hard-drinking bluesman. In fact, Ford, the lead singer in the Delta Big Four had been one of Patton's recent "finds"—and flops. Earlier that spring, Patton had gotten the group an audition with Paramount. They had made their "test" and duly flunked. What vocal ability Ford possessed is uncertain. What *is* certain is that he possessed a Buick. With the front money Laibley had given him, Patton now paid the sanctified teetotaler to be the group's "designated driver." The morning after their all-night practice session, the three men loaded their Stella guitars in Ford's Buick, and they left for Grafton.

10. Calt and Wardlow, *King*, p. 215.
11. Ibid., p. 158.

North of Robinsonville, they visited the Joe Kirby plantation, a place Patton had memorialized in song in his October session. There they picked up one of Patton's girlfriends, a young woman named Louise Johnson, who sang and played piano in a barrelhouse operated by a Liny Armstrong. Brown, who lived on the nearby Harbart plantation, probably had heard her playing and introduced her to Patton, who soon found time for her away from Bertha Lee. House remembered her as being "nice-lookin'... 'bout twenty-three, twenty-four years old." And like her boyfriend Patton, she "didn't do nothin' but drink and play music; she didn't work for nobody..."[12]

Somewhere north of Memphis, the foursome made Ford stop while they bought bootleg whiskey for the long drive to Grafton. The whiskey ensured that the trip would be anything but boring. In Cairo, Illinois, they stopped at a music shop where both House and Patton bought new Stella guitars for twelve dollars apiece.

With the whiskey drinking, things inevitably grew rather boisterous, and after the Cairo stop Patton and Brown began to argue. Although the two men had a long acquaintance of about fifteen years, they had an often contentious relationship. As House put it, "[T]hey couldn't set horses."[13] They squabbled so frequently that House said he could not remember the subject of this one battle. Wheeler Ford had his Buick doing about sixty miles per hour, yet Patton grew so angry that he opened the door to get out. Fortunately for musical history, House blocked his way.[14] Patton then ordered Ford to stop the car so that he and Brown could settle the matter with a fistfight. In House's words, "Willie jumped out first ahead of Charley, and then Charley jumped out with his new guitar." Patton ran after Brown, but stumbled—they had all been drinking since Memphis—and he fell. On his brand new Stella. "He fell right flat on it beside the road," House said. "Just as flat as a patty cake right along side the road. He didn't even get to play one piece on it. And man, he cussed and he swore!"[15]

Patton's mood was in no way improved by having wrecked his new guitar, and soon enough he got into an argument with Johnson. When he slapped her, she had had enough. She climbed into the backseat with House. Then in House words, "That's when it went to happen. Charley,

12. Ibid., p. 216.
13. Interview with Bob West, *Blues & Rhythm*, issue 207, p. 5 (reprint of a 1968 interview).
14. Fahey, "Interview."
15. Ibid.

he's mad. He's sitting in the front. Right along...I commenced to lean-ing over talking trash to her. I say, 'I really kind like you, gal.' And we take another big swallow. So when we got to Grafton, Charley didn't know that I had done made her, see."[16]

There was no African-American population in Grafton, and Paramount's black musicians were, according to most accounts, brought in and out quietly, so as to avoid antagonizing the local citizenry, many of who had recently arrived from Germany and had never seen a black person in their lives. To be sure, some of the blues musicians even appalled some of Paramount's black employees. Aletha Dickerson, who worked as a secre-tary for the record producer Mayo Williams, remembered Blind Lemon Jefferson "with a shudder of disgust."[17] House and his friends, marinated in whiskey since leaving Memphis, could hardly have made a better impression on anyone, white or black. To minimize such uncomfortable encounters, Paramount's black musicians were often boarded in nearby Milwaukee where there existed a small black community. However, when House and his friends arrived in Grafton, they were put up in a local boarding house owned by the Wisconsin Chair Company that was imme-diately next to the recording studio. While recording, their rooms, meals, cigarettes, and drinks were all paid for by Paramount.

In Grafton, House's new romance with Louise Johnson continued to develop apace. When they reached the boarding house, while House was unloading his luggage, an employee handed out three sets of room keys: one to Patton, one to Brown, and one to Louise Johnson. When House asked where to find the man to get his key, Johnson said, "Say, I got *our* key." And House replied, "Oh! Scuse me, honey!"[18]

While he accepted this sleeping arrangement, House was understand-ably worried about how Patton would react. As he recalled years later, his thought was, "Oh brother! It's my old pal's used-to-be woman."[19] This plot twist might have threatened the whole session had Patton played according to the usual script. But he did not. The next morning, he approached House, and the latter, assuming Patton wanted to fight, said, "Now Charlie—what you want I ain't for it right now; I ain't ready for that kinda stuff."

Patton replied, "Oh come here, nigger! I ain't thinkin' about that little old 'tight-haired' woman!"

16. Calt and Wardlow, *King.* pp. 216–17.
17. Samuel Charters, *The Country Blues* revised ed. (New York: Rinehart, 1975), p. 64.
18. Calt and Wardlow, *King*, p. 217.
19. Ibid., p. 217.

House said, "Oh, well ain'tcha? Now listen, Charlie...I don't like it; you'll have to excuse me, look over [i.e., overlook] me for that."

Patton was surprised: "Listen—*listen*, fella! I didn't want her in the *first* place! Now you keep her now and I'll treat you as good as I ever is! Go on and just act like there ain't nothin' happenin.'"[20]

The ease with which Patton passed off a mistress is remarkable, given that he could be very argumentative. Patton was nothing if not mercurial. With romantic realignments settled, recording could begin.

Laibley and H. C. Speir jointly produced all the sessions in a building usually described as a "barn," which was connected by an elevated walkway to the plant where the records were manufactured.[21] Dampness made the acoustics of the studio—a matter that is still far from a precise science now—a problem. Speir complained about the "old rock building," and apparently, some renovations were made between takes during the session in an attempt to improve the acoustics.[22]

By 1930, "state-of-the art" recording equipment was used in the Grafton studio: parabolic microphones, an amplifier, and loudspeaker. All recording was "live." If the musician made an error, he had to do another take. A ten-inch 78-rpm record could hold about three minutes of music, and when ten seconds were left, a light went on to warn the performer that he needed to finish the take. The recording was etched on a ten- or twelve-inch wax disc called the "matrix," which would be plated with metal to make a master for pressing copies. Usually two takes were done. The primary reason was to create a back-up in case the matrix broke. The process of plating the matrix to make a "test" pressing took a few days. A second take also enabled the performer—especially if he or she was a solo performer—to vary the tempo of the song, a factor that might decide which version was released for commercial sales.[23] Finally, when the test pressings were ready, the record company executives listened to them to decide if the record should be released and which version should be used.[24]

---

20. Ibid., p. 217. The entire dialogue is taken from Calt and Wardlow's account. "Tight-haired" probably in the sense of tightly curled 'nappy' hair.

21. Van der Tuuk, *Paramount's Rise and Fall*, p. 150.

22. Calt and Wardlow, *King*, p. 219. Humidity was a particular problem for early microphones. See also Komara, "Blues in the Round," p.10, note 13, on pitch irregularities in Johnson's recordings for which there could have been several causes.

23. The tempo variations between alternate takes are particularly noticeable on some of Robert Johnson's recordings, for example.

24. Twelve-inch 78s were less durable than the 10-inch records, and were less frequently used for blues.

House described the microphone as resembling a "watermelon"—the microphone had a shell around it to improve its reception—and he stated that two were used, one near the performer's mouth and one near his instrument.

Other than recording two takes, there was no crafting of the song. As House put it succinctly: "It worked just like traffic lights. Red light and a green light. And when the green light he'd put it on, it would pop on, you'd start. If he didn't like it, he'd switch that one off and push the red one on."[25]

Prohibition notwithstanding, Paramount made accommodations for the musicians' taste for whiskey. The studio paid a young woman who worked as a waitress in the hotel next door where the musicians were lodged to ferry drinks to the studio. As House recalled, the whiskey was used as an incentive to expedite the recording process: "Anytime that you end a piece, when you end it she's right there with cups about that high. With your whiskey—that old, real good dark whiskey, smell good, taste good, and make you so high you rock like a rockin' chair. She'd be standing right there, waiting for you to come and get it. And the other guy want to hurry up and get to play his piece so he can get his."[26] The result according to House was predictable: "All of us would be high as a Georgia pine." Laibley himself would sometimes have white hillbilly musicians, who after all also hailed from areas where stills were common, bring him "mountain dew" when they came to Grafton.[27]

The first musician to record was Louise Johnson. She laid down two takes of two songs, "All Night Long Blues" and "Long Ways From Home Blues."

It was unusual to have others present in the studio during recording, but House, Brown, and Patton were there when Johnson recorded. "All Night Long" was a raunchy song whose lyrics Johnson cleaned up somewhat for recording.[28] House claimed the men were allowed to be in the studio to encourage her and help calm her jitters.[29] The three men can be heard shouting comments in the background of the recording, and if we close our eyes we can imagine what live blues probably sounded like in a 1930s juke joint. As House remembered it, "We'd all be in the same room. While one was sitting in front of the mike the other one was sittin' over

25. Fahey, "Interview."

26. Ibid.

27. Van der Tuuk, *Paramount's Rise and Fall*, p. 116.

28. See Palmer, *Deep Blues*, p. 81 and p. 83.

29. Calt and Wardlow, *King*, p. 217. Calt and Wardlow dispute this and contend the men's behavior belied a "basic lack of regard" and a "cavalierness."

there...lookin' at him and listenin'..."[30] Shortly after Johnson finished her numbers, House took his place at the microphones to record matrix L-408, "My Black Mama."[31]

Son House's Grafton sides

House recorded "My Black Mama" in two parts that made up the A and B side of a single 78. This song was one of the two pieces that House had learned from James McCoy. The song is—roughly—a twelve-bar blues played in an open G tuning favored by Delta bottleneck players. However, House's lyrics do not fit the conventional metrical pattern of a twelve-bar blues. The standard vocal pattern for twelve-bar blues divides the song into three four bar sections with an A – A – B stanza arrangement (the lyrics usually taking up ten beats of each sixteen beat section). However, when House goes to the subdominant (or more familiarly, the 4 chord), he stretches out the A line with one beat pauses that he emphasizes by snapping the bass string against the fingerboard—a percussive technique that both Patton and Brown also favored. The result shifts what would normally be the second half of the second A stanza into the place of the B stanza, where he again pauses between words and snaps his bass string against the finger-board so as to elongate the line again, thus creating a twelve-bar blues with an A – A stanza structure. Edward Komara has suggested that this feature may point to a work song as the song's origin.[32]

House's powerful performance juxtaposes rapid-fire treble notes played with his bottleneck on the top two strings with bass notes. House had by this point mastered the essential elements of bottleneck guitar, though his approach distinguishes itself immediately from that of Patton. Where Patton's instrumental fills usually echo the melody, House's guitar fills are melodically separate entities. The song's rhythm is driving and propulsive—the piece surges ahead as though leaning forward in such a way that it threatens to topple over. One is tempted to say that the first time House sat down in front of a microphone, he created a piece whose stark

30. Ibid., p. 219.

31. Komara, "Blues in the Round," pp. 9–10, states that what happened after Johnson did her four takes is uncertain because there are gaps in the next eight matrix numbers, L-400 – L-407, except for L-403 and L-404 that are performances by the Broadway Military Band. Komara speculates that there was perhaps a break for some sort of repairs, and before the blues men returned to the studio a marching band was recorded in the interim.

32. Edward Komara, *The Road to Robert Johnson* (Milwaukee: Hal Leonard 2007), p. 25.

juxtaposition of treble and bass perfectly expressed the pattern that characterized his life: the rapid transit from one extreme to another.

House's vocals are even more impressive. Under the pressure of the moment, it seems as if all the bitter disappointments of his twenty-eight years, all the painful failures, frustrations and resentments of his life up to that point gather into a powerful storm that bursts forth in the first words he sings, the angry question, "Black mama, what's the matter with you?" His voice is immediately gripping, fierce, and full of rage:

> Well, black mama, what's the matter with you today?
> Ain't satisfaction (satisfactory?), don't care what I do (2x)[33]
> You take a brown-skin woman will make a rabbit move to town
> Say, but a jet-black woman'll make a mule kick his stable down
> Say, ain't no heaven, say, there ain't no burnin' hell
> Say, where I'm going when I die, can't nobody tell
> Well, my black mama's face shine like the sun
> Oh, lipstick and powder sure won't help her none

House's bitterness and anger speak most clearly in his enunciation of the word "satisfaction." The stress on the third syllable is so strong it seems as though he means to snap the word in two. The lyrics combine "floating verses" such as the "brown-skin woman" verse with House's own creations. They cohere not because they all concern a single subject, but because they all express the same mood of anger and bitterness. In light of House's on-again off-again career as a preacher, the third stanzas are particularly striking in their uncompromising rejection of a fundamental tenet of the religion he had preached.

With slight variations, the lyrics of Part 2 express the same mood. The most expressive of these develop the so-called "death letter" theme. Blues lyrics about receiving a letter that informs the singer of the death or impending death of a loved one had been floating around since at least 1924 when Ida Cox recorded "Death Letter Blues" and probably even before that. Between the Cox version and House's Grafton track there were at least four other versions which also made use of lyrics on the theme: Papa Harvey Hull's "Hey Lawdy Mama—The France Blues," 1927; John D. Fox's "The Moanin' Blues," 1927; Lottie Kimbrough's "Wayward

---

33. As the first two verses are repeated, so too the verses that follow are repeated in the same way.

Girl Blues," 1928; and Romeo Nelson's "Dyin' Rider Blues," 1929.[34] Their popularity testifies to the emotional force they carried for the blues audience. Cox, in particular, mined the theme again and again, following up over the next few years with "Coffin Blues," "Bone Orchard Blues" and "Marble Stone Blues." Lottie Kimbrough's version in "Wayward Girl Blues" substituted the singer's mother for the lover:

> I received a letter, what d'you suppose it read? (2x)
> It said come home your poor old mother's dead

Her lyric is almost identical with the line in House's version. But House's lyrics are closer yet to Harvey Hull's version. House's lyrics begin with a different verse, then take up the "death letter" theme in the second verse, but not with a mother but a lover as the deceased:

> Oh, I solemnly swear, Lord, I raise my right hand (2x)
> That I'm gonna get me another woman, you get you another man
> I got a letter this mornin', how do you reckon it read? (2x)
> Oh, "hurry, hurry—the gal you love is dead"
> I grabbed my suitcase, I took her up the road (2x)
> When I got there, she was layin' on the coolin' board
> Well, I walked the floor 'til I looked down in her face (2x)
> It's a good ol' gal got to lay there 'til Judgment Day

House, as has been noted, would often take other blues singers to task—especially young, white musicians in the 1960s—for stringing together some "floating" lyrics and calling the result a "blues." He was insistent on the point of coherence. But mention of "Judgment Day" in a song that has rejected the existence of the afterlife poses the question of whether his composition met his own standard. To answer that, one must consider what is meant by "coherence" in blues.

It is sometimes said that blues songs tell stories, but this is misleading. In fact, blues contain little narrative per se, a difference that is seen at once when blues are compared to ballads. The point of view of the ballad is third person. In blues, it is invariably first person. And this is not unrelated to the shift away from narrative. A blues song does not really tell the story of how I left Willie Mae, or how I was banished from Dockery Plantation, or how I came to kill Leroy Lee and do time on a Mississippi prison farm, rather, it

34. Komara, "Blues in the Round," p. 10, notes 14–18 contain discographical details.

conveys my thoughts and feelings about those events. The events themselves are alluded to rather than narrated, and blues songs about those events comment instead on the significance of those events from the standpoint of the blues singer—the importance of the shift in the point of view to the first person shows this. If one considers the homily in preaching, the similarity is marked. The preacher does not relate the story of the Israelites' exodus from Egypt, rather he comments on the significance of that story for the gathered worshippers who already know it in its essentials. In other words, a blues song is a secular homily—commentary on a scripture of mundane stories already known to its audience because they have all lived them: love and loss, fleeting pleasures, being broke, moving on.

Coherence, then, is not a matter of narrative coherence, but of thematic coherence. And "My Black Mama"—and, as we shall see, "Preachin' the Blues" too—holds together. What holds it together is the prevailing mood of anger and frustration.

House addressed the theme of religion that surfaced in two verses of "My Black Mama" head on in his next song.

"Preachin' the Blues," like "My Black Mama," was recorded in two parts—masters L-410-1 and L411-1. The verses follow the conventional A – A – B pattern of a twelve-bar blues, but musically it is even more irregular than "My Black Mama" due to House's occasional insertion of additional bars between the A verses—flourishes born of his emotional intensity. More so than even in "My Black Mama," House's emotion seems to overflow the capacity of the song. The treble notes scream, while the bass notes are snapped off like strokes of a butcher knife; the furious energy of House's slide playing on "Preachin'" makes comments about the limits of his guitar technique irrelevant. Again anger is the dominant mood, but now it is mixed with sarcasm and humor, as is seen in the opening verse, a withering indictment of a preacher—and perhaps of House himself:

Oh, I'm gonna get me religion, I'm gonna join the Baptist church (2x)
I'm gonna be a Baptist preacher, and I sure won't have to work

The second verse yielded the title of the song:

Oh, I'm gonna preach these blues now, and I want everybody to shout (2x)
I'm gonna do like a prisoner, I'm gonna roll my time on out[35]

---

35. Another verse, "I wish I had me an heaven of my own, I'd give all you women a happy home" is nearly the same as one in Henry Thomas's "Texas Worried Life Blues."

The verse describes the turning point of his life—embracing the blues—as a conversion and as a form of liberation, as is evident in the allusion to prison. Taking up the blues seemed to have released House from a different sort of prison. The meaning of the phrase "roll my time on out" seems to be to pass one's time as easily and with as little trouble as possible. His most important experiences between 1927 and his arrival in 1930 in Lula are condensed in the verses.

If the song's first two verses tell us *what* House did, the next two tell us *why* he did it:

Oh, in my room, I bowed down to pray (2x)
Say the blues come along and drove my spirit away
Oh, I had religion, Lord, this very day (2x)
But the womens and whiskey, well they would not let me pray

These two verses became House's most famous lyrics. Indeed, rarely are the events in his life mentioned without the latter verse being quoted for the way it captures the pathos of his life.

The song is a remarkable portrait of House's psyche. In it, two attitudes are at war: on the one hand a rejection of organized religion, as in the caustic opening verse; on the other, a painful sense of losing the comfort of religion spoken of in the third verse. The only possibility of reconciliation seems to be to make blues somehow fill the emptiness left by the loss of religion:

Oh, I got to stay on the job, I ain't got no time to lose (2x)
I swear to God I got to preach these gospel blues
Oh, I'm gonna preach these blues and choose my seat and sit down (2x)
When the spirit comes, sisters, I want you to jump straight up and down

There is no way to reconcile the scorn expressed in the song with House's repeated professions of faith. His repeated professions of faith may have been directed mostly at some hardened, impenitent infidel in himself. Whatever the truth of the matter is, it is certainly true that it was only after House became a bluesman that his ambivalent attitude about religion would become for him a full blown conflict whose tension and violence would fuel his drinking—but also raise his musical performances to the level of powerful art.

With these two songs cut in wax, House had recorded his masterpieces. So completely did House stamp his personality on these two songs that not even Robert Johnson's restyled recordings of them, as fine as they are, would replace House's definitive versions. Fittingly, he took a break.

Willie Brown and Louise Johnson recorded next. Brown cut "M&O Blues" and "Future Blues." The songs are based, respectively, on Patton's "Pony Blues" and "Maggie" and show Patton's enduring influence on Brown, which, by and by, would be another channel for his influence on House. Johnson followed with "On the Wall" and "By The Moon And Stars." Then, House recorded again.

"Dry Spell Blues" was again divided into two parts. The first part required four takes, the second two—as Edward Komara says, it was rhythmically "tricky."[36] Its subject was the drought then gripping the middle of the country, and House's tone is quite different from his first two songs. It is sad and pleading. Later in the session Charley Patton recorded a song on the same theme, "Dry Well Blues." Patton's song has a wistful quality, where House's song sounds more desperate. Patton's depiction of the drought is localized—four verses mention Lula—House's lyrics on the other hand are more universal. Patton rues the day, "'Fore I would come to know the day, oh, the Lula well was gone dry." House's vision is apocalyptic:

> It's this dry old spell, everywhere I've been (2x)
> I believe to my soul, this old world is about to end

In Part 2 House, a Job in the Mississippi Delta, sings:

> Oh, Lord, have mercy if you please (2x)
> Make your rain come down, and give our poor hearts ease

Patton recorded three other songs in the session in duets with Brown, "Moon Going Down," "Bird Nest Bound," and "Some Summer Day." Both Willie Brown and Louise Johnson recorded two more songs apiece. Johnson's "On The Wall" and "By The Moon And Stars" were subsequently released by Paramount, as were Brown's "Kickin' In My Sleep Blues" and "Window Blues," but no copy of them has ever been found.

House cut three more songs: "Clarksdale Moan," "Mississippi County Farm Blues," and "Walking Blues."

"Clarksdale Moan" and "Mississippi County Farm Blues," were released as Paramount 13096, but a copy was only found, amazingly enough, seventy-five

---

36. Komara, "Blues in the Round," p. 12. As he notes, Charters relates its "hesitation" to the 'rests' or pauses built into work songs.

years later. Each song in its own way fills out our earliest picture of House as a musician. The former is based on Patton's "Pony Blues" and pays homage to House's hometown with lines like "Clarksdale, Mississippi always going to be my home," and "Nobody knows Clarksdale like I do…" Presumably, House had picked up some of "Pony Blues," one of Patton's basic song templates, while hanging around with him in Lula. He may even have composed some lyrics to fit that song. But it seems likely some of it was improvised in Grafton with House playing what he knew of "Pony Blues," since, after twenty-four bars, he changes the basic "Pony Blues" accompaniment and rhythmically "breaks stride."

The musical ancestry of "Mississippi County Farm Blues" was known years before the record itself was found, because House recorded another version of it for Alan Lomax in 1942 with the simple title of "County Farm Blues." The song is a sixteen-bar blues based on Blind Lemon Jefferson's song "See That My Grave Is Kept Clean." Jefferson's song had been one of those happy "accidents" that kept the record industry profitable, a B-side that became a big seller in 1928. Unfortunately for Paramount (and for Jefferson), he died in December of 1929.[37] According to House, Laibley had asked the musicians if anyone could do a version of the song. Patton and Brown passed. It says something of House's eagerness to exploit the Paramount opportunity that he withdrew to his room where he worked all night with Louise Johnson as a sounding board until he had pulled together a version of it. House's version is played with a bottleneck (Jefferson's is not played with a bottleneck); thirty-two of the bars have only moaning or lyrics of "Lord, lordy lord" etc.,—the 1942 version would add lyrics and show the development of the song over a decade. The song clearly draws on House's conviction and prison sentence—it speaks of killing a man. It was no mean feat for House to compose the song on the spot, and that feat speaks of his rapid development as a musician since 1927—especially when allowing time out for prison.

That House recorded an odd number of songs is itself odd. House himself emphasized that it was important to have an even number of songs when recording since records, after all, always have two sides. "Walking Blues" was apparently done as a "test."

House recorded "Walking Blues" with Willie Brown accompanying him on second guitar, the only time he was accompanied at the session. The song was another House original. It was never released by Paramount and was

---

37. In Chicago under mysterious circumstances.

only found in 1989 on a "test disc." The lyrics are not as personal as "Preachin' the Blues" or "My Black Mama," yet, "Walking Blues" is an equally important part of House's musical legacy. The song became a staple in his live repertoire throughout the 1930s. Indeed, he would record it again for Alan Lomax in 1941. And due to those live performances, the song was heard and learned by Robert Johnson and Muddy Waters. Due to the popularity of their versions, the song became the most covered piece among House's recordings. The song begins with the memorable image of the singer groping in the dark for his shoes:

> I woke up this morning' feelin' 'round for my shoes (2x)
> You oughta know by that, peoples, I must've got the walkin' blues

Another verse personified the blues—something he had already done in "Preachin' the Blues":

> Good morning, blues, blues, how do you do? (2x)
> Yes, if I could, mama, just have a few words with you

Robert Johnson seemed to have been particularly struck by that metaphor and would carry the metaphor even further.

Patton cut the last song at the session with Willie Brown accompanying him, the wistful "Bird Nest Bound." The third verse of the song would prove to be prophetic since the full force of the Depression was yet to be felt:

> Hard luck is at your front door, blues is in your room (2x)
> Trouble's at your back door, what is gonna become of you?

House seems to have been paid forty or fifty dollars per side.[38] Copyrights and royalties were probably not discussed. Musicians generally preferred cash in hand, and Laibley, according to Speir, had learned quickly of the profits that might accrue from copyrights and often copyrighted the songs in his own name—as Speir put it, "Art Laibley was pretty good at that..."[39] House likely made more than three hundred dollars for his

---

38. He told Julius Lester in 1965 that he was paid forty dollars for the session, Lester, "My Own Songs," p. 41. But House told Alan Lomax he was paid thirty dollars per record, John Cowley, "Son House: 1902–1988 an Historical Appreciation," *Blues and Rhythm*, no. 41 (Dec. 1988) p. 8. House may simply have misunderstood Lester's question.

39. Van der Tuuk, *Paramount's Rise and Fall*, p. 128.

work, a sizeable sum indeed and equal to two or three years of income from sharecropping.

Aftermath

The session over, the musicians put their suitcases and guitars in Ford's Buick and drove back to Mississippi. The return trip south was apparently rather more sedate than the trip north, and yielded no romantic escapades, roadside fistfights, or broken guitars.

Back in Mississippi, the foursome played in a barrelhouse on the Kirby plantation near Lula for a brief time, then went their separate ways. House saw Louise Johnson only once after 1930.[40] He thought she had moved to Helena, Arkansas. Another report had her playing in the 1930s on the King and Anderson plantation near Clarksdale. Then she vanished from view. Charley Patton, along with his regular girlfriend at the time, Bertha Lee, moved north to Robinsonville where he stayed for about two months—characteristically, it seems the attraction to that new location was another man's wife. According to House, Patton had taken an interest in the wife of a farmer named Richard Baker. Soon, however, Patton and Bertha Lee moved back down south to Holly Ridge, a hamlet some twenty miles east of Greenville.

In the marketplace—as in music and life—timing is crucial. And despite the blues masterpieces Son House cut in wax at Grafton, his timing for commercial purposes was, through no fault of his own, miserable. The stock market crash in October of 1929 had devastated the market for race records—along with the rest of the economy. To make matters worse, Paramount did little to promote the recordings, possibly because its finances were already severely strained by the gathering depression. As a result, sales of the recordings of all four of the musicians were dismal. Indeed, House's recordings of "Preachin' the Blues" and "Mississippi County Farm Blues" sold so poorly that only one copy of each record has ever been found.

House's contract with Paramount was for four years, and sometime later in 1930 or possibly early 1931, Laibley wrote House a letter asking him and Willie Brown to come back for another recording session. In House's words, Laibley's invitation amounted to, "Why don't you drop everything and come on up here?"[41]

40. Calt and Wardlow. *King*, p. 221.
41. Fahey, "Interview." The remainder of the quotes are also from this interview.

House felt he had to decline: "I wrote him and told him I couldn't make it. I was farming. I had to go to farming... It wasn't enough to live off the money of the next recording." As regrettable as his refusal is for music history, House probably made the right decision, for as he said, "So the next thing I knowed they was going out of business."

By 1931, Paramount had cut its releases in half and fired Laibley. By 1934, the company was bankrupt, and Laibley, after a brief stint selling busts of George Washington, became an insurance agent.

So, in the end, what had seemed a promising opportunity for Son House went for naught. It would be thirty-five years before he would make another commercial recording. Thirty-five years later he would sum up his situation after the Grafton sessions by saying, "I was nowhere. I was in Lula."

CHAPTER 5

Dry Spell Blues

THE 1930S

After their month-long sojourn in Lula, Son House followed Willie Brown to the Robinsonville–Lake Cormorant area. With the judge's warning still echoing in his mind he could not go back to Clarksdale where he had family, and in Willie Brown he had found both a close friend and a musical partner. Indeed, apart from the recordings that survived from the Paramount session, House's friendship with Brown was the most lasting consequence of the Grafton experience. In the north Delta, House and Willie Brown soon dominated the local music scene. But blues alone did not pay enough to support either of them.

As hard as life had been for House and Brown and the other black inhabitants of the Delta before 1930, it became harder yet after 1930 when the Great Depression combined with the drought of 1930–1931 to heap still more adversities on them. Indeed, the Depression began early in the Delta, since cotton prices had been falling for twenty years; the average yearly income of local sharecroppers had fallen from $333 in 1913 to $129 in 1932.[1] The Southern writer Jonathan Daniels saw in this situation the predicament of the entire region: "Everywhere in the South, the poorest men are on the richest land."[2]

Throughout the 1930s, House coped with hard times by holding down two jobs, and until 1934, sometimes even three. His "day job," was once again farm work. He worked in the Robinsonville area on the Tate, Cox, and Harbart plantations—the latter was where Willie Brown lived.

1. Nan Elizabeth Woodruff, *American Congo: The African American Freedom Struggle in the Delta* (Cambridge, MA: Harvard University Press, 2003), p. 153.
2. Jonathan Daniels, *A Southerner Discovers the South* (New York: MacMillan, 1938), p. 136.

His second job was playing blues, almost always in the company of Willie Brown, in juke joints all over the north Delta. They played for whiskey and meals, but often they were also paid cash, although House denigrated the sums he made that way: "No, three or four, five [dollars] or something like that to the high—that's as high as you'd get anytime."[3] Nevertheless, considering the straightened circumstances of the Depression, if a yearly income from sharecropping was one or two hundred dollars, then even three or four dollars for performing one or two Saturday nights a month was substantial.

House said of his musical collaboration with Willie Brown, "So we got to staying together, and got pretty good playing together."[4] Besides being his best friend, Brown was the perfect musical complement to Son House: he was a fine guitar player who did not like to sing, while House had an excellent voice. "Willie was the best guitar player around, although his voice wasn't too strong. He used to play the 'comment' [background] while I did all the lead singing."[5]

Given Willie Brown's musical experience—he had been playing in public since 1916—he must have contributed greatly to House's musical growth. Brown had played with Patton for years, and even though he and House saw Patton intermittently after Grafton, Patton's influence would continue to exert itself on House through Brown. Moreover, Brown was a resourceful musician—House recalled him repairing broken strings with baiting wire. If the string broke over the first or second fret, Brown would tie a knot with the wire and the end of the broken string, then capo past the knot and slack tune the guitar so as to remain in tune with the other musicians. But such thrifty tricks aside, probably the most important musical effect Brown had on House was teaching him to play in standard tuning, which significantly enlarged House's repertoire. He and Brown also played at "white-only" events, something House never mentioned doing before his collaboration with Brown. White audiences did listen to blues, but they would also have wanted to hear their "hits"—songs like "Let Me Call You Sweetheart" that Brown's onetime partner Willie Moore said Brown knew. Performing for white audiences was a sign of their regional status. As House himself recalled, "White people liked our music fine. Anything fast and jumpy went over."[6] The white events also probably

3. Titon, "Interview: Son House," p. 17.
4. Lester, "My Own Songs," p. 41.
5. Cohn, "Delta Bluesman," p. 68.
6. Ibid., p. 69.

paid better, and they must have been less hazardous to their physical well-being.

Charley Patton, who also moved briefly to the Robinsonville area, went back down south in the fall of 1930 to the town of Holly Ridge, which consisted then, as it still does, of two small groceries and a gin. Patton had been thrown off Dockery's plantation the year before, but he still had relatives there, among them an older sister Viola and a half-brother Willie, better known as Son Patton. While Holly Ridge was not too far from Dockery's and Viola, it was far enough for Patton to avoid his half-brother with whom he did not get along very well—"They couldn't 'set horses,'" as House said of them also. But again, Patton's main motive for moving to Holly Ridge seems to have been its proximity to a man named Cliff Toy, whose wife Millie had been Patton's lover twenty years earlier, and who had borne his only known child, a daughter named Willie Mae, but better known as China Lou. Patton, it seemed, still harbored feelings of affection for Millie, and her husband tolerated Patton's presence—which surprised House. However, China Lou didn't think much of her father, according to House, "because he didn't wanna do nothin' but run all over the country and play guitars and pick up with every woman he see..."[7]

House and Brown continued to visit Patton from time to time in Holly Ridge Curiously, China Lou's attitude about her father's carousing and womanizing did not prevent her from taking an interest in House, despite the marked similarity of Patton and House in that respect—as David "Honeyboy" Edwards put it, "Son and Charlie, they was a devil, used to wanna 'clown'..."[8] Soon House became romantically involved with China Lou.

House recalled of Patton's daughter, "Oh, China Lou, she wasn't that old...look like to me...I'd say she was about 20, something like that." China Lou was unmarried, and as House admitted, "That's the reason I went to liking her. She wasn't married."[9]

Surprisingly, Patton encouraged their affair. House said, "Yeah, he knowed it, yeah. He talk in my favor and everything to her." And China Lou responded to House's advances, however as House explained, "...I had so many back up there around Lake Carmen and places, I couldn't bring 'em back with me, but I'd talk trash and make like I's so crazy 'bout 'em and everything..."

7. Calt and Wardlow, *King*, p. 138. China Lou or China Lu sometimes.

8. Ibid., p. 138. Until noted otherwise the following quotes are from Calt and Wardlow.

9. Perls, "Son House Interview," p. 60. All of the subsequent quotes about China Lou are taken from this same interview.

Nevertheless, House had some standards: "I wouldn't tell her I wanted to bring her back, tell her I wanted to get married to her or nothing, 'cause I had too many already. Even the same one I got now, we hadn't got married yet, but I was jumping the broomstick with her just the same."

House's womanizing was hardly unusual for an itinerant blues musician, and he was still rambling in the thirties. Muddy Waters who got to know House in that decade said of him, "He never be still like me." But women were one of the reasons the music profession could be perilous to one's physical safety.

House often remarked about Patton's propensity for attracting trouble on account of women: "Charley was always gettin' in some kind of trouble and then me and Willie would have to jump in and get him out of there. A couple of time we ended up running through a cotton field late at night with buckshot flying around our heads."[10] Indeed, Patton's free ways with other men's wives resulted in a gunshot wound in his leg that left him, in House's idiom, "limpified." Worse yet, in Holly Ridge Patton nearly lost his life for the same reason. One night while he was playing on the Hollyknoe plantation, a woman sat on Patton's lap between songs. When her jealous boyfriend saw her, he pulled a knife and cut Patton's throat. Honeyboy Edwards, who had come to the frolic hoping to play with Patton, learned when he arrived that Patton had been taken to a Greenville hospital. As Edwards recalled, "One of those old guys cut him. It was a deep cut in his vein...a bad cut."[11]

House's behavior—and appearance—must have exposed him to similar dangers. When, years later, the author Edward Komara mentioned him to Robert Wilkin's granddaughter, she said emphatically, "He was a *good looking* man."[12] And as the Patton episode shows, the problem extended beyond the musician's control, since women in barrelhouses and juke joints were just as likely to make advances, but to their boyfriends or husbands it hardly mattered who had begun flirting first. As Honeyboy Edwards recalled, "Some old 'clowny' woman...come up to you...she get a drink or two in her head; she just wanna show herself. She had never seed you before sometimes...but she wanna make people think you done fell for her. Quite naturally their boyfriends or their husbands wouldn't like that...Boyfriend or husband or somethin' say: 'Get rid of that nigger; kill him.'"[13] This was the reason even

10. Waterman, Obituary, p. 49.

11. Calt and Wardlow, *King*, p. 226–27.

12. An anecdote related to the author by Edward Komara. Photographs after 1964 suggest he must have still been a handsome man when he was in his forties and fifties.

13. Calt and Wardlow, *King*, p. 226.

the tee-totaling, mild-mannered Robert Wilkins quit playing blues. In Honeyboy's succinct explanation: "A musicianer, he doesn't have any friends except other musicianers."

It is not surprising then that in recalling the period, House emphasized the dangers to which musicians were exposed while performing at house parties and juke joints. "Them country balls were rough! They were critical, man!" he said.[14] House himself witnessed several murders while he was performing. They were commonplace. "Nearly every other Saturday night or two somebody got stabbed or got shot or something. It wasn't much to it."[15] He described one incident that took place while he and Brown were playing at a house party. A man they called "Horse" was sitting on the floor with his back to the wall and his knees drawn up. A man named Zeb Turner limped in to the house, and House described what happened next:

> He came in the house and said to me, 'Son? Who's that sitting down over there?' I said, 'That's Horse.' He said, 'Oh yeah. That's the so-and-so I want to see.' I said, 'What's the matter, Zeb?' and commenced to moving my chair over. He said, 'Nothing. That's all right.' And he took both hands around that pistol and—Boom! Them owl-head pistols, we called them, didn't have any hammers, you know. Some folks called them 'lemon squeezers.' Zeb squeezed that thing with both hands and the bullet jumped through Horse so quick and hard he didn't realize anything had happened.[16]

Such lethal violence was often overlooked by the white legal authorities. As House recalled: "Whatever guy did it, if he was a good worker—well, whatever white guy he worked for took care of him. They put him in jail, the white man would get in his car and go down there and tell them, 'I need him.' Put in a good word for him. That's what made them kill them up so much. Guy would figure he stood good with 'the man.' 'Mr. Charlie'll get me out.'"[17]

With these hazards and the modest sums earned, it is not surprising that House continued to seek other sources of income. What is surprising, considering his devotion to blues and his friends like Patton and Brown, is that until 1933 or 1934 House's third job was—at least intermittently—

14. Lester, p. 42.

15. Bob West, "From the Vaults: Bob West Interview with Son House." *Blues & Rhythm* 207 (March 2006) a reprint of a 1968 interview, p. 6.

16. Lester, "My Own Songs," pp. 43–44.

17. Ibid., p. 44.

preaching. No doubt his move to Robinsonville initially assisted him in finding a new pulpit in a locality where no one but Willie Brown knew much about his past. He was also helped by the fact that most rural churches could not retain a regular or full-time minister due to the continual exodus of the population to the big cities, so even a truant preacher like House could find empty pulpits. Willie Brown told one mutual acquaintance that whenever House couldn't make enough money playing blues he'd look for a pulpit. The friend quoted Brown, "He'd preach a year, something like that six months again. He could *preach* you know..."[18] On the other hand, other acquaintances said it was Brown who would entice House from the church, so the two could start playing blues again. It probably worked both ways. But this much is clear: Brown had nothing at all to do with the church, and for all the time he and House spent "staying together and playing together" they did not spend any time praying together.

Eventually something had to give. Rumors began to reach the congregation regarding the company House kept and the habits he still indulged. His last pulpit was in a town called, ironically enough, Commerce, and it was there that his blues reputation caught up to him once and for all. Elizabeth Moore, who helped operate a juke joint where House frequently played, put it bluntly, "Them members up there put him outta business."[19]

House's career as a preacher had lasted about seventeen years. His own accounts suggest he had left the pulpit at least once of his own accord in the twenties, when rumors about his drinking circulated. Yet, by his own account, for probably another eight to ten years after he became aware of his hypocrisy, he was still in and out of the pulpit. In other words, for most of his preaching career, he was having difficulty living the life of a preacher. House—who was "a careful observer of human nature," as Robert Palmer put it[20]—must have been aware that at least one of his motives for preaching was less than commendable: he liked the easy money it earned him. As Elizabeth Moore said of House, "He *really* could sing and he *really* could preach."[21] Given the torment he felt about playing blues on account of his religious beliefs, House must have also felt guilty about the money he made preaching, especially when his drinking and womanizing continued apace. Indeed, depending on how one keeps one's

18. Calt and Wardlow, *King*, p. 237.

19. Elizabeth Glynn Moore interview, Gayle Dean Wardlow Collection, Center for Popular Music, Middle Tennessee State University.

20. Palmer, *Deep Blues*, p. 79.

21. Elizabeth Glynn Moore interview.

accounts, both financial and ethical, those activities could have been seen as funded by his preaching. Although this is not to say he did not also have religious motives to keep preaching.

At the same time, decades later he would speak of his experiences with the church with the detachment and humor of someone recalling a youthful amour whose flame has long since gone out—which is curious in a man who never ceased to profess the importance of religion to him.

In 1965, while playing at the University of Iowa, House was asked by folklorists there to relate "folktales." Among the "folktales" he told were two humorous stories about preachers. The first story concerned a boy sent out in the winter cold by his father to find a lost calf. He never finds the calf, gives up, and returns to their cabin to warm himself in front of the fire. But when he gets home, he finds a preacher planted squarely in front of the fire. Seeing the boy sulking in the corner, the preacher asks him how he is, and he replies, "Cold as hell." The preacher scolds him for such language, and then asks him how in any case he would know what hell is like.

> "It's a lot like this place," the boy replies.
> "Why is that?" The preacher asks.
> "Because you can't get near the fire for all the preachers."

In the second story, two preachers are discussing the disappointing results of their revivals. One says that he had a crowd so big that it overflowed the church into the street. But before he could make his collection, the police came along and dispersed the crowd. The preacher says,

> "Now why does God let that happen? They say He is all knowing and all powerful."
> "He is all knowing and He is all powerful," the other preacher says.
> "Then why does He let that happen?" the first preacher asks.
> "Well, I'll tell you why. He just doesn't give a damn."

Both of these mocking tales greatly amused House who could not resist laughing at his own jokes.[22]

It is tempting to say that House kept religion but rejected the church. But that is probably too neat. Despite his professions of faith—protesta-

---

22. The tales were recorded by Harry Oster on April 24, 1965. Some of the tales regarding masters being tricked by slaves found their way onto a record in 1980, "John and Old Master," Flyright, EP-01. At one point a young Asian woman asks House for stories about "crocodiles and poisonous snakes" and House tries to oblige.

tions may also be a fit term—some part of him had finally rejected certain matters of faith that had once seemed fundamental to his concept of "religion." The humorous detachment heard in his recollections and anecdotes implies he was not simply rejecting an institution, after all, but certain attitudes and experiences as well.

And the conflict felt inside may be reflected in the conflicting accounts of his life. He would tell some people that once he quit preaching he never set foot in church again. Yet he also claimed that in the early 1950s he gave up music and went back to the church: "I quit and went right and joined the church in the city where I live now..."[23]

But Elizabeth Moore, who knew him well, said it was really not House's decision to quit preaching: "He went to carryin' on so bad until the church folks didn't want him. They got rid of him an' he run back, then back."[24]

Many a bluesman was condemned by his family for playing the Devil's music—both Muddy Waters and Howlin' Wolf were scorned by their mothers. And many a bluesman would give up blues and become a preacher—Rube Lacy and Robert Wilkins who have already figured in this story gave up blues and ended up as preachers. But Son House was unique. He gave up preaching and took up the blues. And his attitude about blues can only be understood in light of that. Quitting the pulpit—or being driven from it—left a void that House attempted to fill with blues. But his attempt to fill it was never entirely successful, and precisely because it failed, it guaranteed the never-ending anguish that gave his music its power.

House's preaching career in Commerce seems to have ended at about the same time as his last recording session with Patton, a droll episode at H.C. Speir's store in Jackson, Mississippi. Perhaps Patton had gotten wind of House's fizzled career as a preacher, which gave him the idea of billing himself, Brown, and House as a gospel group, "The Locust Ridge Saints," in an audition with Speir. Were there ever three less likely candidates for sainthood?

Speir was still seeking new talent at this time, and indeed he was attempting to find funds to purchase Paramount Records, a possibility that had been broached with people at the Wisconsin Chair Company as early as 1930. House recalled the trip to the recording session in Jackson at Speir's store: "...111 North Farish Street, in Jackson...me and Charley and Willie, we made one together and we. Uh...we called it...'I Had A

23. Goodwin, "Son House: 'You Can't Fool God,'" *Rolling Stone* (December 27, 1969,): p. 16.
24. Elizabeth Glynn Moore interview.

Dream Last Night Troubled Me'…but it was Christian. We made it as a Christian song. And we were playing like that we was sanctified, see, 'cause he wanted some sanctified songs." Speir knew all three men from having been present at the sessions in Grafton in 1930. But Patton attempted to avoid detection by slouching and keeping the brim of a hat low over his eyes. House and Brown were apparently indifferent as to what Speir may have thought. House recalled, "And me and Charley and Willie, nary a one of us wasn't sanctified, but we's making out like it, you know, to make the record. Charley he started that (sings a little)…that's the way we sang it. So on record, people didn't know no better. They figured we's three sanctified guys. We wasn't nothing but ol' whiskey drinkers and blues players."[25]

The "Locust Ridge Saints" episode was the ironic finale of House's career as a preacher.

Shortly before the Jackson trip, probably in late1933, House was also sought again for another recording session involving Patton, this time by W.R. Calaway, a former Paramount executive who had gone over to the American Record Company (ARC). Calaway invited him and Brown to New York for what would turn out to be Patton's last sessions. But, according to H.C. Speir, Calaway was notoriously cheap, and probably this was at most a feeler on Calaway's part to see if he might lure Brown and House to New York at their own expense. Whatever the reality of this "offer," House declined again for obvious reasons.

After returning from the "Locust Ridge Saints" excursion to Jackson, House said he and Brown played with Patton in the area around Holly Ridge and Drew for about three weeks before they returned to Robinsonville. It was to be the last time House and Brown saw Patton.

Not long after they got back to the Robinsonville area House got the news about Patton's death: "So Willie and I went on back to Lake Cormorant where we were living then, and about two weeks after we got back, we got a telegraph from Bertha, that was the girl said to be his wife. The telegram said that Charlie was dead. He was taken with the mumps and they went down on him. And that was the way he died."[26]

Patton died on April 28, 1934, in an Indianola house, not of mumps "going down on him," but of heart disease, a chronic condition probably due to having contracted rheumatic fever as a child.

---

25. Perls, "Son House Interview," p. 60. All of the quotes in this paragraph are from this interview.

26. Lester, "My Own Songs," p. 42. 'Lake Commorant' is obviously Lake Cormorant.

Patton's influence on House was considerable. The next time House was to record, he would cut at least two versions of Patton's standard "Pony Blues," as well as several other songs that showed Patton's traces. Patton's sometimes flippant attitude toward music seems to have made House shake his head—as House would put it, "If you're gonna play 'The Pony Blues,' let all your words [be] something pertaining to the pony." Nevertheless House referred to him with affection: "He was an old clown all right. He was my old buddy."[27] And he did not begrudge giving Patton credit for the critical role he had played in getting him into the recording studio: "Charlie was the big man in the area. Everyone knew Charlie Patton. He made a whole lot of records, you know, and he was the one who got me the contract with Paramount...he was the strongest singer around. He was a fine guitar player too."[28]

Seven months after Patton died, Son House married Evie Goff on November 27, 1934. The Reverend Henry Berry presided over the ceremony in Tunica.[29] With the exception of the ill-fated Carrie Martin episode, all his prior unions were "jump the broom" affairs. The marriage to Evie Goff was to be different.

Goff was four years younger than House, and she brought with her three children by a previous union. Beginning in 1930, she had given birth in quick succession to three children, Beatrice, Rufus, and Sally. When House met her around 1933, Goff was then a cook in a doctor's home near Robinsonville. She and House were soon living together, and House apparently took her more seriously than most of his other girlfriends. At the time of his brief affair with China Lou in 1933, it was Evie Goff's presence in Robinsonville that prevented him from taking China Lou back with him. Goff's three children by her first husband as well as her mother made up the household with her new husband.

Beatrice, the eldest (now Bea or Willie Bea Powell) was the only surviving stepchild when this book was written. She was four years old when her mother married Son House. She had no memory of her natural father and regarded Son as her real father. Her memories of him were entirely positive: "He was good. He was a nice man. A real good father. He raised the three of us." She emphasized that House was gentle with his stepchildren: "He never did scold one of us. Never did whup one of us," she recalled.

27. Titon, "Interview: Son House," p. 20.

28. Cohn, "Delta Bluesman," p. 69.

29. The marriage certificate is in the Tunica County courthouse.

"But he didn't have to do that because the way we were raised, we were raised to respect older people."[30]

According to Bea Powell, her grandmother was very religious, and on that account Son never played blues at home—spirituals sometimes, but never blues. She had no personal memory of hearing him preach, but remembered that he had one very brief association with a church. Likely, it was the one Elizabeth Glynn Moore mentioned as his last pulpit, since, according to Bea, it only lasted about two weeks before they found out that, in her words, "he was a guitar player." And that was that.

Bea Powell's main childhood memories were of House's guitar and his driving a tractor. She also remembered Willie Brown as a frequent visitor to their house, but he never brought his guitar, again out of deference to her grandmother. Brown, she said, lived nearby with his wife and one child. It seemed to her that Son and Willie Brown played somewhere almost every Saturday night. And Evie—despite her mother's attitude and despite her own professions of piety—sometimes went to the juke joints with House.

House was to remain married to Evie for the rest of his life, though there would be at least one lengthy separation. For her part, Evie was to remain remarkably faithful to House despite the challenges his habits must have presented. Somehow the marriage survived the vicissitudes of his blues career, though, not surprisingly, it seems to have been for House a "low fidelity" arrangement. But given Bea Powell's happy recollections of their life in Robinsonville, he seems to have been fairly successful at "compartmentalizing" his life—keeping his drinking and his juke joint buddies, as well as his love affairs relatively separate from their family.

By 1934 then, three events coming close on the heels of each other had in their different ways changed House's life forever: his marriage, quitting the pulpit, and the death of Charley Patton.

By that year, House had left the pulpit once and for all. Indeed, it may well be that he never entered a church again in his life—a surmise that is based on statements House would make many years later to friends in Rochester. And with the death of Patton that same year, Son House became the most important performer in the Mississippi Delta blues. With Willie Brown, he would dominate the local music scene for a decade until 1943.

---

30. Interview with the author, May 17, 2010.

In the juke joints

With the pulpit no longer a possibility, House could pursue his other tastes—at least when he was away from his mother-in-law—without censure: alcohol and blues.

House often made his own whiskey: "We made that old bad whiskey, our own selves. In place of going downtown to the store somewhere, we would do that. We would get it out of our basement and places where we done made it...You know, let it set there, soak in that water and stuff for about at least two weeks, and then it stop blubblin' ('cause it be so hot)..."[31]

When asked what he did with it, he laughed: "We'd run it off and drink it, man! Oh, them that couldn't drink enough, well, they'd sell it to the other ones." But House, it seems, could drink "enough," and he never spoke of having made much money bootlegging.

For the rest of the 1930s and the early 1940s, House made his income by driving a tractor on farms and playing blues in the juke joints of the Delta, not only with Willie Brown, but increasingly with small bands. Both of these things were characteristic of the changes that were coming to life in the Delta.

By the late 1930s, with the mechanization of farms, House was not picking cotton, but driving a tractor. His skill at this job earned him the moniker "Tractor King." When manufacturers brought their prototypes to the Robinsonville area, House would test-drive the new machines. "I could take out one of them harrows that worked eight rows across—pick a bug off of a leaf and never touch the plant!" he would boast years later.[32]

Curiously, House never spoke with as much pride about his music as he did about his skill with a tractor, even though in the same period he was the foremost blues musician in the area.

David "Honeyboy" Edwards first saw House perform in late 1933 or early 1934. Honeyboy said: "I heard they [Son House and Willie Brown] was playing out there at Flowers Plantation out in Coahoma County, up near Robinsonville. I cut on out there and they had a big crowd at the barrelhouse on the plantation. Willie Brown was kind of a big husky fellow; he was heavy." Honeyboy was especially impressed by Brown's

---

31. Titon, "Interview: Son House," p. 14.
32. Waterman, Obituary, p. 49.

guitar playing: "Willie Brown was a great guitar player. That man had some beautiful chords he made in the key of A." Honeyboy also described how Brown and House complemented each other as guitar players, with Brown's more complex chording setting off House's more rough-hewn, vigorous style: "Son House had a rough guitar style on that National guitar of his. He was a rocking, rough slide player. He was a good singer and a good hollerer, a good entertainer with his guitar."[33]

House had switched from a Stella he played at the time of the Paramount session to a steel-bodied National by 1934. For those who could afford them, the National Steels were favored because, with their metal resonators, they were louder than regular wooden guitars and better able to cope with the noisy Delta juke joints. And, of course, being mostly made of steel they were more durable, which also mattered in the boisterous environment of the juke joint. As Bukka White, another Delta bluesman with a similarly energetic style, would say, "I don't play 'em. I stomp 'em."

However, by the late thirties House and Willie Brown were often joined by other musicians. House sometimes played with his younger brother L.J. who became known as "Pump,"[34] due to the way he pumped his leg when he played guitar. House also played frequently with Fiddlin' Joe Martin on mandolin, Henry "Son" Simms on fiddle, Leroy Williams on the harp, and Charlie Ross on drums. A trombone player, Little Buddy Sankfield, was often employed. House and Brown, as a duo and with their musical companions, played all over the Delta and also across the river in Arkansas and up in Tennessee—House was, in the late 1930s, still on the move, still "ramblified." As Muddy Waters recalled, "He traveled through the area and lived on a plantation too—one way across from me. He didn't never be still like me, 'cause he'd do a lot of traveling all over the Delta. And anytime I could get a chance to hear him play, I'd go."[35] While House and Brown and their bandmates played for white audiences at parties and picnics, naturally House's most important audience consisted of the black patrons of the juke joints and house parties.

One of the Robinsonville juke joints where House and Brown frequently played was the Oil Mill Quarters, which was owned by a bootlegger named Nathaniel Richardson. The Oil Mill Quarters was also one of the juke

33. David Honeyboy Edwards as told to Janis Martinson and Michael Robert Frank, *The World Don't Owe Me Nothing: The Life and Times of Delta Bluesman Honeyboy Edwards*, (Chicago: Chicago Review Press 2000) pp. 94–95.

34. And the mysterious young brother "James." (see note 3, chapter 2).

35. Rooney, *Bossmen*, p. 107.

joints where Robert Johnson would turn up to listen to House, frequently sitting on the floor right between him and Willie Brown so as to get the best view possible of how they were playing their guitars.

Johnson had lived in Robinsonville since 1919 when he came to live with his mother, who had married a sharecropper there a few years earlier. Johnson first saw House in 1930 when he, Charley Patton, and Willie Brown were all playing first around Lula and later around Robinsonville. Johnson had already begun hanging out in the juke joints in the area, observing and studying all three musicians.

When Johnson met House around 1930, Johnson was already nineteen years old, but he must have appeared younger than his years for House remembered, "He started his round about between fifteen and sixteen years old...We'd play for Saturday night balls and there'd be this little boy standing around. That was Robert Johnson...He blew a harmonica and he was pretty good with that, but he wanted to play a guitar."[36]

House viewed the young man with the solicitude of an older brother: "When we'd leave at night to go play for the balls, he'd slip off and go over to where we were. His mother and stepfather didn't like for him to go out to those Saturday night balls because the guys were so rough. But he'd slip away anyway. Sometimes he'd even wait until his mother went to bed and then he'd get out the window and make it to where we were. He'd get where Willie and I were and sit right down on the floor and watch from one to the other."[37] Instead of the story that became attached to Johnson in the 1960s of a young man who had sold his soul to the devil for his skill on the guitar, House drew a very convincing picture of a young man sneaking out to juke joints and causing his family to be concerned about his welfare—after all, as House himself had said of the juke joints, "Boy, they were rough!"[38]

Johnson, before he could play the guitar well, often approached House and Brown in the Oil Mill Quarters to nag them about letting him play during their breaks.[39] Johnson would wait until House and Brown set their guitars down to step outside to have a cigarette and then pick up one of the guitars. As House recalled, "And such another

36. Lester, "My Own Songs," p.41. All the quotes in this paragraph are from this interview.
37. Ibid.
38. Cohn, "Delta Bluesman," p. 68.
39. Segrest and Hoffman, *Moanin' At Midnight: the Life and Times of Howlin' Wolf* (New York: Pantheon Books, 2004), p. 58.

Robert Johnson, photo booth self-portrait, early 1930s. © Delta Haze Corporation. All Rights Reserved. Used By Permission.

racket you never heard! It'd make people mad, you know. They'd come out and say, 'Why don't y'all go in there and get that guitar away from that boy! He's runnin' people crazy with it.'" House would have to go back inside and reprimand the young man. "I'd scold him about it. 'Don't do that, Robert. You drive the people nuts. You can't play nothing. Why don't you blow the harmonica for 'em?' But he didn't want to blow that. Still, he didn't care how I'd get after him about it. He'd do it anyway."[40]

But Johnson persisted, and eventually House gave him some private lessons. "He just wanted to learn how to play, so I said, 'You just wait until this is over and maybe Sunday night or Monday night you come on over to the house and I'll give you some little sketches of it.' He called me 'Mr. Son.' He said, 'All right, okay, Mr. Son.'"[41]

Willie Brown also gave Johnson a few lessons, but shortly after that Johnson disappeared for a period of time—probably some time in 1931—and the reason for Johnson's absence was directly related to

40. Lester, "My Own Songs," 1965, p. 41.
41. West, "Bob West Interview with Son House," p. 6.

music. Johnson, House said, was at odds with his stepfather about playing music: "After a while I believe that Robert ran away from home and he came back about six months later with a guitar on his back."[42] It was in a juke joint in Banks, east of Robinsonville, that Johnson reappeared. "We were playing there one Saturday night and all of a sudden somebody came in through the door. Who but him! He had a guitar swinging on his back."

Johnson pleaded with House and Brown to let him sit in, and finally they relented. What happened next was fixed in House's memory: "So I said, 'All right and you better do something with it too,' and I winked my eye at Willie. So he sat down there and finally got started. And man! He was so good! When he finished all our mouths were standing open. I said, 'Well, ain't that fast! He's gone now!' "[43]

As opposed to a deal-with-the-devil story of musical development, House's recollections make it clear that Johnson had taken a year or two at least to develop as a guitarist. It was probably in late 1931 or 1932 that Johnson's guitar playing attained "critical mass."[44]

Once Johnson began performing on his own, House tried to warn him about the perils of working in the juke joints. "The women all liked Robert, he was a good-looking boy, and when he got good enough to perform, I used to tell him, 'When a gal pats you on the shoulder and says, 'Play it again, Daddy,' don't get too excited. She'll probably belong to someone else, and you might get yourself killed.' "[45]

House said he repeatedly warned Johnson about such dangers, and indeed one such warning was shortly before he died on August 16, 1938— quite possibly poisoned by a jealous husband or boyfriend. Then House heard from Johnson's mother: "It wasn't no 'bout to better than two weeks or more that his mother, she got a telegram that he got killed."[46]

Years later, House's memories of the young musician would be selectively mined, embroidered and combined with other accounts by various "bluesologists," and the results would become part of the story of Johnson's deal with the devil at the crossroads, but it is highly unlikely

---

42. Cohn, "Delta Bluesman," p. 69. In another interview House gave the period of time that Johnson was absent as two years.

43. Lester, "My Own Songs," p. 42.

44. See Edward Komara on Johnson in *The Encyclopedia of the Blues* (New York: Routledge 2006), vol. 1, p. 536.

45. Cohn, "Delta Bluesman," p. 69.

46. West, "Bob West Interview with Son House," p. 7.

that House himself ever suggested such a story to anyone.[47] As House himself observed sardonically, "All you got to do is say one word that's untrue, and it will go all over the country in a day or two. But if you tell the truth, it will take ten years to get there."[48]

Muddy Waters, who knew both Robert Johnson and Son House, said of House's influence on the budding musician, "I think Robert got a whole lotta little standpoints from Son House..."[49] Johnson's recordings in 1937 and 1938 showed the extent of House's influence on his music. In his song "Walking Blues," Johnson borrowed the lyrics from House's song of the same title, but set those words to the musical accompaniment of House's song "My Black Mama." Since House's Grafton recording of "Walking Blues" was never released by Paramount, Johnson must have learned the lyrics from House's live performances in the Robinsonville area. Johnson must have also learned the musical accompaniment of "My Black Mama/Death Letter" from House's live performances. Johnson straightened out House's somewhat idiosyncratic musical accompaniment, and in the process created a song that would, by and by, become a blues standard. Johnson also recorded "Preachin' the Blues," as "Up Jumped the Devil," in this instance remaining closer to the House original. Since House's 1930 Paramount records sold very poorly (as mentioned, only one copy of "Preachin' the Blues" has ever been found), it is again likely that Johnson learned the piece from House in person. On the basis of those songs and others that Johnson recorded, it is apparent that he also tried to emulate House's vocal style.

Howlin' Wolf was another young musician who crossed paths with House in Robinsonville. Wolf's upbringing was no less difficult than House's, and he also had his struggle with playing the Devil's music—in fact, his mother would reject him forever for playing blues. House first saw Wolf arrive in Robinsonville on the back of a pickup around 1938. Shortly after that, Wolf began to frequent the same juke joints, including

47. The genealogy of this preposterous tale has been traced by Gayle Wardlow and Edward Komara, in Wardlow's *Chasin' That Devil Music* (Milwaukee: Backbeat Books, 1998), and Barry Lee Pearson and Bill McCulloch in *Robert Johnson: Lost and Found* (Champaign-Urbana: University of Illinois, 2003). See Wardlow, pp. 203–204, and Barry Lee Pearson and Bill McCulloch, pp. 87–92. As Pearson and McCulloch point out, in the late 1960s when House was interviewed by Paul Vernon and was asked about the story, House replied flatly, "I don't want to talk about that." And he remained silent until the subject was dropped.

48. West, "Bob West Interview with Son House," p. 5.

49. *The Voice of the Blues*, edited by Jim O'Neal and Amy van Singer, New York London 2002, p. 159. The interviews were done in 1974, 1980 and 1981, and originally published in *Living Blues* in #64, March–April 1985.

the Oil Mill Quarters, where he was soon sitting in and playing harp with House and Brown. Wolf recalled, "I worked with them two at some of them Saturday night hops. I'd happen up on them at different places, and I'd jump in and play a tune or two with them. They was playing music for dancing mostly, fast numbers to dance to..."[50] Playing together inevitably led to socializing together, and at one point, House, Brown, and Wolf were all dating three sisters. House had been married for four years at that point, but certain habits had apparently persisted.

Despite the demise of Son House's career as a preacher, he was still acquiring disciples—but now they were musical disciples. The most important of them was Muddy Waters.

Waters, who could be considered the most important blues musician after the war, always cited Son House as his most important influence, "...my copy was Son House."[51] Certainly from at least the mid-1930s, Waters often saw House perform,[52] and in his view, "...Son House was the daddy down there then...I thought Son House was the greatest guitar player in the world when I heard him because he was usin' that bottleneck style, and I loved that sound. Man. Son House."[53]

"I used to say to Son House, 'Would you play so and so and so?' Because I was trying to get that touch on that thing he did." Waters, who had been tutored in the use of the bottleneck by a young resident of Stovall's plantation where he lived, went on to say, "When I heard Son House, I should have broke my bottleneck because this other cat hadn't learned me nothing. Once [Son House] played a month in a row every Saturday night. I was there every night, close to him. You couldn't get me out of that corner, listening to him. I watched that man's fingers and look like to me he was so good he was unlimited...I loved Son House because he used the bottleneck so beautiful."[54]

The power and the appeal of House's music in the late 1930s and early 1940s shines through in Muddy Waters' recollections, who said of Son House, "When I was a boy comin' up, that man was king, *king*..."[55]

50. Segrest and Hoffman, *Moanin' at Midnight*, p. 44. The information that House and Wolf dated sisters is on p. 45.

51. Rooney, *Bossmen*, p. 107.

52. Waters, it has been asserted, first saw House perform in 1927 when he was fourteen years old. That seems too early in view of at least two factors, House's newness to blues and his obscurity at that point.

53. O'Neal and van Singer, *Voice*, pp. 159–60.

54. Gordon, *Can't Be Satisfied: The Life and Times of Muddy Waters* (New York: Little Brown and Company, 2002): p. 23, 24.

55. Dick Waterman, Obituary, p. 48.

CHAPTER 6

Jinx Blues

THE 1941–42 FISK-LIBRARY OF CONGRESS SESSIONS

Son House was working on the R.E. Lambert plantation in the first week of September 1941 when it was still hot in the Delta—August hot—when a white stranger pulled up in a Ford, got out, and approached him. He appeared to be in his mid-twenties, and even before he spoke, it was clear he was not a local. He introduced himself as a Mr. Alan Lomax, and he told House that he was affiliated with the Library of Congress and was working on project sponsored jointly by the Library and Fisk University in Nashville. House undoubtedly had never heard of either. Lomax told House he wished to interview him about the blues and also record him playing some songs.

Alan Lomax's account, published more than a half a century later, portrays House as deferential but puzzled: "I'm used to plowin' so many acres a week and sayin' Yessuh and Nussuh to the boss on the plantation, but for sittin' down and talking about my music with some man from college like you, I just never thought about it happenin' to me."[1]

Whether that conversation ever took place, however, is questionable, for Lomax's book is not an ordinary work of nonfiction. Lomax's magnum opus may be rather what John Cowley has termed an "anthropological fiction."[2] Lomax seems to have modeled his book on the work of Howard Odum, most prominently Odum's 1928 book *Rainbow Round My Shoulder: The Blue Trail of Black Ulysses*. Certainly some of the events and conversations that Lomax described took place, but it is not always an easy matter to determine which ones happened and which ones were invented. However, this much can be said, Lomax's portrait of a deferential House

1. Alan Lomax, *The Land Where the Blues Began* (New York: The New Press, 1993), p. 17.
2. Personal communication with the author, May 2010.

is consistent with the way he portrays many if not most of blues musicians in his book, flattered that Alan Lomax has taken an interest in them. And likely House was flattered by the attention of Lomax—but his reaction was probably also more complicated.

Part of House's deference was his wariness at an unfamiliar situation, and his intuition that something new and unusual was afoot was correct. He was about to become a subject in an academic and governmental study, a study that had been conceived more than a year earlier by an assistant professor at Fisk University named John Work and that already possessed a rather complicated history. But it would grow even more complicated, and years after Son House and Alan Lomax had both passed away, people would still debate exactly what happened.

The Fisk University-Library of Congress Study

John Wesley Work III was an African-American professor in the music department of Fisk University in Nashville, a historically black institution founded shortly after the Civil War. Work, a folklorist, had inherited his interest in popular music from his father, who had also been an academic and whose work with the Fisk Jubilee Singers after the college was established raised much of the money for the new college.

In April of the previous year, 1940, a devastating fire in Natchez, Mississippi had killed at least two hundred people, all of them African Americans. John Work knew there would be a commemoration of the tragedy on the first anniversary, and in June of 1940 he took a proposal to the president of Fisk University to record the songs on that occasion and to study their creation and the social contexts of their performances.[3] It was an ambitious proposal, and the president, a white Quaker named Thomas Elsa Jones, and some senior Fisk faculty decided to present Work's idea to the Library of Congress to help finance the project.

At the Library, Work's proposal was sent to Alan Lomax. Lomax, like Work, had inherited his interest in popular music from his father—he had been with his father John Lomax when he discovered a Texas songster named Huddie Ledbetter, better known as Leadbelly, on Louisiana's Angola State prison farm in 1933. Since 1937 Lomax had been the

3. John W. Work, Lewis Wade Jones and Samuel C. Adams, *Lost Delta Found: Rediscovering the Fisk University-Library of Congress Coahoma County Study 1941–1942*, ed. by Robert Gordon and Bruce Nemerov (Nashville: Vanderbilt University Press, 2005), p. 2.

Assistant in Charge of the Archive of Folk Song of the Library of Congress. Lomax liked Work's idea, and discussions immediately began between Fisk representatives and him.

Over the course of the next year, Work's initial proposal would undergo many changes. Other Fisk faculty members were brought in, most notably Lewis Jones, a professor of sociology, and the project would expand and contract as new locations were considered and old ones discarded. Most importantly for Son House, Lomax and the Fisk people finally settled on Coahoma and Tunica counties as the site for the study because of the density of the African-American population there.

In April of 1941, Lomax visited Fisk University to work out the final details of the project. His visit was arranged to coincide with the school's seventy-fifth anniversary, which was to be celebrated with a week of lectures on folklore and black secular music and concerts by black string bands, the latter organized by John Work. By the end of his week at Fisk, Lomax was in firm control of the project that Work had conceived, and Work, like many a hapless junior faculty member, found himself a subordinate in what had originally been his own project.[4]

Lomax and his wife drove to the Delta in August, stopping briefly at Fisk University in Nashville. Lomax's recording equipment, a Presto Model Y unit, consisting of a sixteen-inch turntable, an amplifier, and a speaker, produced recordings on the spot on acetate discs. The unit's power supply had been modified so that it could run on either AC or DC power supply. Like Lomax himself, his recording unit was a presence that could not be ignored. All the various components taken together weighed about five hundred pounds and took up the trunk and back seat of his Ford—so Work had to arrange his own transportation to Clarksdale.

About his method of working Lomax wrote, "Our way of work is simple. From letters and books and word of mouth we hear of someone, perhaps a Vermont woodsman or a Kentucky miner, who knows a store of old folk tunes. We get into our car and go visit him."[5]

---

4. The issue of Lomax's treatment of John Work is a matter Robert Gordon and Work's son discuss at length in their books. However, given the quasi-fictional nature of Lomax's book, its scant mention of Work may be due to other factors. The English singer Shirley Collins who accompanied and assisted Lomax on a 1959 trip through the South was also miffed at the short shrift his book gave her. Perhaps it was just his absent-mindedness, a trait noted by the FBI as early as 1943.

5. Alan Lomax, *Selected Writings*, ed. Ronald D. Cohen. (New York: Routledge 2003), p. 49. First published in *American Girl*, October 1940.

But in Mississippi, Lomax's simple method ran into a few complications. Lomax could not have undertaken the project without Work and Lewis Jones, nor for that matter could Work and Jones have carried out their work without a white "supervisor." But inevitably for Lomax simply being in the company of black men brought him suspicion and hostility—the same experience Perls, Spiro, and Waterman would have more than two decades later. As Lomax wrote to a colleague at the Library, "the community situation was so hot, as well as complicated, that I would hesitate to document it, until I knew the place better."[6]

Not surprisingly, given the origins of the project, tensions between Lomax and Work also quickly emerged. In a letter to another colleague at the Library of Congress, Lomax diagnosed Work's problems: "Work is a good man, suffering from obesity and a desire to write rather than collect music."[7] In his field notes Lomax was harsher yet. Lomax said Work was "... trying to work out his problems—mostly of incompetence, laziness, and the lack of initiative on his part."[8]

Lomax and Work arrived in Clarksdale on Thursday, August 28 and began the next morning by recording some sacred music. Robert Gordon describes Lomax's strategy nicely: "Since churches were easier to find than blues singers—they were less mobile and more sober—Lomax and Work began recording services."[9]

It was highly unlikely that Lomax had heard of Son House before he got to Mississippi. Due to the poor sales of House's Paramount records, only a handful of people outside the Delta knew of him. Lomax apparently located House (and Muddy Waters) by asking for names of the leading blues musicians—or possibly by mentioning Robert Johnson and asking for musicians who played like him or had known him. He had learned of Robert Johnson from John Hammond, who had heard the unreleased masters from Johnson's Texas sessions and had sought him out for his 1938 "Spirituals to Swing" concert at Carnegie Hall only to

---

6. Work, Jones & Adams, *Lost Delta*, p. 319, n. 39. Lomax wrote, "Everywhere we went we were asked point blank, were we or were we not union organizers." The Southern Tenant Farmers Union, founded in 1934 by a group of poor farmers, both black and white, had in the mid-1930s spread through Missouri, Arkansas, and Oklahoma and had made some inroads in the Mississippi Delta. Though the STFU was weakened by 1941, the recent memory of its efforts to organize farm labor remained a bitter one among the planters and the local law enforcement they controlled.

7. The Library of Congress-Fisk University Mississippi Delta Collection.

8. Gordon, *Can't Be Satisfied*, p. 311, n. 43.

9. Ibid., p. 37.

learn of Johnson's untimely death earlier that year. If Hammond's tip about Johnson was the clue that led Lomax to House, there was a certain irony, since House was far better known in the Delta than his protégé Johnson. And more than twenty years later, Hammond's intense interest in Johnson would again, by and by, help to lead people to Son House. Lomax and Work found and recorded Muddy Waters first, and if Lomax and Work had not already heard of Son House, Waters certainly told them about him.

On Sunday, August 31, they recorded "Stovall's famous guitar picker," as Waters introduced himself. As John Cowley notes, Lomax described Waters as "shy" in his notes, which is hardly in accord with Waters' self-advertisement.[10] Again, it seems more likely that what Lomax called shyness was rather the reticence and circumspection of blacks in the Jim Crow South when they dealt with whites, particularly white strangers.

The first song Muddy recorded, the one Lomax called "Country Blues," was based on Son House's "My Black Mama." The riff of that song, as noted before, had been reworked by Robert Johnson and set to the lyrics of "Walking Blues." And Waters knew "Walking Blues" as part of both House's and Johnson's repertoires. When asked about "Walking Blues," Lomax provides the following—possibly apocryphal—conversation in his book: "I learned it from Son House; that's a boy that picks a guitar. I been knowin' Son since 'twenty-nine. He was the best. Whenever I heard he was gonna play somewhere, I followed after him and stayed watching him. I learnt how to play with the bottle neck by watching him for about a year. He help me a lot. Showed me how to tune my guitar in three ways—nachul, Spanish and cross note."[11]

Three days later, on his last day in Mississippi, September 3, Lomax, with the help of directions from some locals, found Son House on a plantation near Robinsonville. Lomax was alone—having shed John Work. In his book, Lomax depicts House as surprised. House probes Lomax's motives

---

10. John Cowley, "Really the 'Walking Blues'" in *Popular Music* v1 (1981): 57–72. Reprinted in *Juke Blues* n1 (Jul 1985): 8–14.

11. Alan Lomax, *Land Where the Blues Began*, p. 411. In interviewing Waters, the tensions between Work and Lomax are evident in the recordings. Work conducted two of the four interviews. In the second, Lomax either cuts him off or the record had reached capacity—Work's voice is never heard again. See *Lost Delta Found*, p. 15. The relations between versions of "Walking Blues" done respectively by House, Robert Johnson, and Muddy Waters are investigated thoroughly by John Cowley in several articles, most importantly, "Really the 'Walking Blues': Son House, Muddy Waters, Robert Johnson and the development of a traditional blues" in *Popular Music 1*, 1981, pp. 57–71.

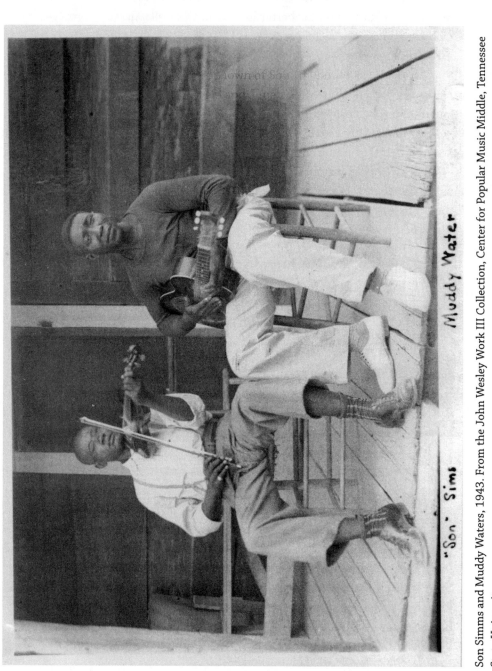

Son Simms and Muddy Waters, 1943. From the John Wesley Work III Collection, Center for Popular Music Middle, Tennessee State University.

for wanting to talk to him and record him, and Lomax explains himself this way, "History wasn't just made by kings and presidents and people like that; we've found out that the people who plow the corn and pick the cotton have had a lot to do with it. My job is to help you get down the history of your people."[12] If this conversation actually took place, we can only wonder what impression such an explanation would have made on House.

When Lomax told House he wanted to record his music, House responded that he would get his band together—by this time he and Brown were also regularly using other musicians. So off they went to assemble House's band, beginning of course with Willie Brown.

Lomax and House drove to the plantation near Lake Cormorant where Brown lived. There they were told that he had gone fishing. House said, "We drove along the levee and I kept singing, 'Willie, Willie, Willeee.' Finally he heard us."[13] After they picked up Brown, they went looking for two more musicians, Fiddlin' Joe Martin and Leroy Williams.

Lomax's account of the recording session begins: "I don't know where Son took me. Down dusty roads, along a railroad track into the back of an aging country grocery store that smelt of licorice and dill pickles and snuff."[14] Where House took Lomax was Clack's Grocery Store which was situated just east of Highway 61.[15] Clack's also served as a commissary and a train station—the railroad tracks of the Illinois Central railroad ran behind the store, across a dirt road.

In *Land Where the Blues Began*, Lomax depicts himself asking House several questions about Robert Johnson, and House's responses emphasize Johnson's rapid progress on the guitar, his good looks and his womanizing, which House took to be his downfall—he told Lomax that he suspected Johnson had been poisoned by a jealous woman. Purely in terms of his musical talent, House was full of praise for his deceased young friend: "That boy could play more blues than air one of us. Folks would say he couldn't, but we know, us musicians, that he was the man. What little I know, I taught him, but he put his own soundin' in it, and sing with it, sing all night."[16]

---

12. Lomax, *Land Where the Blues Began*, p. 17.

13. Cohn, "Delta Bluesman," p. 69.

14. Lomax, *Land Where the Blues Began*, p. 17. Lomax only mentions Martin and Williams in his notes.

15. Not the present day Highway 61. Old 61 runs roughly parallel to the new highway about a half a mile west of where Clack's Grocery once stood.

16. Lomax, *Land Where the Blues Began*, p. 16.

But again it is unlikely any such conversation took place. According to his field notes, Lomax expressed some interest in Robert Johnson, and House told him the now familiar story of how Johnson had followed him and Brown around to listen to them play. And that seems to have been all that was said about Robert Johnson in 1941. Probably, decades later when Lomax got around to writing his book, he was simply trying to capitalize on Johnson's fame—he was by then perhaps the most famous bluesman who ever lived—and so Lomax worked more of Johnson into his narrative with another well-known bluesman in his book who was indisputably connected to him.

Lomax's description of House in his 1941 field notes is brief: "...he is 39 and learned to play from an old boy in Clarksville [sic] called Lemon because he played so many of Blind Lemon's pieces—learned about 1926—always made up his own songs rather than play those of other people—no stories, just separate verses."[17] The reference to "Lemon" was to Willie Wilson. The date for taking up music which House gave Lomax, 1926, is the earliest in all his accounts.

Lomax recorded House performing five songs, four of them with his band—Willie Brown on guitar, Fiddlin' Joe Martin on mandolin, and Leroy Williams on harp. There is nothing in Lomax's book or his archived field notes at the Library of Congress about the song selections, and it seems House played what he wanted. House and his band rocked through "Levee Camp Blues," "Government Fleet Blues," and "Walking Blues." On "Delta Blues" House was accompanied only by Leroy Williams. It was so hot that the musicians removed their shirts. Between songs they passed around a bottle of corn liquor.

Lomax's discs, unlike commercial discs, could accommodate fifteen minutes of sound on each side, and three of the five songs ran well beyond the usual three-minute limit of a 78-rpm record. "Delta Blues" was more than five minutes long, while "Government Fleet Blues" and "Walking Blues" each lasted almost seven minutes. Lomax, as a result, was capturing something that no commercial recordings ever captured, the Delta blues live, as they sounded when they played for dancers in the Oil Mill Quarters in Robinsonville. The musicians, to judge by their encouraging asides, were in high spirits—no doubt, assisted by the "corn"—the whiskey—too.

---

17. Field notes and correspondence, Library of Congress-Fisk University Mississippi Delta Collection., Washington D.C. "Clarksville" is not a mistake. Clarksdale had once been known as that, and blacks continued to use that name occasionally. The age House gave Lomax again confirms the 1902 birth date.

"Levee Camp Blues" and "Government Fleet Blues," despite their titles, were basically two takes of the same song which was a fixture in House's repertoire. The lyrics describe a time when House worked on a levee gang and a woman who on payday waits at the landing for the boat that carries him. Once she has his money, she leaves him. On "Government Fleet Blues" another voice—likely Willie Brown—chimed in with comments. The entire foursome played on these two songs and "Walking Blues." On "Delta Blues," House is accompanied only by Williams on the harp. The lyrics are a lover's protest whose second verse sums up the singer's frustrations:

> Look here, darling,what do you want me to do (2x)
> I've done all I could just to get along with you

Only on "Shetland Pony Blues," a version of his friend Charley Patton's most famous piece, did House perform by himself, probably because the song is rhythmically complicated. He would record yet another version of it the next summer—it had also become an essential part of his repertoire. Two survivors from that era, Walter Jerry Brown and Nancy Holmes, who saw him perform before the war said that "Ride My Black Pony" was their favorite song by him.[18] The mood of House's version differs markedly from Patton's recorded version. Patton's song has a jaunty and sly sexual humor about it. House's versions have a brooding almost aching quality—again, the difference between the two interpretations seems to epitomize the two men's different approaches to blues in general.

But the highpoint of the session was the rollicking version of "Walking Blues" that House and his band rolled out for Lomax. House and his friends stormed through the song—the tempo of the Clack's Grocery version is faster than the Paramount "test" that House and Brown recorded in 1930. Just after two minutes into the song, a train can be heard rumbling past, blowing its whistle, and indeed Son House rolled through the song like a locomotive. And while his vocal on the Paramount version is good, on the 1941 version he sings verses with more swagger and more confidence, coloring the notes with more variety than he did in the Grafton version—one definitely hears the effect of more than a decade of performing in his vocals. Put simply, "Walkin' Blues" rocks.

---

18. In an article in the Memphis *Commercial-Appeal*, June 18, 2007, by line Penny Wolfe. Brown was listed as House's 77-year-old son-in-law, but he was his 'step'-son-in-law having been married to one of Evie Goff's daughters by her first marriage. Even that relationship is complicated since both of Evie natural daughters, Bea and Sally, moved to Detroit in the late forties.

Lomax also recorded a few other songs involving various combinations of Fiddlin' Joe Martin, Leroy Williams, and Willie Brown. The two songs most often anthologized are Martin's "Four O'Clock Blues" and Willie Brown's version of the chestnut "Make Me A Pallet On The Floor." Martin crooned "Four O'Clock Blues," which sounds like a vaudeville blues from the 1920s as interpreted by Delta musicians.[19]

When House and his friends finished their last song, Lomax went in Clack's and bought them a bottle of Coca-Cola. Willie Brown grabbed it first and downed it. Then Lomax packed up the recording equipment and drove off, leaving barrels of dust behind his Ford.

In October, House sent a letter to Lomax—the letter was written for House by someone else since the difference between the neat hand in which the body of the letter is written and House's signature is plain. The letter, dated October 30, 1941 reads:

> Dear Mr. Alan Lomax I received and realy [sic] appreciated your writing me about those records we made Listen Mr. Lomax since those records will not be published I would be glad for you record one or two of them and send me I would like very well to my sister and brother one if even I would have to pay for them I would like to have the one I and Leroy Williams made with guitar and harp So answer soon Your Truly Son House[20]

House's references to his sister and his brother are puzzling. It is the first mention of a sister, and the existence of only two brothers—Rathel and L.J.—was ever confirmed. Rathel had disappeared long ago and his reappearance was very unlikely, and according to House's stepdaughter Beatrice Powell, L.J. died in the late thirties. Probably House was simply using the terms in a looser sense for kin of some sort,—cousins perhaps—of whom he had many. Whatever the case may be, Lomax replied in a letter dated, November 12:

> Mr. Son House
> Route 1, Box 8
> Robinsonville, Miss.

19. See Wirz's discography at http://www.wirz.de/music/housefrm.htm. These songs are still left off most compilations of the Fisk-Library of Congress recordings dedicated solely to Son House.

20. Field notes and correspondence, Library of Congress-Fisk University Mississippi Delta Collection.

Dear Son: Don't let my first letter discourage you, because I think some day your blues will bring you a reward. In the meantime I will be glad to send you a copy of one of your records. If you want additional copies, these can be furnished at $1.50 per 12-inch acetate disc.

> A friend of mine may drop in to see you some time soon.
> Please give him all the help that you can.
> Sincerely Yours,
> Alan Lomax
> Assistant in Charge
> Archive of American Folk Song[21]

Who Lomax's "friend" was is unclear. But on Christmas Eve, Lomax wrote House inviting him to come to New York to perform with an unspecified group of singers who, Lomax assured him, were "very nice people" and who *might* pay him.[22] Lomax suggested that commercial recording opportunities might follow but said that there was no money to pay for House's travel expenses to and from New York. Not surprisingly, House declined this offer.

In between Lomax's two letters to House, an event occurred four thousand miles away that would have an impact on both men's lives. On December 7, the Japanese attacked Pearl Harbor. When Lomax heard news of the attack, his immediate reaction was characteristic: he took a recording machine out into the streets of Washington D.C. to capture the reactions of passersby.

House also did his part, composing a patriotic song about the war effort. Meanwhile, events were gathering that would change his life.

July, 1942

In the spring of next year—just about the same time Son House was writing his patriotic song—Alan Lomax found himself dealing with the FBI as a result of a letter from an anonymous informant who claimed Lomax had "Communist sympathies." So the FBI began to investigate the folklorist, mostly focusing on his arrest in a demonstration while he was

21. Ibid.
22. Ibid. However, I first found it in John Cowley's obituary: "Son House 1902–1988: An Historical Appreciation. *Blues & Rhythm*. p. 9.

a freshman at Harvard ten years earlier. Lomax gave a sworn statement to an FBI agent on April 3. As a result of their investigation, the FBI would conclude in their report that Lomax possessed "an erratic, artistic temperament," "a bohemian attitude," and—most damning of all—he had "no sense of money values..."[23] As if that was not enough, his grooming habits were yet another concern. In June the FBI attempted to get Archibald MacLeish, then the head of the Library of Congress, to discipline or dismiss Lomax, but MacLeish dismissed the FBI's report instead. Still, the determination of the J. Edgar Hoover and his minions to protect Americans from such subversive influences as "Make Me a Pallet on the Floor" and "Froggy Went a Courtin'" is impressive.

His job saved for the time being, Lomax returned to Mississippi the next month on July 17. This summer, however, John Work was not with him. Instead Lomax brought with him a Brazilian assistant Eduardo. And now the indefatigable Lomax lugged his ponderous recording machinery around in the back of a brand new Hudson Super 6.

In his 1942 field notes, Lomax says that House took him to meet Robert Johnson's mother, but whoever the woman was, she was definitely not Robert Johnson's mother. In his book, Lomax placed this episode after the 1941 recording session, but his field notes make it clear that this visit occurred *before* the 1942 recording session--a mix-up on Lomax's part that has long been known. After visiting the woman who was not Robert Johnson's mother, Lomax recorded Son House in Robinsonville. This time House performed alone for Lomax, recording ten more tracks: "Special Rider Blues," "Low Down Dirty Dog Blues," "Depot Blues," "American Defense," "Am I Right Or Wrong," "Walking Blues," County Farm Blues," "The Pony Blues," and two versions of "The Jinx Blues."

In view of the fact that the previous summer, when Lomax said he wanted to record him, the first thing House did was gather his band, one must wonder if this was by design or by chance. Were Brown, Martin, and Williams simply unavailable, or did Lomax indicate that he only wanted to record Son House himself? Taking into account that Lomax was, as one writer put it, a "somewhat regressive defender of old ways and styles,"[24] it is not out of the question that he may have expressed a preference to House to play alone, which would have suited Lomax's idea of how a "folk

23. Ted Gioia, "The Red-rumor Blues," in the *Los Angeles Times*, (April 23, 2006). Lomax's FBI file was several hundred pages in length.

24. Gary Giddins in his review of Lomax's book, *New York Times Book Review*, (July 4, 1993) p. 9.

blues" ought to be performed.[25] However, Lomax's field notes are sparse and give no indication one way or the other.

The first song House recorded in 1942 was "Special Rider Blues." When Lomax questioned him after recording it, House told him he learned the song from Willie Williams in 1928 in Mattson—he meant his early mentor Willie Wilson. Songs with such a title had been around for more than a decade. In 1930 the piano player Little Brother Montgomery recorded "No Special Rider," and Skip James recorded "Special Rider Blues" the same year (on guitar). House's version—which, oddly enough, leaves out the line "I ain't got no special rider here" that gives the song its name— sounds somewhat like James' song, but the two men would not cross paths until both had been rediscovered in 1964. House may have heard James' recording, or learned it from someone else, perhaps even Robert Johnson who was certainly acquainted with Skip James' records. Stephen Calt has also suggested that his song is influenced by the widely performed Patton song "Pea Vine Blues."[26]

"Low Down Dirty Dog Blues" combined two Leroy Carr titles recorded in the late 1920s and early 1930's: "Low Down Dirty Blues" and "Low Down Dog Blues." The song is a complaint to a woman whose feelings towards the singer have been poisoned by slanders.

"Depot Blues" was another Patton-influenced piece that draws on the "Pony Blues" template. The opening stanza, "I went to the depot and looked up on the board..." was found in Tommy Johnson's "Cool Drink of Water Blues" as well as many other songs.

The next blues, "Walking Blues," should have been called "Death Letter Blues." When Lomax asked its title, House replied "Girl I Love Is Dead," adding that he composed it about ten years earlier and recorded it for Paramount in Grafton. He also gave Lomax the Lula back-story for the session and told him that the musicians received thirty dollars a record from Paramount.

Despite its mislabeling, the song showed the evolution of the Death Letter theme in House's music since his use of it in Paramount's "My Black Mama." All the Black Mama lyrics extraneous to the Death Letter theme had been taken out. The song now was solely about the singer

---

25. Angered at the appearance of the Paul Butterfield Blues Band with electric guitars at Newport in 1965, Lomax gave the band a very condescending introduction, and the band's manager Albert Grossman confronted him. The two men ended up grappling in the dust behind the stage.

26. See Stephen Calt's notes to the 1968 Yazoo reissue "Mississippi Moaners."

receiving news in a letter of the death of a lover. However, the melody differs from both the 1930 "My Black Mama" and the 1965 version, (called "Death Letter"). Those two songs have the same accompaniment and the same melody. The accompaniment to the 1942 is a proto-boogie. It combines the bass line of "Jinx Blues" with a Patton-like riff, and indeed it sounds somewhat like Patton's "Moon Going Down."

"County Farm Blues" is the further development of the 1930 Grafton track "Mississippi County Farm Blues"—the sixteen-bar song that House composed in his Grafton hotel room when the Paramount producer Art Laibley asked for a song like the Blind Lemon Jefferson hit, "See That My Grave Is Kept Clean." Since the Grafton session, the lyrics of the 1930 version had been developed and refined. They contain some of House's most evocative and moving images.

In 1942's "County Farm Blues" begins:

> Down South when you do anything that's wrong (3X)
> They'll sure put your down on the county farm

But it was the verses about "Captain Jack" that brought the misery into the sharpest and most frightening focus:

> Put you down under a man called Captain Jack (3X)
> He'll sure write his name up and down you back

When the song ended, House responded to Lomax's question about when he wrote it: "About three years ago. That's a song in Spanish A." What House meant by having composed the piece three years earlier is uncertain; possibly it was three years earlier that House rewrote the song's lyrics.

House recorded yet another version of "Pony Blues" in 1942, which he told Lomax he learned from Willie Brown. It is somewhat slower, and its mood seems less erotically charged, less urgent than the 1941 version.

The last blues pieces House recorded were two versions of "The Jinx Blues." This has been identified as a Willie Brown song, which seems related to Patton's "Maggie." The fill after the second A verse is virtually the same as that of "Highwater Everywhere," Part 1. Lyrically the song is one of House's standouts. The third and fourth verses of the first take, sometimes attributed to Willie Brown,[27] are justly famous:

---

27. Calt and Wardlow, *King*, p. 143.

You know the blues ain't nothing but a low down aching chill (2x)
If you ain't had 'em, honey, I hope you never will
The blues, the blues is a worried heart disease (2x)
declare the woman you be lovin,' man, is so doggone hard to please

House's rendition amplifies the bleak mood to proportions that transcend the issue of the departed lover. The song is one of his masterpieces, the sort of brooding, lustrous gem that only he could have cut.

Two of the ten songs House recorded were not blues. "Am I Right Or Wrong?" is a rag-flavored piece, a cousin of Patton's rag "Shake It And Break It," and is unlike anything else House had recorded to this point for Paramount or Lomax.

"American Defense" is even more curious. In between Lomax's 1941 visit and his return in 1942, America had entered World War II, and House in a wry moment of patriotism composed a waltz-time song about the war effort whose melody is taken from "Polly Wolly Doodle." After recording the song, House told Lomax he had composed it about three months earlier—about the same time the FBI was trying to determine if Lomax was a Red. The lyrics have a droll humor that most people do not associate with House's music:

You can say yes or no, but we gotta win this war
Because General MacArthur's now afraid
There won't be enough chaps to shoot a little game of craps
Because the biggest of them all will be dead

But the chorus has a wistful quality with a resonance in a time of seemingly perpetual war:

No use to shedding no tears, no use to having no cares
This war may last you for years

"American Defense" and the rag inspired "Am I Right Or Wrong" show how the twelve years House spent playing with Willie Brown expanded his repertoire. House's interviewers in the 1960s tended to concentrate their inquiries on blues, and these two recordings provide the only tantalizing evidence of other sorts of material that House may have performed.

At some point during the session, the manager of the plantation showed up and confronted Lomax. In his field notes, Lomax wrote: "Had a run in with the manager of the plantation Son rents on. He was extremely insulting and hostile. Finally after the recordings were over I drove to Tunica with him and we went to the Deputy Sheriff's office and had an hour's debate—all the attitudes. Will have to [be] discussed in another place. Clarksdale that night."[28]

The next entry reads, "July 18—Spent this day until 3 getting my affairs straight with the law."

That day, July 18, Lomax was detained in Clarksdale by the sheriff of Coahoma County, a man named Greek Rice. Someone had told Rice of Lomax's visit with House, and Rice warned Lomax about going on any plantation without permission of the owner. Lomax dropped the name of his "employer," Archibald MacLeish. But the sheriff, apparently unacquainted with MacLeish's poetry or his position as Librarian of Congress, was unimpressed, and it took word from an FBI agent and the intervention of Lomax's immediate superior at the Library, Harold Spivacke, to extricate Lomax from the clutches of the local constabulary.[29]

After he pried himself loose from Sheriff Rice, Lomax went onto record Muddy Waters again, David "Honeyboy" Edwards, and several other musicians before he headed back to Washington.

Some listeners consider the 1941–1942 recordings to be inferior to House's 1930 Paramount sides, but comparison of the latter with Lomax's recordings is to some extent an "apples and oranges" operation. House in the late 1930s and early 1940s was playing with a small band a good deal of the time. Some of the Fisk-Library of Congress pieces—"Pony Blues," "Jinx Blues," and "County Farm Blues" especially—show that House could still play a more intricate finger-style guitar, but such a style would have been lost in an ensemble. From this standpoint, House's manner of playing on the Lomax recordings was not a decayed form of his 1930 technique, but rather a stylistic adaptation suited to the context of a small band. This much is certain: House's performances with the ensemble in

28. Lomax, Alan. Field notes and correspondence, Library of Congress, Washington D.C.

29. The account of this incident and, indeed, of his interviews and recordings of House in his book is almost hopelessly muddled. In his book Lomax has the incident begin after he had recorded House and his band—in Tunica in 1941—yet in a few pages we are in Clarksdale in 1942 with the sheriff reminding Lomax, "There's a war, you know." Lomax combined both the 1941 and 1942 trips into a single narrative. So Lomax makes it seem as though the incident began while he was recording House and his friends in Robinsonville. The major flaw in Lomax's narrative ought to be apparent to anyone who carefully reads the section "Tunica Blues" in Chapter 1. In his account Lomax begins with Son House, Willie Brown, Fiddlin' Joe Martin and Leroy Williams outdoors behind Clack's Grocery, two pages later the same people are all inside a barrelhouse and he quotes House saying, "That's somebody honking *outside*," (my italics).

September of 1941 offer the best evidence on record of the powerful music one would have likely heard in a Mississippi juke joint in the late 1930s and 1940s.

For Son House, the 1941 and 1942 recordings came near the end of the first part of his musical career and did nothing to extend it. Lomax simply archived them, and they would sit in the archives of the Library of Congress unnoticed for nearly twenty years. Lomax knew of House's move to Rochester, since House corresponded with him, hoping that some sort of break might come from the recordings. But that break would not come for twenty-two more years.

To be fair, Alan Lomax soon had other pressing concerns. The next year, 1943, the war accomplished what the FBI had tried and failed to do: he lost his position at the Library of Congress, a victim to war-time budget stringencies. Shortly after that, Lomax found himself in the military. In the Army, the folkmeister set to work trying to sell the brass on a scheme to bolster troop morale with folk songs. After the war, he would spend most of the 1950s in England, more or less hounded out of the United States by the FBI due to his subversive attitude and poor grooming habits.[30]

That same year, 1943, Son House left Mississippi. He headed north, landed first a job in a foundry, and then found a job with the railroad. He would pass the next twenty-one years of his life in musical exile, in the shadows of long, dreary winters and short, hazy summers.

---

30. Gioia, "Red-rumor Blues." Gioia says the FBI suspected Lomax's "poor grooming habits came from associating with the hillbillies who provided him with folk tunes."

CHAPTER 7

Eclipse

1943–1964

When Son House left Mississippi in 1943, he might well have fallen off the face of the earth. But this he did not do. Instead he moved to Rochester, New York, where, in the years between 1943 and 1964, he lived in almost total obscurity. Indeed, what is known of his life in that period is so slight that inference, surmise, and speculation are unavoidable. The hard facts about House's life during these decades reduce themselves to this: two addresses in Rochester city directories, two other residences gleaned from correspondence, three confirmed employers, the names of two girlfriends, a police report, and the cursory notes on the exterior of an envelope that contains a grand jury proceeding from October 1955.

The reasons for this sorry state of affairs are several. The first is the nature of the interviews done with House after his rediscovery in 1964. The interviewers were mostly young, white blues aficionados—not journalists or academics—and for these interviewers a period in which House all but ceased performing and even playing was of little interest. A second reason for the dearth of information is House himself. He had an amusing phrase he would use to dismiss much of the blues music of the 1960s. "It's not the blues," he would say. "It's just a lot of monkey junk." The blues so dominated House's life that a period in which he all but ceased playing blues may well have seemed to him simply so much "monkey junk," and therefore not worth talking about in any detail. There is, yet, a third possibility. House may not have wanted to talk about this period because the most significant thing he did in this period was not something he wanted to share with anyone.

Nevertheless, a few facts about House's life in this period have been established, and these can be seen in the larger context of black migration and the history of the African-American community in Rochester. Aside from his music, most of what we know about his relocation and subsequent work fits the larger pattern of what is usually called the "Great Migration"— the movement of African Americans from rural, agricultural communities in the South to urban communities in the North and the South, a migration that began in earnest with World War I and continued into the 1960s. The move north meant for House—as it did for other southern blacks who migrated to northern cities—a great transformation of his life. He left a small rural community for a much denser urban community. He left farm work for industrial work. And he left music.

Rochester, New York held the same attraction for Son House that larger cities like Chicago and Detroit held for southern blacks: its industries offered better paying and less onerous work than the work available in the agricultural South. Northern cities also offered, in some degree, relief from Jim Crow—though, to be sure, there was no relief from racism per se.

House's first job was in a foundry manufacturing armor plating for tanks and bombers. As a result of World War II, industrial employment in Monroe County, in which Rochester is located, nearly doubled between 1939 and 1943, going from 68,000 to 120,000. For blacks, and members of other ethnic groups like Italians who had also faced discrimination in an over-whelmingly WASPish city like Rochester, the war created unprecedented opportunities for employment. Industries that might have discriminated against minorities had lost workers to the armed forces and could no longer afford discrimination—at times, bigotry gives way to an even more brutal force—capital.

Despite the luster of the city having been a home to Frederick Douglass in the nineteenth century and an important stop on the Underground Railroad, when Son House arrived in Rochester the black population of the city was still quite small. It was not until the 1950s that the number of blacks would grow significantly. In 1920 there were only 1,579 black people in a total population of 295,750. Two decades later, that number had increased to 3,262 in a total population of 324,975. In 1950, when the Rochester population had peaked at 332,488, some 7,590 were blacks. Then came the real growth; by 1960 there were 23,586 blacks in a total population of 318,611.[1] The decline in the total population suggests that "white flight" had already begun. That the illustrious progressive history of the city (which included Susan B. Anthony as well as

1. The statistics come from Norman Coombs unpublished paper, found at: http://people.rit.edu/nrcgsh/arts/rochester.htm

Douglass) counted for little by the time House arrived is seen in another statistic. In 1964, the year Waterman, Spiro, and Perls found House living at 61 Greig Street, Eastman Kodak, which then employed more than 10 percent of the city's population of 300,000, still would not hire blacks for anything but janitorial positions.[2]

Son House offered—as usual—two explanations of why he left Mississippi. They are not mutually exclusive, but they are different. The first was the motive he shared with every black person who left the South: as he told John Fahey, "I just got tired of the mess they's putting down for years and years. I said it's time I'm getting out of there. As old as I'm getting, I'll soon be dead. Live in this stuff the rest of my life?...What it was it was low wages, and wasn't treated as a human being should be."[3] The preacher was not a prophet however. House was not soon dead. In fact, in 1943 he had forty-five more years left to live—he hadn't even lived half his life.

House provided more details about this first explanation in the Julius Lester interview, saying it was a letter from a friend that spurred him to move to Rochester: "It was along about 1943 when I moved to Rochester. A friend of mine had moved up there and was working for a firm they call Simelton and Gold [sic]. They were making some kind of war equipment and he wrote and told me about them and what good wages they were paying. So I went on up. I worked on that job for a payday and then I quit. I didn't like it too well."[4]

The name of the firm, mangled in the interview transcript, was actually Symington-Gould, a foundry that made armor plating for tanks and the gun turrets on B-29s.

But House also offered a second, quite different motive for leaving Mississippi, a much more personal reason: to get away from his wife, Evie. When pressed and asked why he chose Rochester he told John Fahey in 1965: "Now I'll tell you truth about it. This wife I got now, I married her in 1934. And here's what happened. I had—just to tell you all the truth—I had a sweetheart woman. Her name was Daisy Mae Ketchum. She was a cook for the white folks. Her and my wife got in a fight. She [Evie] caught me dead to the right one Saturday night. I had a Chevrolet car, and I was actin' big shot in the little old place they call Robinsonville. This woman was there and my wife was there. All right, another old tattlin'

2. From the Kodak Historical Collection 003, Rush Rhees Library, University of Rochester.
3. Fahey, "Interview."
4. Lester, "My Own Songs," p. 44.

woman—I had been goin' with her, but I quit her. Well, this woman, she's mad about it. And she goes and tells my wife, 'Say, this woman Daisy says he's gonna take her home,' and I hear 'em talkin'..."

Fahey did not pursue the matter, but House later told Stephen Calt that he followed Daisy Ketchum to Rochester. He left Evie, her mother, and her three children behind in Robinsonville. How long House and Ketchum were together in Rochester is not known, and Daisy Ketchum seems to have left no trace in Rochester.

After his brief stint in the foundry, House landed work with the railroad: "So then I got a job with the New York Central out to East Rochester in the dispatch shop where they make box cars and things like that. I got a job as a rivet-heater and kept that about two or three years." Then a much better opportunity presented itself. "I got a promotion from the railroad company and they sent me over to Buffalo to get signed up for a job as a porter. There was a big fat colored guy over there doing the hiring at that time, so I got right on and stayed with that job ten, eleven years."[5]

Documents from the Railroad Retirement Board do not exactly match House's story. His first job may have been seasonal: The railroad documents only show him working for the railroad at the Despatch Shop in East Rochester as a "carman" during the summer months from 1944 to 1946: Then, eleven years later, in May and June of 1957, he is listed as working for the New York Central in the category of "extra gang and Section Men."[6] Until 1958, all the porters on the New York Central were actually employees of the Pullman Company. In July of 1958, the New York Central ended its contract with the Pullman Company and began staffing its own trains.[7] The Pullman job apparently offered itself in 1946, and House probably worked the job for most of the next decade. A position with the Pullman Company, it should be said, was considered a good job in the African-American community in Rochester.

House's initial residence was in the Seventh Ward just north of downtown Rochester at 24 Oregon Street, an address mentioned in an undated letter from House to Alan Lomax in the archives at the Library of Congress. Despite House's stated resolve to stay away from the church, his new home was, ironically, located squarely between two churches. Immediately next door was the Aenon Baptist Church at 22 Oregon, and only a few

5. Ibid., p. 44.

6. Documents obtained from the Railroad Retirement Board, January 17, 2008.

7. Some records for the Pullman Company are in an archive at the Newberry Library in Chicago, but no mention of an "Eddie J. House" is found in them.

24 Oregon Street, Rochester, NY, Fall 2009. Photograph by Daniel Beaumont.

doors further south at 6 Oregon Street was St. Simon's Episcopal Church.[8] The tract map shows the "location of social institutions," and in the key to the map the name of each church is followed in parentheses by "Negro." The growing presence of blacks in the neighborhood is also seen in the fact that two other "Negro" churches were located in it—the Church of God and Saints of Christ at 452 Ormond Street and the New Bethel Methodist Episcopal Church at 29 Leopold Street. In Rochester, as in Mississippi, religion—like the devil—was all around House.

A document produced by the Research Department of the Council of Social Agencies, Rochester, New York, provides a picture of House's new home.

The district had once been notable for a significant Jewish presence—it contained four synagogues—but according to the 1940 census this district already contained what for Rochester was a very high proportion of blacks. The pattern of blacks moving into what had previously been mostly Jewish neighborhoods occurred, of course, in many other cities, most notably Harlem. Blacks constituted just over 20 percent of the population

8. *Rochester, New York: A Graphic Interpretation of Population Data By Census Tracts*, published by The Research Department of the Council of Social Agencies, Rochester, New York, 1942, Census Tract 12 in Ward 7. All of the statistics and facts about the neighborhood that follow are taken from this page.

of the district when House arrived. The average rent of $20.41 in the area was less than half of that in the wealthier neighborhoods of the city, which explains why poor blacks leaving the South would have landed in this district. The document also shows that the African-American population was proportionally much younger than the rest of the city; more than three-quarters of the population was under the age of forty-four—House was forty-one when he arrived. That proportion reflected the larger migration—migrants tended to be young.

The housing statistics drawn from the 1940 census also reveal the character of the neighborhood in which House had taken up residence and what his new life must have been like. House's address was only four blocks from the New York Central Railroad station, so after he began working for the railroad he could have walked to his job. The block he lived on had a total of sixty "dwelling units" of which only two were occupied by their owners—a typical ratio for the neighborhood.[9] Most of the buildings on his block had been built between 1900 and 1919, while all the buildings across the street had been built in the previous century. On his block nearly half of the units—twenty-eight of the sixty—were listed as "needing repair or no private bath." In other words, House moved into a deteriorating quarter, a ghetto in the making. But it was still an improvement over the sharecroppers' shanties of the Delta.

According to his step-daughter Bea Powell, House sent for Evie about two years after he got to Rochester. Apparently, he and Daisy Ketchum had split up in the meantime. Evie apparently possessed nearly limitless reserves of patience. Bea Powell and her younger siblings stayed in Mississippi with their grandmother for another three or four years, then in the late 1940s they all moved to Detroit.

Sometime probably in 1951 or early 1952, House also convinced Willie Brown to move to Rochester. House sent him a ticket and some money. Brown moved in with House (and Evie presumably), and House helped him to get a job at the railroad yard in East Rochester. Once Brown was in Rochester, he sent for his girlfriend, a woman named Rosetta. But they were not together long before they had a falling out, and Brown sent her back to Mississippi. House provided some amusing details about their break up to Stephen Calt.

House, Brown, and Rosetta were in House's apartment one evening when the latter said that she had let a man "suck her" (in House's words)

---

9. Block 11 in census tract 12.

one night on a Mississippi levee—that, is, perform oral sex on her. House commented something to the effect, "Gee, I didn't know you liked that sort of thing," and Rosetta replied, "I do! Now more than ever!" This was too much for Brown. He exploded and told her he was taking her to the bus station and sending her back to Mississippi.[10] But according to House, Brown not long after that began to complain of homesickness, and soon he announced he was going back to Mississippi as well. As House put it, "I said, 'Well, Bill, you going to try and find Rosetta now.' 'Aw, naw,' he said. I said, 'Cut it out. That's what you're thinking about.' So he left and went on down."[11] House waggishly noted to Calt that Brown must have developed a liking for the sexual activity he had so vociferously denounced.

House made at least one trip back to Mississippi to visit his close friend, probably in the late fall or early winter of 1952. House told Julius Lester he used a two-week vacation to make the trip: "So I went down to see him. He had just had an operation for ulcers, and every time he'd eat a meal, he'd have to lay down flat on his back for thirty minutes. Well, after the different guys heard I was there, they all wanted me to come and play for them. 'Son House is here!' And they gave extra parties and everything, and Willie would go and play with me."[12]

But according to House, their musical reunion soon proved fatal to Brown: "The doctors had told him not to drink anymore, but he'd be with me and the fellas would come around offering me whiskey, you know. I'd turn it up and Willie would look at me drink it. He knew how we used to do, and he'd want a drink so bad. He'd say, 'Let me taste a little of that.' I'd say, 'Bill, you know what the doctors said.' He said, 'I'm going to try it anyhow. It look so good.' So he'd take little nips, you know."[13]

In January of 1953, not long after he got back to Rochester, House received a telegram from Brown's girlfriend, Rosetta. Willie Brown died on the last day of the year.

The death of his closest friend and his musical companion for more than two decades was the blow that caused House to stop playing music entirely. Looking back, House put it this way: "I said, 'Well, sir, all my boys are gone.' That was when I stopped playing. After he died, I just decided I wouldn't fool with playing anymore. I don't even know what I did with the

10. Stephen Calt generously shared his notes of this conversation with the author.
11. Lester, "My Own Songs," p. 44.
12. Ibid.
13. Ibid., pp. 44–45.

guitar."[14] Of his friendship with Brown, House said simply, "We were closer than brothers."

Brown's death affected House deeply, and while he attributed his quitting playing music to his friend's death, at the same time, musical styles in blues had been changing quickly after the war. Under the influence of swing and big band music, a smoother, more polished style of blues gained popularity—such as the music of Louis Jordan and T-Bone Walker—especially in the urban North. And even if House had wanted to continue playing, the black population of Rochester would not be large enough to support a club scene for a few more years. With all of these things working against him, quitting the blues must have seemed an obvious decision for House after Brown's death in December of 1952. As his neighbor and friend in Rochester, the blues musician Joe Beard put it, "…all of his friends started to die off—he got scared!"[15]

But House did not renounce all of his habits. Probably sometime in the early fifties House had another extramarital romance.[16] The young woman, Louise McGee, worked in the soda fountain in a Woolworth's, and she was likely many years his junior.[17]

House mentioned McGee to Stephen Calt in the 1960s, and he would commemorate his affair with her in the song "Louise McGhee" which he would record in 1965. Apparently the romance ended badly as far as House was concerned—McGee must have dumped him—for he would tell Calt later, "I couldn't afford to drop a bomb on her, so I made up a song instead."[18]

When House and McGee got together is uncertain, as is how long their affair lasted. But in the 1955 city directory McGee is listed as an employee of the decidedly upscale department store E. W. Edwards at 144 Main Street

14. Ibid., p. 45.

15. As quoted in my video documentary on Joe Beard, "So Much Truth: the Life and Music of Joe Beard," 2004.

16. A second possibility is that their affair took place later, say 1957, after House left the railroad once and for all. House would say that, at some point prior to his rediscovery, he worked at a department store and McGee worked at a Woolworth's department store. House probably worked for the department store after he ceased working for the railroad which appears to have been around 1957. In this scenario, their affair might have begun when he met her in the department store where they both worked.

17. A search in the city directories between the years of 1943 and 1964 yielded only one reference, in the 1955 directory, to a "Louise McGee." But it is almost certainly the same person since her address of 9 Leopold Street was just around the corner from 24 Oregon Street, House's first known address in Rochester.

18. Quoted in the liner notes by Stephen Calt to "Son House–The Real Delta Blues: 14 Songs from the Man who Taught Robert Johnson," Blue Goose 2016, 1974.

East—a much better employer than a Woolworth's. That same year, 1955, it is also known from court documents that in the fall, House was not working on the railroad, but rather was on Long Island (as shown later in this chapter), a long ways from Rochester. If McGee did not tire of House's drinking and his marital situation, her "upward mobility" may have induced her to ditch an older man who had lost a good job (temporarily it seems), an older man redolent of boozy memories of Mississippi and long dead musicians. Something like the Daisy Ketchum episode may have happened again, with House leaving Evie and leaving town. Although, this time, Louise McGee did not go with him.

By 1955 House had moved a little over a mile away, to 161 Atkinson Street, on the other side of the Genesee River, in the Third Ward southwest of the city's downtown.[19]

Two years later, in 1957 House left the railroad. Why he left is unknown. He may have quit, been fired (for drinking?), or been laid off. The date suggests being laid off is the best explanation. By the late 1950s, the New York Central, like other passenger trains, was losing business to automobiles. His last short stint with the New York Central coincides with a time when the railroad cancelled its contract with the Pullman Company and for a short period paid the porters itself.

After leaving the railroad, House was reduced to working at a series of menial jobs. The first newspaper article published after his rediscovery stated that he had "... been working off and on at various jobs: a cook and porter in a State Street restaurant, in a railroad shop in East Rochester, a department store."[20] Armand Schaubroeck, who operated a coffeehouse where House would perform in the 1960s, heard that House had worked in a Howard Johnson's restaurant as a cook or a dishwasher. He may also have worked for a veterinarian, shaving animals to prepare them for surgery. The Lawrence Cohn article stated that House worked as a barbecue cook and as a private chef for a gangster in his Adirondack redoubt.

House may in fact have been connected with a mobster. There was the Rochester of Kodak and the University of Rochester—the Rochester of respectability—and then there was another Rochester, a shadier version that accommodated activities that made life in the stuffy respectable city tolerable. The mob was a part of the city's life until quite recently, and there were, at least into the 1970s, a significant number of gambling operations—indeed, an

---

19. The address is found in a court document dating from 1955.
20. "Hunt For 'Blues' Singer Ends in City," *Times-Union*, July 6, 1964, p. 4B.

intermittent local mob war over the control of these operations stretched over three decades. House remained a patron of bars and gambling joints that were either on the fringes of legality or beyond it entirely. According to Joe Beard, House liked to gamble, and in one account, one of his "jobs" after the railroad years was as a sort of factotum for a man who ran a floating card game. House fetched beers for the players and performed other small tasks that kept the game going. That House would have gravitated toward such places and "jobs" is, of course, quite consistent with his haunts in Mississippi.

The first reference to "Eddie House" in the city directories only comes in 1964, when he was listed as residing at 86 Adams Street, about two blocks from the Atkinson Street address. Again Third Ward housing statistics in the 1960 census also reveal something of the conditions of his life there— more than a quarter of the housing units were either "deteriorating" or "dilapidated."[21]

In the spring of 1964, House and Evie moved to the Greig Street apartment house, where Perls, Spiro, and Waterman found him in June. 61 Greig Street is also a Third Ward address, only a few blocks from his Adams Street address.

86 Adams Street, Rochester, NY, Fall 2009. Photograph by Daniel Beaumont.

21. *U.S. Census of Housing: 1960 Rochester, N.Y.* published by U.S. Department of Commerce, p. 2.

61 Greig Street, Rochester, NY, circa 1970. Courtesy of the Rochester Municipal Archive.

61 Greig Street, Rochester, NY, Fall 2009. Photograph by Daniel Beaumont.

All of House's residences in these two decades were in those parts of Rochester where the city's burgeoning black population was concentrated, in neighborhoods that were segregated, overcrowded and suffering from the neglect of landlords. By the summer of 1964 these harsh conditions would contribute to an explosion.

This is just about all that is known of Son House's life for the period of twenty-one years between 1943 and June 23, 1964—with one significant exception. The exception is a strange and violent episode on a corporate farm on the eastern end of Long Island, New York.

The Cutchogue Labor Camp, October 8, 1955

"Migrant Admits Fatal Stabbing" read the headline of a brief story that appeared in the Monday, October 10, 1955 edition of Newsday. The story described how a migrant worker on a large potato farm on the eastern end of Long Island had been arrested in the early hours of Saturday, October 8 with a bloody kitchen knife in his possession. The arrest came thirty minutes after another laborer had died in a nearby hospital from a knife wound to the heart. When a policeman found the suspect, a fifty-three year old black man, near the entrance to the farm, he told him, "I did it."

The victim, a much younger man, had entered the older man's cabin and asked for money. When the suspect said he had no money, the victim had replied, "I'll look for myself, old man—" and started searching the cabin. Then the older man lunged at him with a seven-inch kitchen knife and stabbed him in the heart. The victim staggered out of the cabin, and three fellow workers took him to the Central Suffolk Hospital in Riverhead where he was pronounced dead.

The suspect was arraigned early Saturday morning for manslaughter. He waived examination and was held for the grand jury.

The Cutchogue Labor Camp was the largest of many corporate farms in Suffolk County on the eastern end of Long Island, on the North Fork, the smaller arm of the island after it branches into two peninsulas. Besides growing potatoes, the Cutchogue Labor Camp had "grading barns" where the potatoes were graded and sorted. The first barn had been built in 1927. The last barn closed in 2005. The farm was one of several that employed thousands of black migrant farm workers in the 1930s, 1940s and 1950s, at which point the Long Island suburbs creeping eastward began to encroach on the potato farms. In those peak years, the black employees usually hailed from South Carolina and Georgia. They were housed in barracks and fed as cheaply as possible—the huge farms, which supplied the New York City market, reproduced something like the conditions of the Mississippi Delta on Long Island. But the planters had been replaced by corporations like I.M. Young and Agway.

When the Cutchogue Labor camp finally closed for good in 2005, a *Newsday* journalist, Steve Wick, described the work on Cutchogue and the other farms in this way: "The job of the contractors, who were nearly always southern-born black men, included finding workers to bag the potatoes, which involved bringing men and women north on buses, then deducting food and housing costs from their wages. The workers from the Cutchogue grader said many of these young black men and women were "Shanghaied"—brought north against their will from rural towns in the South and forever separated from their families..."

According to Wick, conditions on the farms were miserable: "Everyone here agrees that just a few years ago the camp was filthy and unlivable, the food little more than slop served on dirty plates. As with other work camps, alcohol and drug abuse was rampant, fights common."[22]

On October 8, 1955, Son House was a laborer at the Cutchogue Labor Camp. It is impossible to connect his presence there with what is known of his life in Rochester in this period—how or why he landed in such a miserable place is a complete mystery.

At 12:52 AM that day—early Saturday morning—the Southold Police received a call from Cutchogue to send police immediately to the farm. A few minutes later, according to the handwritten police report, "three colored men," Nathaniel Miller, Jimmie Williams, and John Mack Brown, showed up at police headquarters and reported that they had taken a badly wounded man to the hospital, but the victim, Willie Junior Patterson, was dead on arrival from a knife wound to his heart. By 2:30 AM detectives had been sent to both the labor camp and the hospital to investigate and take statements. Soon, one of the labor camp's managers, Henry Wolf, called the police to say that a "colored man" was at his door, asking him to call the police because he had stabbed someone to death. That man was Son House.

By the time patrolman Robert Hogan reached Henry Wolf's residence, House had left. A few minutes later, Hogan found him in some scrub woods behind his shack which was near the main entrance to the farm.

---

22. Steve Wick, *Newsday*, April 24, 2005.

In his coat pocket, House had the bloody knife he had used to stab Patterson.

At 6:30 in the morning, House was arraigned before Judge Ralph W. Tuthill on a charge of manslaughter, first degree, of Willie Junior Patterson, a nineteen-year old migrant farm laborer from South Carolina. House waived examination at the arraignment. No bail was set, and House was sent to the county jail. Nine days later on October 17, a grand jury listened to testimony from the sheriff and House, and then dismissed the case, apparently accepting House's argument of self-defense.

The grand jury record remains sealed, with scant information about who testified written on the outside of the envelope. Alcohol may have played a role, given the late hour, Patterson's behavior, and House's own perennial drinking habit. Some dispute may have already existed between House and Patterson, but more likely House was targeted because he was significantly older than the rest of the farm's population. House's Mississippi origin may also have made him stand out among the other migrant workers most of whom came from the Carolinas and Georgia. House must have seemed an obvious target. But as a man who had killed before, he was not an easy one.

House's stepdaughter Bea Powell was completely unaware of his ever having worked on Long Island. While Bea lived in Detroit, she never visited Rochester. Her mother Evie had always gone to Detroit to visit her and her two siblings. After House left Mississippi in 1943, Bea would not see him again for over three decades, by which time the story of the killing on Long Island was long buried.[23]

Oblivion, part two

Aside from the violence of a few minutes after midnight on October 8, 1955 the man Muddy Waters remembered as "the king" wandered for two decades in a wilderness of humble jobs, alcohol, and apathy. House was, like many, pursued by demons—the conflict between religion and music, his womanizing, and his drinking—but the incident at the Cutchogue Labor Camp is a very different kind of demon. House sang about the killing of Leroy Lee in Mississippi and his time in prison in his 1930

---

23. From statements in the obituaries published after Son House died, it is clear that the rest of the family in Detroit knew even less than Bea Powell about his life, especially in this period. Bea Powell herself did not know when Willie Brown died until I told her.

recording "Mississippi County Farm Blues," and that story became part of his biography. Not so, the killing of Willie Patterson. House seems to have only mentioned this as a mumbled aside to Stephen Calt in 1965.[24] But for that brief confession, like so much else in House's life, it would have vanished. Although he had escaped prosecution by the law for this second killing some twenty-seven years after the first one, he did not escape prosecuting himself. This was a deed that could not be laid at the doorstep of the blues. House instead sought refuge in oblivion. But it was an oblivion that was not to last.

In 1962, seven years after the killing of Willie Patterson at the Cutchogue Labor Camp, there were signs that House's situation was about to change—though he was almost certainly unaware of it. Two reissues of some of his prewar recordings came out that year. The first contained three of House's Fisk-Library of Congress tracks. The second contained the Paramount tracks "My Black Mama," Parts 1 and 2. Then, the next year, 1963, two more compilations appeared, one including "Preachin' the Blues" both Parts 1 and 2, the other featuring six more of the Fisk-Library of Congress tracks. That same year, in the liner notes of the Columbia Records Robert Johnson reissue, House was mentioned as a major influence on Robert Johnson. Son House was about to reemerge.

24. Credit is due Ted Gioia here. More than forty years after House's "hushed" admission to him, Calt's recollection surfaced in Gioia's *Delta Blues: The Life and Times of the Mississippi Masters Who Revolutionized American Music* (New York: W. W. Norton, 2008), p. 85. It is possible House was alluding to the Long Island killing when he said to John Fahey of the killing of Leroy Lee in Mississippi, "Well, the *first time* I had to get in trouble..."

CHAPTER 8

Father of the Folk Blues

1964–1970

In the spring of 1964, Joe Beard moved into an apartment at 67 Greig Street to become the building's superintendent. Beard, then twenty-four years old, was an electrician who had, since the previous year, been playing bass guitar in a band with his friend John Ellison.[1] But Ellison wanted to play soul music, and Beard's first love in music was the blues. It had been that way as long as he could remember.

Beard was born in Ashland, Mississippi, a hill country hamlet about sixty miles southeast of Memphis that was then home to a few hundred souls. Despite its small population, Ashland counted among its residents a number of important musicians, and blues had been all around Beard in his childhood. Nathan Beauregard, a blind musician born not long after the Civil War, was the town bard. Beauregard lived with Beard's family intermittently, and Joe was one of the children who guided him around town. Beauregard would perform songs like "Spoonful," "Bumblebee," and "German Blues" in front of the town store or on someone's front porch while Beard and his friends the Murphy brothers, Dan, Floyd, Melvin, and Matt, crowded around to listen. The Murphy brothers were already adept guitar players as children, and when the family moved to Memphis after the war, the brothers quickly established themselves in the city's music scene. Floyd played guitar on Junior Parker's seminal Sun Record hit "Mystery Train," and in his teens Matt (later Matt "Guitar" Murphy) was already playing with Parker, Howlin' Wolf, and Ike Turner. Soon, Joe Beard and his family also moved to Memphis and, through the Murphy brothers, Beard met most of the important musicians in that scene, people like Wolf,

---

1. Ellison would go on to compose "Some Kind of Wonderful" with the Soul Brothers Six for Atlantic Records, a song that would be covered by many musicians.

Roscoe Gordon, and B.B. King—B.B. dated Beard's older sister for a time, and sometimes when he took her out to dinner, Joe would tag along.

The Murphys and the Beards left Ashland, but Nathan Beauregard stayed on, like one of the jinn bottled up by Solomon for eons, living on well past what can really be called "old age," until his life came to resemble the myth of the blues itself, patient, undying, and indomitable. Beauregard's musical breakthrough would not come until he was almost one hundred years old. Then, like a genie in the Arabian Nights loosed by a chance passerby—in this instance, a Memphis hippie—he would perform at the Memphis Country Blues Festival, make recordings, and appear on the television screen of Joe Beard in Rochester, New York, who gazed in mute astonishment at the flickering image of the ancient man singing "Spoonful Blues" on the public television station.

In the spring of 1964, a few days after Beard moved into his Greig Street apartment, he was sitting on the front steps of his building one evening playing his guitar when a lanky, soft-spoken older man approached him. The man listened to Beard play a blues song. When Beard finished the song, the gentleman told him that he had played blues in Mississippi before the war, and he mentioned some musicians with whom he had played—Charley Patton, Willie Brown, Robert Johnson. For Beard, whose schooling in the blues began in earnest in post-war Memphis, the names Patton and Brown were indistinct forms in the Delta haze. But the last name, Robert Johnson, caught his attention.

As a teenager in Memphis, among the many musicians Beard had seen perform was one Elmore James who had played with Johnson and had made one of Johnson's songs into the best known bottleneck blues ever, "Dust My Broom." And another of Beard's favorites, Muddy Waters, was also much influenced by Johnson. So, now as the older man recounted stories to him about Charley Patton, Willie Brown, Robert Johnson and himself, Beard began to realize that his neighbor must have been a musician of some stature. As Beard said, "He told me all these things, but I had no idea because I had really never heard of Son House—I'd never listened to him or Charley Patton. I knew of Robert Johnson, but I didn't know that he was associated with Son House. But then Son told me all these stories about him and Robert Johnson and Charley Patton. And, you know, I never was one to say, 'He doesn't know what he's talking about'—I never accept a person that way."[2]

---

2. Interview with the author, November 10, 2000. Unless otherwise indicated, all quotations of Joe Beard are taken from this interview.

Joe Beard. May 2010. Courtesy of the *Democrat and Chronicle*.

With their common interest in the blues, Beard and House quickly became friends. As Beard recalled, "He found out I played guitar, that I had guitars, and that's when we really started to see a lot of each other." That spring the two men began to spend their evenings passing the guitar back and forth, either on the steps of their buildings or in Beard's living room, playing songs for each other—House had not owned a guitar in years.

"Son loved to hear me do the acoustic thing alone," Beard recalled. "He would sit in my living room, and just ask me to do certain things that he loved to hear me do. There's a thing that I play on the guitar that Nathan Beauregard used to do, and he loved that...The song was called 'Mellow Peaches.'"

As the weeks passed, Beard learned more details about House's life in Mississippi. From their evenings playing music, it was evident to Beard that House remained proud of his musical career. It soon also became evident to him that very few people in Rochester knew of House's musical career in Mississippi. In fact, to this point there had probably only been four: his wife Evie, his girlfriends Louise McGee and Daisy Ketchum, and one other woman, a distant cousin who had also come from Robinsonville. Beard made five.

His new friendship with the young musician must have meant a lot to House. He had not worked regularly in a few years, and he spent much of his time either sunk in the gloom of Greig Street, apartment number 9, or cadging money for alcohol. Beard's friendship reopened a box of memories that House had more or less stashed away in a closet for years.

Yet, despite the abiding interest in the blues that House showed in their conversations, it was clear to Beard that his friend considered his musical career over. As Beard put it, "He knew that his life experience with the blues and the music would always be a part of him. But he had no thoughts of ever getting back into it again until Dick Waterman came along." It was pure happenstance that House met Beard and began to play guitar with him not long before the arrival of Perls, Spiro, and Waterman, and yet there is a providential air about it. House's new musical friendship with Beard showed that the blues still mattered to him, and without this he could not have revived his professional career. Shortly after his rediscovery, when House was asked if his neighbors knew about his musical career, House replied, "Most of them don't even know if I could blow a whistle." But after the arrival of Perls, Spiro, and Waterman, the small circle of people in Rochester who knew of House's past fame was about to become significantly larger.

Just two weeks after Perls, Spiro, and Waterman arrived on his doorstep, House had another unusual visitor, a young woman named Betsy Bues. Bues was a twenty-three years old rookie reporter for Rochester's afternoon daily, the *Times-Union*. She had graduated the previous year from the College of New Rochelle, a downstate Catholic college for women. After she followed the stairway to apartment number 9, 61 Greig Street, she found herself facing a black man from Mississippi who was forty years older than herself, an ex-preacher, an alcoholic, a convicted killer, and a bluesman. Nothing in the curriculum at the College of New Rochelle could have prepared Bues to make sense of the man who occupied apartment 9.

On July 6, the *Times-Union* ran Bues' story. It was the first story in Rochester—or anywhere in the mass media, for that matter—about the reappearance of Son House.[3] The story was accompanied by a photograph of House, sitting sideways on the steps of the Greig Street apartment. He smiles and holds what the story says is a borrowed guitar. The headline beneath the photograph read, "Hunt For 'Blues' Singer Of Thirties Ends in City." As the single quotes around the word "Blues" suggest, Bues and her editor must have thought that most of their readers would be unfamiliar with the term, and she took some pains in the article to describe the sort of music designated by the word:

3. In the mainstream press at least. Phil Spiro's article in the folk scene magazine *Boston Broadside* was dated June 24, although Spiro and his two friends were still in Rochester on June 24.

A search for a "country blues" singer of the past ended in Rochester last week.

The searchers, Richard Waterman of New York,[4] Philip Spiro of Cambridge, Mass. and Nick Perls of Fire Island, were looking for Eddie (Son) House who reached fame in the late twenties.

The men, "blues" hobbyists, are interested in locating singers of the 1920–30 era, and hope to bring back the "country blues." These blues were sung by southern Negroes. Many of the songs were slow laments about the plight of the Negro or about life in general.

The men searched in Mississippi, in Memphis, Tenn., and in New York.

They wound up in a third floor walk-up apartment at 61 Greig St.

There lives Son House with his wife, Evie.

He didn't have so much as a guitar to strum. But he was the Son House who recorded on the Paramount label from 1928–1932 with Charlie Patton, Willie Brown, and Blind Lemon Jefferson, well known in the "blues world."

The blues era was a short-lived one however, and House, like many others, drifted out of sight in the early 30's.

House says he is the only one left of the original four. His discoverers are encouraging him to try to make a comeback.

"That's what I want to do," he says. "I think it's great. I'm going to try to make it as great as I can. And I think I can."

House was scheduled to be the subject of a story in *Newsweek* magazine this week.

House, a Negro of slight build, is now 62 years old.

He was born in Clarksdale, Miss., the son of a deacon at Alan Chapel, a Baptist congregation, who was also named Eddie. That's where the "Son" came in.

Before taking up singing, House was an assistant minister in Alan Chapel.

He went to New Orleans in the mid-20s and came back to Mississippi with a guitar under his arm. "I taught myself how to play," he says.

From 1928 to 1932 House recorded on the Paramount label with the three other singers. Around that time he recalls there was a group of four gospel singers also with Paramount who became famous by singing "Four And Twenty Elders On Their Knees."

House's foursome split about 1932 and he went back to Mississippi. He married Evie Goff in Lake Carmen where she was a cook for a doctor.

4. Waterman was living in Cambridge, Massachusetts at the time.

Times-Union, July 6, 1964.
Courtesy of the *Democrat and
Chronicle*.

EDDIE (SON) HOUSE . . . on steps of his Greig Street apartment.

Hunt for 'Blues' Singer Of Thirties Ends in City

By BETSY BUES

A search for a "country blues" singer of the past ended in Rochester last week.

The searchers, Richard Waterman of New York, Philip Spiro of Cambridge, Mass. and Nick Perls of Fire Island, were looking for Eddie (Son) House, who reached fame in the late twenties.

The men, "blues" hobbyists, are interested in locating singers of the 1920-1930 era and hope to bring back the "country blues." These "blues" were sung by southern Negroes. Many of the songs were slow laments about the plight of the Negro or about life in general.

The men searched in Mississippi, in Memphis, Tenn. and in New York.

They wound up in a third floor walk-up apartment at 61 Greig St.

There Son House lives with his wife, Evie.

He didn't have so much as a guitar to strum. But he was the Son House who recorded on the Paramount label from 1928 until 1932 with Charlie Patton, Willie Brown and Blind Lemon Jefferson, well known in the "blues world."

The blues era was a short lived one, however, and House, like many others, drifted out of sight in the early 30's.

* * *

HOUSE SAYS he is the only one left of the original four. His discoverers are encouraging him to try to make a comeback.

"That's what I want to do," he says. "I think it's great. I'm going to try to make it as great as I can. And I think I can."

House was scheduled to be the subject of a story in Newsweek magazine this week.

* * *

HOUSE, a Negro of slight build, is now 62 years old.

He was born in Clarksdale, Miss., the son of a deacon at Alan Chapel, a Baptist congregation, who also was named Eddie. That's where the "Son" came in.

Before taking up singing, House was an assistant minister in Alan Chapel.

He went to New Orleans in the mid-20s and came back to Mississippi with a guitar under his arm. "I taught myself how to play," he says.

From 1928 to 1932 House recorded on the Paramount label with the three other singers. Around that time, he recalls, there was a group of four gospel singers, also with Paramount, who became famous by singing "Four and Twenty Elders On Their Knees."

House's foursome split about 1932 and he went back to Mississippi. He married Evie Goff in Lake Carmen, where she was a cook for a doctor.

"I stole her right out of the doctor's kitchen," recalled House.

* * *

HE CAME to Rochester in 1943 and has been working off and on at various jobs; a cook and porter in a State Street restaurant; in a railroad shop in East Rochester and in a department store.

He has been unemployed for three years. But since his discoverers arrived, he has been practicing up on a borrowed guitar and hoping to make a comeback.

He keeps the telegrams they sent close by his chair. House said he expects to be contacted again July 17.

"I thought I was too old," he said with a smile, "but I guess not."

Do the people in his apartment house know of his past fame? "Most of them don't even know if I could blow a whistle," he said.

Father Keck   Father Car

Father Keck New McQuaid Head

Rev. Robert Keck, S.J., ha taken over duties as princip of McQuaid Jesuit Hig S 'ool, replacing Rev. Co nelius J. Carr, S.J.

The appointment was mac recently by the Rev. James Shanahan S.J. provincial the Buffalo province.

Father Keck has been teacher of religion and Lati at McQuaid the past tw years.

Father Carr has been supointed supervisor of sec ondary education for Buffal province. He is stationed Canisius College, Buffalo.

SA
WOMEN'S
DRE
★
20% to
ALL SIZES and WID
GENES
Open Daily
9:30 - 9:30

"I stole her right out of the doctor's kitchen," recalled House. He came to Rochester in 1943 and has been working off and on at various jobs: a cook and porter in a State Street restaurant, in a railroad shop in East Rochester, and in a department store.

He has been unemployed for three years. But since his discoverers arrived, he has been practicing up on a borrowed guitar and hoping to make a comeback.

He keeps the telegrams they sent close by his chair. House said he expects to be contacted again July 17.

"I thought I was too old," he said with a smile, "but I guess not."

Do the people in his apartment know of his past fame? "Most of them don't even know if I could blow a whistle," he said.

Like Nick Perls' red Volkswagen, the *Times-Union* article is also a period piece. Bues' uncertainty about the things House told her was apparent not only in her attempt to explain to her readers what "blues" as a musical term meant but also in a few innocent and fanciful errors—for example, the blues "super group" of Charley Patton, Willie Brown, Son House, and Blind Lemon Jefferson that broke up in 1932. Still Bues' article contained at least one piece of information found in no other article or interview—the name of a church near Clarksdale to which House's family belonged.[5]

If Bues was somewhat perplexed by House, House too must have been somewhat perplexed by her. We can be reasonably certain that he had never been interviewed by a twenty-three year old white woman recently graduated from an all-women's Catholic college. On the evidence of the article, he omitted some colorful details from his life story in his responses, no doubt, so as not to rattle Bues' sensitivities. When Bues recollected the encounter years later, her main impression of House that day was his air of uncertainty about what was happening.[6] Lomax's sudden appearance in September of 1941 was improbable. But at least in 1941 House was still an active musician. Twenty-three years later, long after he had been out of music, three young white "folklorists" appear and propose to revive his musical career. Then, a young white reporter visits and questions him about things that occurred more than thirty years earlier. Events since June 23 exceeded mere improbability by several orders of magnitude. House must have wondered if he was waking or dreaming.

5. The name is incorrectly given as "Alan" in the article. There is still an Allen's Chapel in Marks, Mississippi. The information that House gave her that he was in New Orleans in the mid-1920s was also significant, since such a date does not conflict with other parts of his early chronology in the way that a period in New Orleans usually does in interviews done later in the 1960s.

6. Personal correspondence with the author, 2008.

July 14, the day after the *Newsweek* issue with the story of House's rediscovery appeared on the newsstands, the *Times-Union* ran a second story about him. The brief article read:

> "'Blues' Singer Making Try For Comeback"
> Son House may be on his way to making a comeback.
> The Negro "country blues" singer of the 20's and 30's who was recently rediscovered here will appear at the Newport Folk Festival, Newport, R.I. later this month.
> A festival official confirmed two bookings for House: at the Blues Workshop Friday, July 24, and at a concert Sunday, July 23. The festival runs from July 23 to 26.
> House's agent is Richard A. Waterman of Cambridge, Mass., who reports that the singer also will appear at the Philadelphia Folk Festival in August and at the Unicorn Coffee Shop in Boston next month.
> Waterman said that House is with him now in Cambridge. House and his wife have been living at 61 Greig St.

Besides time running in reverse between Friday and Sunday, the editor was still putting quotes around the word "blues." The music, the man, the world of pre-war Mississippi—it was all still very novel, still quite strange.

Soon the newspaper would have a story about a cultural encounter between black and white of another sort in House's neighborhood. And this time it would make the front page.

The Rochester riot

On Friday, July 24, one month after Waterman and his friends met Son House, and eighteen days after Betsy Bues visited him, the anger over conditions in the black community in Rochester boiled over.

That Friday evening the "Northeast Mothers Improvement Association" sponsored a street dance in the Seventh Ward at the intersection of Joseph and Nassau—just a few blocks from House's first Rochester address. This was then, and remains, the heart of the black neighborhood in the Seventh Ward.[7] At 11:30, one of the chaperones at the dance called the police about a drunken young man. Some policemen tried to arrest

---

7. This intersection is only four blocks from the first known address of Son House, 24 Oregon Street.

the young man, who was black, and the crowd, also mostly black, interfered with the arrest. The officers called for help. When a K-9 unit was brought on the scene, the sight of the dogs ignited a riot.

Joe Beard was playing at a club called the Brick Wall out on the west side of the city that evening, and when he came home, he heard sirens and saw police cars streaming towards the Seventh Ward on the east side of the river. But his neighborhood was quiet. It seemed to him some sort of local disturbance.

The next morning Beard read the headline on the front page of the Rochester morning newspaper, the *Democrat and Chronicle*: "Negro Mob Riots Here." He became, as he put it, "a little concerned."[8]

On Saturday night, the violence spread to the black neighborhood in the Third Ward where Beard and Son House lived. Beard had no gig that night, which proved to be a good thing. As it grew dark, he heard the sounds coming from the far end of Clarissa Street where the bars and clubs were located, a low rumble with sirens wailing above it. He could not have gone anywhere—police in the street kept everyone indoors.

A white man was killed on Clarissa Street that night. On Sunday afternoon, a helicopter surveying the damage crashed into a house on Clarissa Street and three more people died. That same day, the governor of New York, Nelson Rockefeller, sent the National Guard to Rochester, and finally, on Sunday evening, they quelled the violence. A local minister and activist, Franklin Florence, said of the violence, "... they didn't look at this as a riot, they looked at it as a rebellion."[9]

Son House's Greig Street apartment was near the center of the violence on Saturday and Sunday, and we may well wonder where he was during the riot. He was safe—though not sound. Despite its proximity to his apartment, House saw none of the violence, because he spent all three days in a hospital in Newport, Rhode Island.

On Thursday July 23, Nick Perls and Dick Waterman had driven House to Newport to perform at the Newport Folk Festival which began that day and ran for the next three days—the same three days when the rioting in Rochester took place. As soon as they pulled onto the festival grounds in Perls' red Volkswagen, they promptly ran into one of the festival grandees, Alan Lomax.

8. Personal conversation with the author.

9. In the documentary *July'64*, directed and edited by Carvin Eison, produced by Chris Christopher.

House, according to Waterman, was something less than overjoyed by their reunion after twenty-two years. When he saw Lomax coming towards them, he said to Waterman, "Here come that old booger Lomax."[10] Lomax asked House if he was still living in Rochester, which "stunned" Waterman who asked if Lomax had known that House had been in Rochester since the early 1940s. Lomax replied, yes, he had known, and Waterman asked why he had not informed others so that House might have had a chance to record again. Lomax's response according to Waterman was, "After I recorded him, it wasn't any of my business what he did with his life. My job was to record him for the Library of Congress. I didn't care what he did after that."[11]

By evening, however, House had other more pressing concerns than his relations with the folk music impresario. He was in an emergency room with abdominal pains, and from there he was admitted to the hospital. House missed the riot—but he also missed the entire Newport Folk Festival.

On Sunday—the same day the violence in his neighborhood subsided—House was released from the hospital. House and his community would begin to patch themselves together and move forward.

Rehab

After House got out of the hospital, Waterman brought him back to Cambridge. When the trio found him at 61 Greig Street, House had a tremor in his hands. With his tremor controlled by means of carefully calibrated amounts of alcohol, House got down to the task of dusting off his old repertoire that he had not played in years.

Before Al Wilson's intervention, Waterman and others would recall that House could only play slow blues, but Joe Beard remembers it differently. Beard said emphatically, "No, he could still play—he just didn't own a guitar." It would seem, although Wilson and Waterman did not know it, that Beard had already in his own way been preparing the ground for their work. The real issue was not really whether House could still play, but *what* he was going to play.

---

10. Dick Waterman, *Between Midnight and Day* (New York: Thunder's Mouth Press, 2003), p. 37.

11. Ibid., p.37. However, Phil Spiro would later say that it was pointed out to him that, "Lomax had a lot of problems around 1964 and was probably not aware that people were looking for Son." Personal correspondence with the author, February 28, 2009.

Al Wilson played guitar with him every day for a period of about two weeks, and encouraged by Wilson, House was able to quickly pick up much of his repertoire, including the most important pieces as far as his new folk blues audience was concerned: "Preaching the Blues" and what had become his version of "My Black Mama," the song he now called "Death Letter Blues." And that was precisely the goal of Wilson's musical rehabilitation of House. What songs House might have played and what instrument he might have chosen to play them on had he been left to his own devices is a moot question, since left to his own devices—or vices—he probably would have never performed professionally again. House had to reproduce his prewar songs as closely as possible, since the folk circuit mostly featured blues musicians who had gotten out of music and thus not evolved musically. The contrast with a musician like Lonnie Johnson helps to illustrate the situation. Johnson, who had never ceased playing and was now playing an electric guitar, scandalized people in the folk scene by stating that he preferred to play an electric guitar, and as if that was not bad enough, he also wished to play current hits like "I Left My Heart In San Francisco" as well as blues.[12] Such expectations were not confined simply to the rediscoveries. When Muddy Waters first toured England in 1959, certain critics and fans were disappointed when he played his Telecaster despite the fact that he had been playing in bands with electric guitars and amplifiers for a decade. Then, when he returned a few years later and tried to appease the critics with an acoustic guitar, the audience's expectations had changed, and they were disappointed again.

And House's own tastes might have changed. A music store owner in Rochester, remembered House coming in with what must have been his first royalties to look for a guitar. When the owner tried to show him some vintage National Steels, House said he "didn't want that junk," and instead he pointed to a candy-apple red electric guitar with three pick-ups. But from the standpoint of marketing him on the coffeehouse and festival circuit, Son House playing an electric guitar was not what the folk music audience wanted to hear. They wanted to hear "Preachin' the Blues" on a National Steel, and ultimately that is what they got.

The next month, August, marked the real launch of House's second musical career. That month he played the Unicorn Coffee Shop in Boston

---

12. Elijah Wald, *Escaping the Delta*, p. 242. Recall too Phil Spiro's remarks: "We also consciously or unconsciously tried to shape the music that they played on stage ... I wonder now what would have happened if we had just left them alone instead of telling them what songs to sing and what instrument to play them on." Von Schmidt and Rooney, *Baby*, p. 198.

and the Philadelphia Folk Festival. Thereafter, for the rest of the 1960s, Son House's revived career under the management of Dick Waterman consisted of three elements: touring, recording, and giving interviews.

Son House on tour, on record

In the fall of 1964, House played at the University of Chicago and Indiana University. He also began working that fall and the following winter on the East Coast coffeehouse circuit, places like the Café A Go Go and the Gaslight Café in New York City, the 2nd Fret in Philadelphia, and Club 47 in Cambridge, and for the next five years, he would play in these sorts of venues at least twice a year.

The same winter of 1964–1965, Waterman was also working on a recording contract for House. Some of the other rediscoveries had already signed or would soon sign recording contracts: Mississippi John Hurt signed with Vanguard; Bukka White signed with Takoma, a label founded by young blues initiate John Fahey. House also had offers from such labels, but it was to Waterman's credit that he bypassed the lesser labels which would have meant folkloric oblivion for his client. Waterman had met John Hammond, Columbia's longtime jazz and blues producer, at the Newport Festival the previous summer, and that meeting, coupled with Columbia's release of the first Robert Johnson album a few years earlier, had given him hope that House might sign a contract with that label.[13] Once again, it seemed Robert Johnson—from beyond the grave—might help his musical mentor.

In late winter or early spring of 1965, House and Waterman met with Hammond in New York. Hammond asked if House knew that the Fisk-Library of Congress sessions in 1941 and 1942 had come about due to his influence on Alan Lomax. That was undoubtedly news to House, but given his sentiments at his reunion with Lomax, House must have received it with genial indifference. Hammond then brought up Robert Johnson and said that he had always wanted to record him. But since Johnson was dead, he would be thrilled to record House. The three quickly agreed that House would sign a contract with Columbia for one record.

Afterward, Waterman took House to a bar to celebrate his new contract. When Waterman proposed a toast to Hammond, Son House lifted his bourbon and said with sardonic humor, "Here's to Robert Johnson . . . for

13. Waterman, *Midnight and Day*, p. 37.

being dead."[14] Thirty-five years after his Grafton session, House had signed a contract with the biggest and most prestigious record label in the country and was returning to the recording studio. The contract was for one record—with an option, as we shall see—and House received a $1000 advance. A very respectable sum at that time.

On May 12, Columbia Records issued the press release: "Columbia Records has signed country-blues singer Son House to an exclusive recording contract."[15] As a Columbia recording artist, Son House was now in the company of such hit makers as Bob Dylan, the Byrds, Paul Revere and the Raiders, and Barbra Streisand. By design or by chance, Columbia's publicity department was a little tardy with their announcement. The session actually took place a month earlier in New York City on April 12–14.

In early April, House played at the Ontario Place coffeehouse in Washington D.C. A few days later, he went in the studio in New York City for Columbia. It was a measure of the seriousness of the project that Hammond, who had worked with such artists as Bessie Smith, Count Basie, Bill Broonzy, and Bob Dylan, took it upon himself to produce the record.

Lawrence Cohn, one of the "blues mafia," who subsequently would have a long career with Columbia reissuing classic jazz and blues, was present at the session. As Cohn recalled, the studio was set up like a "small club," and there were actually more people present than there were on many of the nights when House played in Greenwich Village coffeehouses.[16] Twenty-one tracks were recorded over the three days. When the album was issued, it contained nine songs. Side 1 contained "Death Letter," "Pearline," "Louise McGhee," "John the Revelator," and "Empire State Express." Side 2 consisted of four tracks, "Preachin' Blues," "Grinnin' in Your Face," "Sundown," and "Levee Camp Moan." Al Wilson played second guitar on "Empire State Express" and harmonica on "Levee Camp Moan." Dick Waterman wrote the album notes, which mentioned The Beatles, The Righteous Brothers, The Supremes, Peter, Paul and Mary among others. Besides the alternate takes, seven other tracks were unreleased: "President Kennedy," "A Down The Staff," "Motherless Children," "Yonder Comes My Mother," "Shake It And Break It," "Pony Blues," and "Downhearted Blues."

The sound and fury of the Grafton track, though muted by the passage of time, were still evident in "Death Letter." "Sundown" and "Levee Camp

14. Ibid., pp. 37–41.
15. Not quite as "exclusive" as they might have wished, as would soon become apparent.
16. Lawrence Cohn, in Letters, *Blues Unlimited*, Vol. 148–49, p. 6.

Moan" were reworkings of material familiar from the 1941–42 sessions, revisiting themes found in "Levee Camp Blues," "Low Down Dirty Dog Blues," and "Jinx Blues." The musical accompaniments on all of these are virtually the same—it was one of House's favorites. On "Levee Camp Moan," Al Wilson played harmonica accompaniment, rather after the fashion of Leroy Williams in 1941. "Pearline" was unlike anything House had recorded and sounded unusually sweet for the blues.[17] "Louise McGhee" was the slow blues that House composed about the Woolworth's soda fountain employee who had dumped him. "John the Revelator" is the well-known gospel song that House invariably performed unaccompanied—as he does here—in his 1960s concerts. "Empire State Express" was, like "Pearline" and "Louise McGhee," a new song. Like the other new songs, it shows House—like most adept composers—reusing and recombining old pieces to make "new" material. In musical terms, it is a "down the staff" version of "Maggie"—again showing the enduring influence of Patton on House, and indeed, Al Wilson's guitar accompaniment makes it especially reminiscent of Patton's tune "Moon Going Down." In House's own prewar repertoire, it resembles "Jinx Blues" and to a lesser extent the 1942 song labeled "Walking Blues" which is really another version of "Death Letter Blues." The title, of course, refers to his time with the New York Central, and House's new lyrics about that train were "retrofitted," so to speak, with a good many older floating verses about trains.

Side 2 of the LP began with House revisiting "Preachin' the Blues," now simply called "Preachin' Blues"—which gives it the title of Robert Johnson's version. House's 1965 Columbia version was noticeably slower than the Grafton track and, while lacking the demonic ferocity of the latter, somehow still remained an intense rendition of the central dilemma of his life. "Preachin' Blues" was followed by the most bizarre song House ever recorded, the strange solo vocal "Grinnin' In Your Face."

"Grinnin' In Your Face" was musically irregular, which is probably why House performed it without instrumental accompaniment. Some of the lyrics read:

> Don't you mind people grinnin' in your face
> Just bear this in mind, a true friend is hard to find
> Don't you mind people grinnin' in your face
> You know your mother will talk about you

17. It resembles somewhat the opening notes of "Bedside Blues," recorded in Memphis in 1930 by the otherwise unknown Jim Thompkins.

> your sisters and your brothers too...
> You know, they'll jump you up and down
> They'll carry you all around and round
> Just as soon as your back is turned
> They'll be trying to crush you down
> Just bear this in mind...

The piece conjures up a bad dream taking place inside a fun house. Grinning faces loom in front of you, threatening and malevolent. The surreal song hints at some gloomy recess in House's personality from which he observed his fellow humans with considerable suspicion. It is compelling, unsettling, and just plain weird all at the same time.

The Columbia session was to be House's last studio recording. The day after the Columbia sessions ended, House traveled to Ohio where he played a concert at Oberlin College. A recording of some of the songs he played there would also appear in 1981.[18]

The next month, May, House was touring the West Coast. His biggest date was the third annual UCLA Folk Festival, which he played on opening first night, May 14. An article in the *L.A. Times* the day before the event spoke of House as the festival headliner. The article had a picture of House playing a song while the chairman of UCLA Folklore and Mythology Group held a microphone to him; the headline was: "Blues Singer Will Be Folk Festival Feature." The article began, "Son House, blues singer from the Mississippi Delta, will be one of the stars at the opening concert of the third annual UCLA Folk Festival..." The next evening, House was the headline performer at Royce Auditorium.

By coincidence, while House and Waterman were in Los Angeles, they learned that Howlin' Wolf was also in town taping an appearance on the ABC television show *Shindig*. The show's producers had asked the Rolling Stones to appear, and the Stones told them they would do the show if they would get either Muddy Waters or Howlin' Wolf to appear on the show with them.

House and Wolf had known each other well in the Delta. As we have seen, House first met Wolf sometime in the mid 1930s when Wolf, who was eight years younger, arrived in Robinsonville on the back of a pickup truck and began to play in the local juke joints.

---

18. The songs are listed on the CD "Son House in Concert" as "It's So Hard," "Judgment Day," "New York Central," "A True Friend Is Hard To Find," "Preachin' the Blues," and "Change Your Mind." Their relations to his recorded songs are fairly easily discerned.

House and Waterman found the studio and managed to make their way to the set. Wolf, who had been rehearsing with the *Shindig* house band, was sitting in one of the theater seats when he saw House enter. Astonished, Wolf hurried down to greet his old friend, who he had not seen since they played together in the Oil Mill Quarters in Robinsonville more than twenty years earlier.

The Rolling Stones, who were huddled on the stage between rehearsing numbers, noticed Wolf's enthusiastic greeting, and Brian Jones came over and tapped Waterman on the shoulder. "Excuse me," he said, "Who is the old man that Wolf thinks is so special?"

Waterman told him he was Son House, and Jones nodded, "Ah, the one that taught Robert Johnson."[19]

Two months later, on June 17, 1965, at the first and last New York Folk Festival, House performed in Carnegie Hall—the honor that had eluded his young friend Robert Johnson twenty-seven years earlier. Once again he was reunited with another Mississippi native and friend who he had not seen for more than twenty years, Muddy Waters, who was also on the bill. Muddy, since he had toured England in 1959, had been playing increasingly to white audiences. When House found Muddy backstage and approached him, one of Waters' band members mocked House's loose-limbed gait. Waters got up and scolded the young man, "Don't you be mocking that man...When I was a boy comin' up, that man was king. King! If it wasn't for that man, you wouldn't have a job. Because if it wasn't for him, I wouldn't be here today..."[20]

The month after the New York Folk Festival, Son House returned to the Newport Folk Festival, and this time he managed to stay out of the hospital and actually perform. It was also the year at Newport that Dylan shocked the folk movement by taking the stage playing an electric guitar with members of the Paul Butterfield Blues Band backing him. House could have watched his old friend Alan Lomax wrestle in the dust with Albert Grossman who took exception to Lomax's rude introduction of the Butterfield Band. An album of performances from that year's festival that was released by Vanguard later that year included two of House's songs, "Death Letter," and "Sundown Blues." Most of House's recordings after the Columbia album were like this, live performances. The exceptions were the numerous bootlegs made with House.

19. The anecdote is found in the biography of Howlin' Wolf by James Segrest and Mark Hoffman, *Moanin' at Midnight*, (New York, Pantheon Books 2004) pp. 226–27. Also in Bill Wyman's *Rolling With the Stones* (London, DK Publishing 2002), p. 186.

20. Waterman, Son House Obituary, p. 48

Son House and Howlin' Wolf, Los Angeles, CA, 1965. Courtesy of Dick Waterman

Avalon Productions

While House played at Carnegie Hall in June, he and Waterman stayed a few blocks away in the Henry Hudson Hotel. And it was there in the bar of the hotel that Waterman formed his own management company, Avalon Productions. Besides House, Waterman was soon managing other rediscoveries such as Mississippi John Hurt, Bukka White, Sleepy John Estes, and Skip James. Waterman worked with a list of 512 colleges he obtained from a booking agency. By his own account, he wrote letters, night after night, on his Underwood manual typewriter to these schools and to folklore societies. Once House began to perform, Waterman collected favorable reviews and included copies of those. The result was about five years of fairly steady bookings for House on the college, coffeehouse, and folk festival circuits.

House's deal with Waterman was a handshake agreement, with Waterman taking 10 percent of the fee. Initially House was paid sums in the range of $50 to $75 per show. Waterman recalled that House earned $115 for a show at Wayne State University in Detroit in the spring of 1965, and that led to better fees. Among Waterman's artists, only Mississippi John Hurt, whose gentle—say it, unthreatening—manner made him a college favorite earned much more money, about $500 to $600 a show. However, by the late 1960s House was often making $200 to $300 per show at colleges. Working two or three tours a year, House probably earned a few thousand dollars a year between 1965 and 1970. In present day dollars, this means House went from earning about $300 per show initially to $1200 to $1500 for his college dates.

House was Waterman's most difficult artist. Waterman's foremost concern was his client's inclination to liquidate his assets—if House had a guitar, he would pawn it to buy alcohol. So he could hardly be entrusted with the National Steel he used in his performances. As Waterman put it, "I tried to mask it and conceal it while he was alive, but he was a total, hopeless alcoholic."[21]

However, since House could not and would not perform without alcohol, the task of managing his consumption of alcohol fell to Waterman. "He could not be left on his own all day," Waterman recalled. "There was an incredible amount of pressure that comes with being with someone who is a total alcoholic and is devious and is looking to find a way to get a bottle to get drunk. And it was up to me to safeguard the gig…if he got out of your sight and found a bottle, there was no 'take a sip' or 'take a swig.' He would simply drink the entire bottle."[22]

In a very real sense, Waterman became a kind of surrogate spouse, someone who fulfilled the functions of Evie when House was on the road away from her.

Except for his appearances in Rochester and western New York, Waterman was, of necessity, House's constant companion. Even on the tours that took House all the way out to the West Coast, Dick Waterman

---

21. Waterman, interview, 2009. When Waterman was not present, he sent instructions about alcohol. See, David Feld, *Blues Access* (Winter 1993): p. 14: "Waterman made sure we had some money for House and told us exactly what kind of alcohol to give him, how much and when."

22. Waterman, interview, 2009.

drove him, and long silent hours on the road passed with Waterman behind the wheel, all the while rationing House's alcohol intake by means of little airline bottles of gin. In order for either man to make any money, accommodations and meals necessarily were cut-rate. When House played at Oberlin College in the fall of 1964, for example, he and Waterman stayed in a dormitory room that one of the students gave up for their use for the night.

To keep his wayward client occupied, Waterman sometimes took him sightseeing. When House performed in a folk festival at Swarthmore College in 1965, which is just outside of Philadelphia, Waterman took him to see the Liberty Bell. House had never heard of the Liberty Bell however, and as far as Waterman could tell it failed to make much of an impression on him.

Shepherding his boozy star took a toll on Waterman. "That was real work," he said. Despite the fact that the earnings from touring must have been a significant piece of income for House and Evie, strangely enough, according to Waterman, neither seemed to care that much whether he worked. As Waterman put it, "If I found work for him, and came and picked him up, and took him out on the road, that was okay. If I left him alone, and didn't call, and didn't come—that was okay too. Neither one had any strong feelings on it, one way or the other. And Son had no feelings of being a well-known artist. He had no sense of celebrity."

Others who knew House in this period had other, somewhat different views however—as will be seen.

Son House Live

In 1965, House played colleges like Wayne State University, Grinnell College, Oberlin College, and other folk festivals like the Swarthmore Folk Festival and the Mariposa Folk Festival in Toronto. House also played clubs in Montreal and Toronto that year, and *Downbeat* published a review of his performance at the Toronto club, the New Gate of Cleve. The reviewer for *Downbeat* wrote: "The final set of his week-long appearance at the New Gate of Cleve was something that will live in the minds of those who heard it as long as they live."[23]

When House played at the Gaslight Café in Greenwich Village in 1965, there was present in the audience a college student named Brian Williams who had come with a friend to hear the Delta bluesman for the first time. Williams would later move to western New York, where he would become

23. John W. Norris, *Downbeat*, Vol. 32, no. 24, (1965): p. 38.

Son House, Philadelphia, PA,
1965. Courtesy of Dick
Waterman

well-acquainted with House and often play music with him. Indeed, Williams would also become a professional musician himself, playing the upright bass in a variety of musical contexts, blues, swing, and rockabilly, and he would credit Son House with changing his style on the instrument.

At the time however, Williams was a callow nineteen year old, and though he had already seen such rediscoveries as Mississippi John Hurt, Skip James, and Bukka White play, none of these musicians had quite prepared him for the experience of Son House.

House was on a bill that night with a young, white singer-songwriter named Tom Paxton. Paxton would go on to write songs covered by musicians as varied as Mel Tormé, Willie Nelson, and Pat Boone, but his style of music had absolutely nothing to do with Son House. Indeed, a more incongruous double bill is difficult to imagine—it was the sort of "mouse-frog" nuptial that occurred now and then under the rubric of "folk music."

While Paxton played his set, House sat in a corner of the room, smoking and placidly biding his time. He was the only black person in the club, and as soon as Williams caught sight of him, he ceased paying attention to Paxton. He was wearing a white shirt and Williams sensed that despite his weathered look, he was very concerned about his appearance. But there was something else in House's physical appearance that set him apart: "Obviously he had been through a hell of a lot in his life. His body movements and his facial expressions showed that he lived a hell of a hard life. So before he uttered a word I knew there was a different kind of character."[24]

When Paxton finished his set, House took the stage with his National Steel guitar, which he proceeded to tune. As Williams put it, "...my ear was telling me that even when he felt it was in perfect tune, it was still out of tune. But that didn't seem to bother him very much."

When House began to play the guitar, he pressed the slide down so hard, that it knocked against the frets as he ran it up the neck—he violated not only the canons of European music, but in its way even those of blues, if indeed such exist. And the note the slide finally produced was in Williams' words, "kind of 'in the vicinity of.'"

House leaned his head back, and his eyes rolled up until only the whites were visible, and—he began to sing. Williams soon realized that he was watching some sort of psychological transformation: "He was getting in touch with something inside of himself that was so foreign and so alien to anything I knew or understood as a nineteen-year-old kid that I was captivated by it. If I think back, I can remember a number of the songs that he did, but the lyric of the song was hardly what I was getting out of it at that moment. It was just kind of looking into somebody's soul, way deep down in a space that was so unfamiliar to me that I knew I was having an experience at that moment that I was never going to forget."

Some of House's musical skills had diminished by the 1960s—the tempo at which he performed "Preachin' the Blues" in 1965 is far slower than that of the 1930 Grafton version—but somehow the emotional power of his performances had not ebbed.

The Gaslight was, fortunately for House, located next door to a bar called The Kettle of Fish—and as Williams observed, "Son House loved to take a drink, for sure." When House had finished with his first set, as Williams recalled, "he put his guitar in the case, and he pretty much disappeared right out of the coffeehouse and was at the Kettle of Fish, knocking 'em back." Williams and his friend were so entranced by what they had seen, they followed House to the Kettle of Fish and, from the other end of the bar, watched him with rapt attention as he knocked back one drink

24. Brian Williams was interviewed by the author and University of Rochester student Jessica Steele on April 28, 2002.

after another. His drink was straight gin, room temperature. Even House simply drinking was more interesting to Williams and his friend than Tom Paxton performing.

One can hardly overemphasize how utterly foreign a musician like Son House was to Williams—and how utterly foreign Williams and his young white audience must have been to House. When House and Willie Brown had performed blues before 1943 he played for a completely black audience who danced to his music in the raucous atmosphere of a Delta juke joint. After 1964, House performed by himself for almost entirely white audiences who sat in rapt silence listening to him in coffeehouses and college auditoriums. Such a passive response unnerved some of the rediscoveries. Skip James complained, "Sometimes they just look at me like I was...I don't know what—a bear or something."[25] But while House was performing, he was too immersed in himself to notice such things.

Newport 1966, Europe 1967

The next year, 1966, House played the Newport Folk Festival again, and this year Evie went with him, and together they sang a spiritual. And at the 1966 festival House once again became involved with folk music's unflagging demiurge, Alan Lomax. Lomax's latest brainstorm was to recreate the atmosphere of a Mississippi juke joint in, of all places, Rhode Island, and then film the results—a sort of prototype House of Blues before the House of Blues. But Lomax's pioneering prototype had one enormous advantage over the later mass-market model: it would have real blues musicians in it, among others, Skip James, Bukka White, Howlin' Wolf, and Eddie "Son" House. To this end, Lomax rented a house, created a performance space, and stocked a bar with liquor in an establishment where some of the festival performers were staying. Lights, action!

Lomax, it must be said, was successful in creating an atmosphere in which the performers were at ease. House is loose and amiable in Lomax's movie—very loose and amiable, and not surprisingly, his performance of "Forever On My Mind," shows the effects of the well-stocked bar. But then House was compelling simply being himself. Rather like Brian Williams at the Kettle of Fish, Lomax and his camera sometimes followed House even when someone else was performing.[26] And, in fact, the most interesting

25. Calt, I'd Rather Be the Devil, p. 275.
26. Mark Humphrey in his notes to the video Devil Got My Woman: Blues at Newport 1966, (Cambridge Mass: Vestapol Productions, 1996) p. 20: "Lomax's continued fascination with House is evident in scenes where his camera follows a tipsy House around as someone else is performing."

Son House, Newport Folk Festival, 1966. Courtesy of Trey Stadler.

sequence of the film, at least as far regards House, is not his performance, but a conversation that ensues between him and Howlin' Wolf.

From their time together in Mississippi, Wolf certainly knew of House's habits. Some of these Wolf shared, notably his taste for women, but not his addiction to whiskey. Now, a year after their *Shindig* reunion, a tipsy House repeatedly interrupted Wolf when he was attempting to introduce his song "Meet Me in the Bottom," and in the film, one can see the warmth of the previous year's reunion dissipate when Wolf could no longer ignore House's drunken banter. Wolf gestures at House and says, "See, this man got the blues right now. See, that's where the blues come from. Because he has done drunk up all of his."

Son mumbles a reply, and Wolf says, "I'm telling you like it is." Again Son's reply is unclear, but he mentions something about problems, and Wolf picks up on this: "Of course, of course, my man. You know the problems—" Son seems to say, "You might not be broke." Wolf replies, "I was broke when I was born. That's the reason I'm howlin.'"

Son mumbles again, and Wolf finally says, "Well, you see. You had a chance with your life, but you ain't done nothin' with it. Seeing, you got to have the blues."

Son says, "I don't want no woman—"

Now Wolf cuts him off, "We ain't talkin' about the women. We're talking about the life of a human being. How they used it." Son again mutters something, and again Wolf cuts *him* off, "Seeing you don't love but this one thing, and that's some whiskey. And that's plumb out of it."[27]

Wolf at length concentrates, ignores House, and proceeds to do a measured and intense take of "Meet Me in the Bottom," his version of the old Mississippi standard "Rollin' and Tumblin.'" Wolf's vocal style was so influenced by Charley Patton that the ghost of House's boon companion in the Delta looms over his performance, and the song, along with the drunken repartee and scolding, becomes a strange reunion of the three men.

In 1967, besides his usual venues of coffeehouses and college campuses, House toured Europe as part of what was called in deference to the times, the American Folk Blues Festival. The tour's performers ran the gamut of blues styles. Resurrected acts like Son House, Bukka White, and Skip James were on the bill with Hound Dog Taylor, Koko Taylor, and Little Walter. Sonny Terry and Brownie McGhee were on their "umpteenth British visit" as one critic put it. Hound Dog Taylor and Koko Taylor were young acts, apprentices almost, before a critical audience who had seen powerhouse acts on previous tours like Muddy Waters, Howlin' Wolf, and Sonny Boy Williamson backed by the cream of the Chicago blues musicians. Little Walter "mumbled" according to Paul Oliver and was a little "ragged" and "a little off form" according to two other critics—he would be dead within four months.[28] The real draw, however, was Son House.

Paul Oliver wrote then, "Son House is to Charlie Patton as King Oliver was to Buddy Bolden; his contemporary, part-successor and wearer of the crown." Bob Groom in *Blues World* said House was "the man everyone was there to see."

27. *Devil Got My Woman: Blues at Newport 1966*, 1996.

28. Paul Oliver in *Jazz Monthly* (Dec. 1967): p. 10. "ragged" acc. to David Illingworth in *Jazz Journal* (Dec. 1967): p. 10. "a little off form," acc. to Bob Groom in *Blues World* 18 (Jan. 1968).

House faced expectations that were almost impossible to meet. One reviewer wrote, "It was with some trepidation that we watched him feel out his beautiful National steel guitar." Oliver wrote, "His hands shake with ague and one could not imagine how he could find the notes, so that the moments before he began were clouded with apprehension."[29] Yet—somehow—he delivered.

A reviewer wrote: "As Son broke into the opening bars of 'Death Letter Blues,' all doubts vanished. It is difficult to describe the transformation that took place as this smiling, friendly man hunched over his guitar and launched himself, bodily it seemed, into his music. The blues possessed him 'like a low-down shaking chill' and the spellbound audience saw the very incarnation of the blues as, head thrown back, he hollered and groaned the disturbing lyrics and flailed the guitar, snapping the strings back against the fingerboard to accentuate the agonized rhythm. All this might sound highly melodramatic but that is how it really was...After thunderous applause Son concluded his performance with a magnificent version of 'Empire State Blues,' a lineal descendant of Willie Brown's "'M. & O. Blues.'"[30]

Paul Oliver described House's transformation when he performed in a similar way: "Then his head was thrown back, his eyes rolled under the lids and he sang loudly and forcefully in a manner that seemed inconceivable after his barely inaudible speech. *Death Letter, Levee Camp Moan, Empire State Express*—the years rolled away and one was transported by the mesmeric rhythm of the guitar under the flailing fingers, the singing brass ring sliding on the strings and the powerful, musical voice."[31]

While the recordings House was to make after 1964 would spread his name wider, it was really his live performances that left a deeper impression—an impression for those who saw him that still remained vivid decades later.

The next year, 1968, House's comeback took him all the way to national television, when he appeared on a CBS program called *Camera 3* accompanied by Buddy Guy.[32] He had come quite a ways from the train depot in Lula.

Perhaps the best film of House performing was made a year later in Seattle in November, 1969. Amazingly enough, it came right after a hospitalization and surgery. A few weeks later he would tell an interviewer: "Jesus, I been

29. Bob Groom, *Blues World* (January 1968). Oliver, *Jazz Journal*, p. 10.

30. Bob Groom, *Blues World*, (January 1968).

31. Paul Oliver in *Jazz Monthly*, (December 1967), p. 10.

32. Shortly after this, Waterman would also be managing the duo of Buddy Guy and Junior Wells, who, like many other blues acts, were increasingly playing for white rock fans.

sick. I just come out of the hospital to come over here...See they split me open once and a little mistake was made. So they had to go over it a bit."[33]

The Seattle Folk Society booked House for two nights, November 15 and 16. The first night's performance, done on a soundstage, was filmed.[34]

It is almost certain that House had had something to drink before performing in Seattle, nevertheless, in the Seattle footage House seems somewhat guarded, especially at first. He lowers his head somewhat, though this may simply have been due to him trying to spy the audience beyond the stage lights. He was not in his element the way he was among his peers in Newport. In the Newport "juke joint" everyone in the room with the exception of Lomax was black. We never see the audience in Seattle, but likely it was mostly—if not entirely—white.

The film begins with House performing an extraordinary version of "Death Letter." He then sets his National aside and stands up to perform "John The Revelator." When he finishes that, he sits down again and delivers the long well-rehearsed monologue on religion that always served to introduce "Preachin' the Blues".

This "homily" was an essential part of House's repertoire. When he first performed in a Cambridge coffeehouse shortly after June 23, 1964, Al Wilson had fretted about House subjecting the audience to an "incoherent and rambling sermon" about the Bible, God, and the Devil. But based on House's later recorded and filmed performances, these "sermons" seemed remarkably consistent, really set pieces themselves. The same themes and phrases recur e.g., "You can't hold God in one hand and the Devil in the other." House was not rambling. He seemed to know exactly what he wanted to say:

> The truth about it, I was brought up in the church from a little boy on up. And I didn't believe in no blues or none of it—I was too churchy. I didn't believe in that. I talked against it. And I really was called to preach the gospel. And that's why I knowed it so good. I didn't have to read the books so much. It come from above (gestures upwards)—now this is the truth. It's not a lie. This is the truth. And I was taught all them things (taps his head). I knowed everything about the King James version of the Bible. Thirty-nine books in the Old Testament, twenty-seven in the New, which makes sixty-six

33. Goodwin, "Can't Fool God," p. 16.
34. *Bukka White & Son House: Masters of the Country Blues*, John S. Ullman, producer, Ronald Ciro, director (New York: Yazoo Video, 1991).

books. And four hundred and fifty thousand words. And I knew 'em—I didn't have to go to school to learn it, 'cause the school teacher that is teaching school at that time, he didn't know how to say his alphabets three ways, as far as that goes [chuckles]. Well, now this is the thing come from God. A lot of people don't believe in God and don't think it's possible. But it is. I'm sitting here playin' the blues. And I play church songs too. But you can't take God and the Devil along together. 'Cause them two fellas, they don't—they don't, uh, communicate together so well. They don't get along so well together. 'Cause one believes in one thing, and the other believes in another. The Devil, he believes in another way, and God believes in a different way. Now you got to separate them two guys. How you goin' do it? You got to follow one or the other. You can't hold God in one hand and the Devil in the other. You got to turn one of 'em loose. Which side you thinks the best? Well, this one—I didn't give up. 'Cause I was regenerated and borned again. I was born in sin, now I got to regenerate myself to realize what a great creator is. I look around, I see yonder something man didn't make. That thing over yonder man didn't make. Say, there must be somebody else somewhere else. Then He said, "Let us make man in Our image and likeness and give them dominion..." All right, 'let's make him like us...' Now who is 'us'? One person can't be 'us.' So, not one. It takes another one. Well, anyway, I don't wanna go along too much here with time. But any, after I went to doin' wrong, I know right ain't wrong. Wrong ain't right. You gotta be one or the other. Your friend or enemy—it's God and the Devil. So you can't sit straddlin' the fence. You can't hold two—you got to give up one side or the other. To make it plain. So, well, I went to doin' a little wrong, but I didn't give up God. So I says, 'Well since I give up and goin' back to playin' I'll make a piece about, oh, "The Preachin' Blues," 'cause I preached for a long time...I said, "Well, I'll make a piece about 'Preachin' the Blues.'"[35]

Then he gave an impassioned rendition of "Preachin' the Blues."

The final song was another spiritual, performed as usual without guitar accompaniment, "I Want To Live So God Can Use Me." The footage, while grainy and dark, was his best performance caught on film. When he performed in Berkeley a few weeks later, Michael Goodwin wrote in an article for *Rolling Stone*, "...the Mississippi blues ring out with an intensity that will, with his passing, never be heard again."[36]

35. Ibid.
36. Goodwin, "Can't Fool God," p. 14.

Beginning with his 1965 performance at Newport, a series of recordings would be drawn from House's live performances. In 1967, Verve issued an album containing House's "Levee Camp Moan," recorded at the Café a Go Go on August 9, 1966. This was added to songs Skip James, Bukka White, and Big Joe Williams recorded at the Café in November of the same year. In 1968, Fontana issued an anthology from the American Folk Blues Festival tour of 1967 containing "Death Letter" recorded by House in October of that year at the Kongress-Halle in Berlin.[37] At the same time, House's prewar recordings both for Paramount and the Library of Congress, were regularly appearing on new anthologies. Johnny Parth's label Roots, based in Austria, issued two recordings in the sixties. The first was made in 1964, but issued two years later; side two of the record contained Robert Pete Williams. In late 1969, Parth issued another album, *The Vocal Intensity of Son House*, made in Rochester by Steve Lobb in September of that same year. The latter recording was the subject of a heated dispute between Parth and Waterman—the disputes that had begun with the rediscoveries were still going on. And all of these recordings were augmented by a steady stream of private, bootleg recordings, most of them made in Rochester when House was away from the watchful eye of his manager.

Besides touring and recording, Son House's resurrected career transformed his life in other ways. House was reunited with old friends from Mississippi, and through touring he also came to know other musicians like John Hurt, Skip James, and Lightnin' Hopkins. He also came into contact with a new generation of young musicians, both black and white, who were avid members of his new audience. Musicians like Al Wilson, Buddy Guy, Stefan Grossman, Taj Mahal, Woody Mann, Rory Block, and Bonnie Raitt all got to know House, sometimes picking up techniques from him, but all influenced in some way by his unique approach to the blues.

But the changes in his life after June 23, 1964 that resulted from his revived career—the touring, the recording, the new income from both activities, and the connections and reconnections with other blues musicians—were not the only changes in his life. Just as striking were the changes in his life in the city where he lived, Rochester, New York. Although he continued to live with Evie at the same address, 61 Greig Street, after his second career was launched and had brought him additional income, almost everything else in his life there changed.

37. But titled "Got A Letter This Morning."

CHAPTER 9

He Was Who He Was

THE FINAL ACT OF SON HOUSE

The two stories published in the *Times-Union* on the heels of Son House's rediscovery in June of 1964 were followed by another story in the newspaper the next spring about his recording session for Columbia Records. The May 29, 1965 edition carried the story, "Son House Records Blues Again." A year after his rediscovery, House had become nothing less than a celebrity in Rochester. He had gone from well-nigh total obscurity to becoming one of the city's more renowned residents—a musician who toured the United States and who had signed a recording contract with the most prestigious record label in the country.

The stories in the local newspapers brought House to the attention of the young music community in Rochester, and soon a phenomenon began that would be a feature of his life for the rest of his years in Rochester: the pilgrimage of young, blues fans to 61 Greig Street. Scores of them came to ask him questions and to listen to him tell stories about Charley Patton, Willie Brown, and Robert Johnson. Many, if not most of them, were aspiring amateur musicians who brought guitars and—if they wanted to hear him play—brought liquor, too. They hoped not only to learn the history of the music from a living practitioner, but also those musical techniques specific to Delta blues. Some of these aspirants learned some music from him, and some of them simply hoped to somehow get his blessing, as it were—to acquire that ineffable something that would make them worthy and able to play the blues. Of the latter, most would probably have done better to follow B.B.'s sage advice and practice their scales. But among the young music community who came to seek out the bluesman was someone with ambitions and designs beyond those activities, a young man named Armand Schaubroeck.

The Adventures of Armand Schaubroeck

It would have been poetic justice if it had been Armand Schaubroeck who rediscovered Son House. But as both House and Schaubroeck could have attested, justice, even of the poetic sort, is a scarce commodity in this world. In 1964 Schaubroeck had recently gotten out of prison, and already at eighteen was well along his way to becoming as original a character in his own right as Son House was in his.

At seventeen, Schaubroeck had been sentenced as a "youthful offender" for burglary to three years in the reformatory in Elmira. After serving a year and a half of the sentence, Schaubroeck was paroled, and he returned to Rochester where he began selling guitars out of his mother's basement. By 1970, Schaubroeck, along with his younger brothers Blaine and Bruce, would have enough money to buy a building to house their expanding business, called, as it still is, The House of Guitars. The building was a former Grange Hall on Titus Avenue in Irondequoit, a suburb just north of Rochester. After settling a lawsuit with the city of Irondequoit, they would open the store at that location in 1972. That establishment would grow over the next four decades absorbing and annexing neighboring structures to provide more space for the brothers' burgeoning collections of instruments, records, and musical memorabilia, until the store also became a labyrinthine museum, whose walls and ceilings were covered with the signatures of the thousands of famous and not-so-famous rock 'n' roll musicians who visited the store.

Along the way, Schaubroeck and his brothers would branch out into many other loosely related activities. They began doing their own whimsical television advertisements. An advertisement with Armand jumping up and down in a bunny suit became a local legend.[1] In the late sixties, when a group of local conservatives put up a series of billboards reading, "Beautify America. Get a haircut," Schaubroeck countered with his own billboards proclaiming "Help Keep America Free. Let Your Hair Grow."

A recording studio would eventually be built beneath the music store. By and by, Schaubroeck would launch a rock 'n' roll band called Armand Schaubroeck Steals, which was also the title of his debut album. That album caught the attention of Andy Warhol who wanted to use it as the

---

1. And now, with the Web, not just locally. It can be viewed on Youtube. Indeed, Armand himself has acquired an international cult-following on the Internet. When I informed him of some of the sites I had found that posted articles about him, he simply smiled and said, "Cool."

Armand Schaubroeck, 1978. Courtesy of Armand Schaubroeck.

basis for a Broadway production—a Warholian "Hair"—and discussions were noted in a 1968 Billboard article.[2] But when Warhol was shot in June of 1968, his slow recovery delayed the project, and it was ultimately shelved. Nevertheless, that album and four subsequent albums have become cult classics: *I Came To Visit But Decided To Stay, Ratfucker, Shakin' Shakin'*, and *Live At The Holyday Inn*. The liner notes to his fourth album *Shakin' Shakin'* stated that all the songs were "written by Armand Schaubroeck right after they were recorded."

However, in 1966, the location of the store was just across the Stutson Street Bridge from Rochester in the suburb of Charlotte. And there Schaubroeck and his younger brothers pursued yet another sideline: they decided that Rochester needed a coffeehouse scene where blues and folk music could be featured. Accordingly, they took over the space next to the Charlotte store and opened up a coffeehouse, briefly called The Black

---

2. Warhol arranged for Schaubroeck to see John Hammond at Columbia Records to get Columbia's backing (they would release the soundtrack album). Hammond simply listened to Schaubroeck, now and then inserting a noncommittal, "hmm." When Schaubroeck finished, he said, "So, tell Andy 'No'?" "No! No!" Hammond replied, "Tell him I'll get in touch with him."

Candle, soon to be known as Studio 9. When the Charlotte town authorities told them they would have to close it because it had only one restroom, Schaubroeck and his brothers simply knocked a hole in the wall to provide access to another bathroom in the music store.

Once he had Studio 9 up and running—after a fashion—Schaubroeck found out from a young aspiring blues player named Jerry Porter that the Delta bluesman Son House had been found living in Rochester about two years earlier. Porter said he had been visiting House at 61 Greig Street, and he suggested that Schaubroeck book House to play at Studio 9. Schaubroeck was enthusiastic. He was into the blues and the coffeehouse was drawing few people as it was.

Schaubroeck made several trips to Greig Street before he finally located House. Of his first impression of Son House, he said simply, "You could tell he was the real thing."[3]

Schaubroeck found he had to do quite a bit of talking to convince House to play, meeting in him at first the same reluctance that others noticed: "When I talked about playing at the coffeehouse, he seemed somewhat suspicious of us at the beginning, like we might have been up to something, or maybe it was somewhat of a mistrust for white people—for good reason probably." But Schaubroeck kept talking, eventually convincing House that his interest and his offer were genuine. "As time went on, he learned we were really fans, that we were in awe because he was the last of the living twenties Delta blues guys ... basically a generation before Robert Johnson. We knew that, and we knew who he was, and we were familiar with his music. So we just kept talking until he said he'd do it."

By this time, almost two years after his rediscovery, House's reputation in Rochester had grown to the point that his local debut attracted considerable attention. Schaubroeck left nothing to chance, however, and bought advertising space in one of the local newspapers, and the result surprised him: "We advertised in the *Democrat and Chronicle* ... and the place was crammed. This was very unusual for the place, because it was usually dead."

The first appearance by Rochester's new celebrity drew an unusually diverse crowd: besides college students, there were faculty members from the Eastman School of Music, and businessmen in suits and ties. Some of the students from the Rochester Institute of Technology filmed the show with 8mm cameras.

3. Interview with the author, April, 2002 Unless otherwise indicated, all quotations of Armand Schaubroeck are from this interview.

The crowd watched in silent awe as House played the same song for eight or ten minutes. Indeed, as Schaubroeck said, "He used silence. He'd hit a couple of notes and stop. And he'd use that."

Faced with a new audience who, in stark contrast to the juke joint audience, expressed their appreciation by rapt silence, House had found a way to exploit their silence in his performance for dramatic effect.

When he finished a song and applause filled the coffeehouse, he would step over to Schaubroeck and ask, "Got something to drink?" But the alcohol did not hinder House's performance at Studio 9 that night as far as Schaubroeck was concerned: "He was right on...he was fantastic. Just powerful. Today's bands just sound wimpy next to this guy."

After that initial engagement, House played at Studio 9 several more times, but, like Waterman, Schaubroeck always had to deal with House's seeming indifference or reluctance. However Schaubroeck had a rather different idea about the cause of that reserve: "You had to get Son House in the mood to play too, otherwise he wouldn't do it...I don't know that it was shyness. I think it was more a worry, 'They're not getting it.' He was not a shy person. He'd blurt it right out, whatever he wanted. He was tough. He was a tough guy. He'd been through some stuff."

As might be expected, relations between the two men, one young and white, the other old and black, could be easily disturbed, and Schaubroeck made at least one misstep in his dealings with the bluesman. When he learned that Evie played organ in her church, he suggested to House that perhaps the two of them could perform together sometime. House took umbrage at Schaubroeck's impertinent suggestion and snapped, "I'm the goddamn musicianer in this family—" Schaubroeck years later would laugh at the memory, "It didn't go over well! Who the hell am I to bring that up, you know? I mean, he was his own man for sure." House's visceral reaction in this instance lends support to Schaubroeck's sense that his reluctance about performing for his new audience was not simply indifference.

Ironically enough, one item, more than all the others in Schaubroeck's resumé, helped to improve relations between the two men. At some point House learned that Schaubroeck had done some time in prison, and then his respect for the young man increased: maybe he knew a few things after all.

Nevertheless, through all of their dealings, House's attitude toward his young, white fans remained as Schaubroeck said, "If they want me that bad, let 'em come and get me." Thus, more often than not, when Schaubroeck booked House to play at Studio 9, there was a search involved. "Sometimes he wasn't home, and we'd have to go club to club finding him." In one such search Schaubroeck recalled, "There was a corner bar, and we went to go in and get him, and I remember the owners—they were very polite to us—but they said, 'You better not go in there. No white person has ever been in there before. We'll tell him you're out here.'" Schaubroeck agreed and waited on the sidewalk outside. After a few moments House came out of the bar and listened as Schaubroeck reminded him of the gig at the coffeehouse. As soon as Schaubroeck stopped talking, House said, "Well, I gotta have another drink first—" Schaubroeck said, "We'll get you a drink, Son. There's a lot of people who really want to see you. They're at the club waiting, you know, and you promised you'd be there. Here's the money."

House weighed this, looked at the money, pondered the matter a little more, and then relented.

House also appeared to Schaubroeck to be ambivalent about the enthusiastic response of his young audiences. "He wasn't impressed with the whole thing. Sometimes he liked it when the kids really went wild for him, you know. But I don't think he felt everyone really understood his times, and his era, and what it all meant for real to live it." Where others saw a quiet and somewhat indifferent old man, Schaubroeck saw someone else, a very independent man. As he put it, "He was going to do what he wanted to do when he wanted to do it."

Schaubroeck certainly saw a different side of the man who Joe Beard recalled as "a real gentle person, a real understanding guy." The fact that Beard was an "insider"—a fellow black musician and Mississippi émigré— probably accounts for much of this. Schaubroeck was white and wanted to hire House to perform, while Beard, who himself was already performing around Rochester, was content to play music with him informally and let House relax in his living room. Yet, Schaubroeck also saw a rather different side of Son House than Dick Waterman, a young, white music fan like himself. House seemed to reveal certain facets of his character to some people, and other facets to other people—how else to account for the disparity of opinions about him? Yet Schaubroeck's relationship with House still stands out. With most of his young fans, House ignored them, or was deferential, or tried to use them to obtain liquor. House sensed something different in Schaubroeck from most of his young admirers—because Schaubroeck was different. He was full of creative energy, and he had many irons in the fire besides hiring House to perform in his coffeehouse. The fact that they had both spent time in prison probably signified something larger to House about the way Schaubroeck stood out from the mass of adoring young fans. From the way he treated Schaubroeck and the way he spoke to him, it seems he regarded him as a kindred spirit in some way, a peer even—when he got his first royalty check, one of the first places he went was to the House of Guitars.

For his part Schaubroeck found House unique as well: "He was who he was. And there was no one else like him to me. He could do whatever he wanted. And he did."

"See that ye fall not out by the way"

House could do whatever he wanted—except control his drinking. And by the end of the decade, it was beginning to have unpredictable and ultimately disastrous consequences both for his performances and his health.

In January of 1969, House was to perform at Rochester Madison High School as part of a program called "Project Uplift." The idea was to highlight the achievements of the black community so as to instill pride in young African-American students. The focus of the evening was the blues. The evening began with the poet Don L. Lee[4] addressing a crowd of both blacks and whites about the history of black music, about jazz, gospel, and soul music as well as blues. At one point, Lee asserted rather tendentiously that "only black people can play blues." He repeated the old canard that Bessie Smith died because a Clarksdale hospital refused to admit her after her automobile wreck. After this dubious prologue, Son House was introduced.

House began with his own discourse about the blues—the same speech he always made, but he was extremely inebriated. He began to play a very slow blues, but soon lost his way in it. Then he fell to tuning his guitar— but this time without the guidance of Waterman or Schaubroeck he was, again, lost. In his drunken state, even this proved to be too much for him, and after a few minutes he was led from the stage. His removal caused some furor in the audience. Part of the audience thought he should be removed—for his own sake probably—and part of the audience resented his removal. Lee took the stage again and reproved the audience, telling them that Son House had been trying to teach them something, but they were not capable of understanding it.

---

4. Lee would change his name to Haki Madhubuti in 1973. His poetry in black vernacular was a major influence on the Last Poets.

Lee ignored—or tried to obscure—the reality that House was simply too drunk to perform with a riposte about the white audience's inability to comprehend the blues. But one salient fact remains: had it not been for burgeoning white interest in blues, Son House would have never performed or recorded again after 1943, and then Don Lee could not have sung his praises.

As lamentable as the episode was, and as embarrassing for those who cared about Son House, it had no consequences for House who was almost certainly oblivious to what happened and likely had no memory of it. One year later, however, another bout of heavy drinking would land him in a rather worse place, a snow bank in Plymouth Circle.

Late one frigid night in January 1970, after an evening of drinking in a bar on Clarissa Street, House headed home on foot for apartment 9 on Greig. But he did not make it. While crossing Plymouth Circle, he passed out and collapsed in the plowed snow by the curb. He lay there for several hours until a passerby discovered him and called an ambulance. The ambulance took him to Strong Hospital where he was admitted from the emergency room and treated for exposure and frostbite. It was almost a miracle that he survived at all.

House spent several days in Strong Hospital, and when Joe Beard learned of his mishap, he visited him. "He had drank so much so he just passed out there," Beard recalled. "They find him in the middle of the night and takes him to the hospital. His hands was all frostbitten. He was in the hospital for quite awhile. Because, you know, he had laid there in the snow, and his hands had got frostbitten—his hands looked terrible."

Just about a week later, on February 6 and 7, the rock band Delaney and Bonnie and Friends was booked to play Fillmore East. British rock star Eric Clapton had gotten to know Delaney and Bonnie Bramlett when they opened for Blind Faith the previous year and had informally joined their band, Delaney and Bonnie and Friends, when Blind Faith disbanded. Clapton, needless to say, brought in his train a huge following of his fans, and Delaney and Bonnie were regularly selling out shows on that tour— and, indeed, the Fillmore East date sold out very quickly. As the February dates approached, Clapton and Delaney Bramlett told rock impresario and Fillmore East owner Bill Graham that they wanted to have Son House on the bill with them, so Graham called Dick Waterman. But Waterman, who had lately learned of House's condition, had to turn down Graham's offer. As a result of his Plymouth Circle misadventure, House missed what would have undoubtedly been the biggest performance—and payday—of his career, losing out on the ringing endorsement of Eric Clapton, an endorsement that would have sent legions of Clapton's fans to the record stores in search of Son House's recordings.[5]

It must be testimony to the strength of House's constitution that this mishap was not the end of House's active musical career. There would be yet one more tour of England.

Montreux & England, 1970

"Old and well stricken in old age," by late spring House had, nevertheless, recovered sufficiently from his icy debacle to perform publicly once more.

In June, House flew to Europe with Waterman, and on June 20 he performed in Switzerland at the Montreux Jazz Festival. A scheduled date in Vienna had to be cancelled due to "traveling difficulties and Son's indisposition."[6] So they flew to London and embarked on a tour of Great Britain.

The four-week tour of Great Britain was to be House's last tour anywhere, and his British audience was well aware of this. The English writer Alan Balfour wrote, "The appearance of Son House in Britain that year was almost certainly the last time most would get to see an artist so important and so influential in the history of the blues." Indeed, the punning headline in the music journal *Melody Maker* announcing the tour was even blunter: "Your Last Chance to See the Son."

Balfour would write, "There had been a certain loss of dexterity since his 1967 tour, perhaps to be expected in a man nearly 70, but what his fingers lacked in precise picking was more than compensated for by his spine chilling voice and eerie slide playing."[7] Although time was undoubtedly taking its toll on him, probably the loss of dexterity was also due to the more or less permanent effects of frostbite on his fingers. Bob Groom, editor of *Blues World*, wrote, "Last winter he suffered very severe frostbite damage to his fingers—they have lost their pigment and turned white and one is permanently bent over—but he has persevered with them and,

5. Conveyed to the author by Dick Waterman in a conversation in Oxford, Mississippi in October 2002.

6. Bob Groom, *Blues World*, August, 1970, p. 3.

7. Alan Balfour, notes to the reissue album of live recordings made on this tour. "Son House: John the Revelator," Sequel NEXCD 207, U.K. 1992.

with difficulty and some discomfort, he has continued to play his own guitar accompaniments."[8] Groom spoke of House's "dogged determination" to go on with the show.[9]

Given the valedictory character of his tour, critics were prepared to be generous. As Paul Oliver said of House that summer, "For blues enthusiasts, the living witness to the Mississippi tradition, he is virtually set apart from normal critical appraisal. Playing partner to Charley Patton and Willie Brown, of Robert Johnson and Muddy Waters, he is a key figure in the story of Delta blues with a timeless reputation."[10]

House opened the tour on June 26, playing in "the fading Victorian splendor" of St. Pancras Town Hall.[11] According to Balfour, "House's opening concert performance was greeted by standing ovations; which was to be the case where ever he played during those four weeks."[12] For the next three and a half weeks, he played dates all over England and Scotland.

Two nights later, on June 28, House played at Lancaster University. Before the show, House was interviewed on the university's closed-circuit television station.

House began his show with a long discourse on the blues, after which he "stunned the audience with a magnificent version of 'Death Letter Blues.'"[13] The toll of time and his habits was evident in the fact that House had to rest after about four numbers. After a fifteen minute break, filled by "a singer of tropical tunes,"[14] House returned to perform a long version of "Sundown" and an unaccompanied spiritual. With those two songs, he had reached his limit. His physical weakening was evident to Groom, who had accompanied House and Waterman to the show, and who had seen him on the 1967 tour.

On June 30, he played the 100 Club in London, and he recorded four songs, "Between Midnight and Day," "I Want to Go Home on the Morning Train," "Levee Camp Moan," and the spiritual, "This Little Light of Mine."

8. Groom, *Blues World*, p. 3.

9. One of the more famous photographs of House was taken in 1970 by Giuseppi Pino while House was in Montreux. In it House cradles his face between his hands and stares directly at the camera, and it seems some discoloration—possibly the result of frostbite—can be seen on the little finger of his right hand. The passage of time seems apparent compared to the photographs taken of in 1964 and 1965. The furrows and shadows in his brow, and his cheeks seem deeper and darker than they were four years earlier.

10. Paul Oliver, *Melody Maker*, October 3, 1970 p. 24.

11. Balfour, liner notes, "John the Revelator."

12. Ibid.

13. Groom, *Blues World*, p. 4.

14. Ibid., p. 4.

On the first two titles, Al Wilson, now a guitarist in the rock band Canned Heat, accompanied House on harp. "I Want to Go Home on the Morning Train" is especially moving. Wilson's harp was so attuned to House's vocal and guitar that by the second verse one senses Wilson's playing actually propelling House forward. On the next song, "Levee Camp Moan," a second career standard that House performed at every date, the sound is so acute that we hear the sounds of the House's guttural straining of his throat in between his utterances. The audience too seemed more relaxed than his American audiences usually were. On the gospel number "This Little Light of Mine" they clapped along enthusiastically. When the songs ended, the scraping in his throat as he catches his breath was audible, and one realized how much of his physical being he had poured into the performance.

On July 6, House performed at the BBC's Playhouse Theatre in London, and producer John Walters also recorded this session. It was subsequently broadcast five days later, on July 11, on John Peel's Top Gear radio program.[15] On July 13, House was filmed on short notice in the evening in a West End loft. He performed two blues and three gospel songs for a small audience, and he was also interviewed. It seems only a brief portion of the film ever was shown on BBC television many years later in 1985.

The next night, House played the 100 Club again, and he recorded four more songs, "Death Letter," "How to Treat a Man," "Grinnin' in Your Face," and "John the Revelator." On "How to Treat a Man," the English blues musician Dave Kelly played second guitar.

An album titled "Son House: John the Revelator" containing the recordings made at the 100 Club was issued on the British label Liberty that same year. Comparison with his performances on record in 1965 and on videotape in 1968 reveal him to have slowed somewhat, and he had lost some of the nimbleness in his fretwork—and yet House remained a powerful performer. For, if his guitar playing suffered due to his snowy accident, his voice was still powerful, still laden with anger and passion forty years after Grafton. His audience could not remain unmoved—Alan Balfour wrote, "... it was all but impossible to obtain any detachment."

The recordings were faithful to the context of his performance by including House's spoken introductions to the songs. According to David Evans' notes for the reissue, the idea was—in keeping with the post-Sgt. Pepper's cultural milieu—to produce a blues "concept album." In Evan's

---

15. And subsequently rebroadcast a month later on August 9—all of the information about the recordings comes courtesy of Alan Balfour.

words, the album was to be "a Blues Bible written by Son House, running from the Genesis of The B.L.U.E.S. to the ending of *John The Revelator*."[16] House's commentaries, which are at times fairly lengthy, did in fact make it something of a "concept album"—and also show that what Al Wilson and others on the heels of his rediscovery had taken for mere rambling, must be regarded as part of Son's performance. His opening remarks on the meaning of the blues, titled "The B-L-U-E-S" (as House habitually spelled the word out) run over three minutes and establish the theme—the blues are about loss. House's other speeches explain different things about what the blues meant to House.

The comments that follow the first song reveal, in ways both humorous and poignant, how House, who undoubtedly had had a few drinks, viewed his alcohol habit. The monologue titled "Thinkin' Strong" begins with remarks he always made about God and the Devil and the struggle between them, but on this occasion in an oddly comic vein: "God and The Devil don't work together so well. I'm scared to trust 'em like that!" [audience laughs] "Cause, you know, one guy he started a song about 'Lord have mercy' when he come to die." Then dramatizing a different viewpoint, House says "I don't want that. I want to have some of this mercy now!" The audience responds with laughter, and it becomes apparent what "mercy" means to House as he begins to talk about his alcohol habit: "I tell you the truth now. I been drinking this medicine ever since . . . twenty-seven, I think it was." The voice of Waterman off-microphone is heard to say, "—eighteen twenty-seven," and House bursts into laughter. When he gathers himself, he plays along jokingly, "Something slipped my remembrance there! Oh, yeah!" Then he says matter of factly, "A habit is a habit, y'all. Sometimes it looks like you can't do without a thing. Just let you . . . the way you look at it, you just can't do without it. That old word 'can't.' 'Just can't.' Well, anything you get in your mind, and your mind tell you, that you can't do without it. Don't try!" [laughter] "Because you'll sure fail. That's right. But when you think you can, you can pretty well— you can come more near doing it then, when you're thinking you can, than if you think you can't. Because some people I used to hear them say, tell the others something happened, 'Say, man, you know, my mind told me not to do that thing. If I'd a just followed my first mind! My mind told me something was gonna happen.' Say what? 'Yeah! If I just followed my first mind.' Well, that's the very one you oughtn't to follow. Now that's true!

16. In his liner notes to the 1995 Capitol Records reissue, p. 27.

Don't never follow your first mind. Cause that's the one that's wrong. Cause the Devil beats God to you every time. [laughter] He sure do! The scripture says something about it, 'Think twice, and speak once.'"

A curious idea for a believer, that the Devil is much faster than God. House's reputation was that of a gloomy man who struggled with the Bible, the bottle, and the blues all of his adult life, but the monologue reveals he could look at even these topics with humorous detachment. Or perhaps it would be more accurate to say that he *had* to look at them with some irony and detachment if he was not to lose his mind—or worse.

House's London speech reveals why he captivated audiences in a way that other talented musicians like Mississippi John Hurt or Lonnie Johnson did not. His words are not those of a rambling drunk, though drunk he may have been, rather in them he somehow expresses an entire vision of life. For House, the blues were part of that vision, an agonized vision—a struggle between the desire of the all too human son and the implacable law of the father, religion. It would be difficult to name a blues musician whose life had not had great hardships, but in Son House his audience sensed someone— and not without reason—who had seen hell and lived to tell about it.

Following the fifteen-minute-long "How to Treat a Man," the elegiac mood is further emphasized when House, responding to the crowd's enthusiastic applause, alludes to dying: "I enjoy all of you. All you good, nice people, yeah, I enjoy all of you. May the good Lord be with you. And maybe we can live for many, many more. Yeah, we don't know when. We don't discuss...But we're glad to be here now. Be happy and enjoy each other, and be happy. Okay..."

The unmistakable tenderness in his farewell is all the more sharpened, somehow all the more poignant, when one remembers the suffering and violence that roiled his own life.

House finished his set with two second career standards, his own private apocalypse, the strange and unsettling "Grinnin' in Your Face" and "John the Revelator." Then Dick Waterman took the microphone and said, "This is his last appearance in England. He's going back home to America to a well-earned retirement."

There was more applause, and then the applause faded and died.

Rochester 1970–1976

While the tour of Britain was House's last tour, it did not mark the end of all public performances. When House returned to Rochester in late July

1970 one constant in his life after June 23, 1964 resumed: the visits by young, white blues fans. It must be said that among House's motives for accommodating the stream of young, white pilgrims who made their way to Greig Street, alcohol must have been an important one. Their visits provided his habit with free booze—as Joe Beard alluded, "His wife got so tired of peoples bothering him, bugging him, you know."

A guitar lesson that House gave to a young man named Trey Stadler was typical. Stadler, when he was in his teens, had seen House perform in 1966 at a Rochester coffeehouse. That same year he had attended the Newport festival, where he ran into House and Evie in the town center and introduced himself. After the festival, they all traveled back to Rochester on the same Greyhound bus. About seven years later Stadler, who had been practicing on a guitar for a while, called up House to ask if he could come over for "a guitar lesson."

Stadler found House sitting in his apartment with a warm Miller's beer beside him. Evie allowed him to drink beer in the apartment, and House preferred his beer warm. Stadler brought the photographs from Newport with him as a way of reconnecting with House. When he showed House the photograph of himself and Evie in the town square of Newport, House became very excited and called to Evie to come at once.

Stadler let them keep the photograph, and then he began to play guitar for House. After awhile House took a turn with it. And that was the "lesson." Stadler paid House five dollars. House looked at the money and immediately asked Stadler to take him to the store—the liquor store, of course. Stadler got his car and pulled up in front of the apartment, and House came down the steps in Stadler's words, "lickety-split" and jumped into his Celica. At the liquor store, House bought a bottle of fortified wine, Mogen David 20–20, which he consumed on the spot in Stadler's car. And that led to a peroration about God and the Devil—and Stadler himself had a devil of a time ending the guitar lesson.

But among all of the musical pilgrims who came to pay homage in this period, two would stand out, John Mooney and Brian Williams. Probably no one among all of his young fans absorbed more music from House than Mooney. Mooney had left home in the small town of Mendon south of Rochester when he was still a teenager and started playing blues. Soon he crossed paths with Joe Beard who, next to Son House, was the most important blues musician in the region by this time. Beard had spent about a year in Chicago in the late sixties; it was a musical apprenticeship in blues, during which he met old friends from Memphis like Matt Murphy, and made new acquaintances like Muddy Waters, Buddy Guy, and Junior Wells. Chicago acts traveling back and forth between the East Coast and Chicago often played in Rochester, and Beard usually performed with them.

Mooney, with his interest in blues, could not have found a better mentor than Beard, and by 1968 he started playing in Beard's band. Beard worked for himself then as now as an electrician, and Mooney sometimes even worked as his assistant—indeed, his relationship with the older man developed to the point that for a period of time he even lived with Beard and his wife Mary.

Mooney said: "Joe and I had been playing together for a year or two, he said, 'You play so much Son House stuff, you ought to meet him.'" Beard arranged for Mooney to meet House at his place, a fact that set Mooney apart from the rest of the Greig Street pilgrims who lacked an introduction from a credible blues musician. "So we got together at Joe's house and played some. Son was just amazingly loud. I remember the windows rattling in the panes from his singing."[17]

Not long after Beard had introduced him to Son House, Mooney also met Brian Williams. Williams, as we have seen, had observed House perform at Gaslight Café in Greenwich Village in 1965, and subsequently a few more times at coffeehouses and folk festivals. Then in the late sixties he moved to western New York where he began playing upright bass in a string band called the Swamp Roots String Band. One of their regular gigs was at a bar called the Cottage Hotel in Mendon, a small town about ten miles south of Rochester. Mendon happened to be Mooney's hometown. One night Mooney asked the band if he could sit in during their breaks, and Williams and his bandmates agreed. Mooney played blues with a bottleneck, and after he had sat in a few more times, Williams asked him where he had learned to play like that. Mooney told him that he had been playing with Son House on Greig Street and learning from him. Williams was surprised to learn that House was still alive, and they made arrangements to go to Greig Street together.

Soon Mooney and Williams were performing blues as a duo, and Williams was taking his bass fiddle along when the two visited Son House. Usually they took House over to Williams' apartment, which was not far from the Third Ward where House lived. In order to get him to play, however, it was always necessary to "prime the pump," in House's words, to

---

17. Daniel Beaumont, "He Was His Own Man For Sure," *Living Blues*, September–October 2003, p. 37.

provide alcohol. When House saw Mooney and Williams at his door, he would invariably ask them, "Did you guys bring any 'primer' with you?"

This, not surprisingly, caused tensions between the two young musicians and Evie. "She was never really happy about it," Williams said. "If she knew that we were going to be taking him away, she was not very happy with us. She didn't *not* like us. She just didn't like us coming around, and she knew that we were bringing 'primer' with us, because that was the only way that we could really get him playing. Now maybe he would have played anyway, but I think he sort of held out. Like, 'If you want me to play, bring some primer along.'"

It seems that among the young musicians who played with House only Joe Beard was exempt from this condition. Indeed, the subject *never* arose between the two men. Beard recalled, "He never asked me to buy him a drink. In all the time we spent together, and I would take him out to clubs to hear music, he never asked me to buy him a drink. And if I told him I thought he'd had enough to drink, he'd say, 'I think I have.' And when I took him out, that was fine with Evie. She would say, 'I know you'll look after him.'"[18]

But Williams and Mooney felt they had little choice but to acquiesce. As Williams recalled, "So we would do that, and in retrospect we probably shouldn't have encouraged him. But he would go through a lot of booze over the course of an afternoon of playing. And like I said before, I don't know if that was taking him to any worse a place than he was already at...But certainly I think it allowed him to maybe go to that place where he could play blues. Whereas if he hadn't have had a couple of drinks first, he might have felt too self-conscious to go to that other 'bad' place."

However, House did not simply play blues, he would also perform spirituals with Mooney and Williams—but always while he was drinking.

Mooney's recollection of window panes rattling in Joe Beard's living room when House sang says much about the way House threw himself into his music no matter whether he was in Beard's living room, a coffeehouse, or in front of 10,000 people at a blues festival. Evidently the power and the fury were still inside even after 1970, but it was simply too draining for House to unleash them for an entire evening. So in the years between 1970 and 1975 House would often join Mooney and Williams at Rochester venues like the Wine Press, the Genesee Co-op and the Red Creek—a patron on one of those occasions at the Red Creek recalled

---

18. Personal conversation with Joe Beard, April 5, 2010.

seeing the bluesman dancing by himself, the only soul on the dance floor, lost in his own world. But House no longer had the strength to play a complete set and would instead play a couple of songs between their sets.

House's close relation with Mooney and Williams supports what Armand Schaubroeck said about House's attitude toward his young, white following. But it was not simply about performing, it was about allowing greater access to himself. House made distinctions among the young whites who approached him. If he was unimpressed by their knowledge of the blues, he accepted the alcohol and was pleasant, but removed. They might not have known it, but he was impatient with some of the young blues fans pretensions about blues. He would speak of them calling some composition a blues, "...they always had some little old junk, some funny little old word. Some kind of funny something that didn't mean nothing."[19] That "funny something," he was adamant, was not blues. But in the case of Schaubroeck, Mooney, and Williams—people who knew more about the music—for all of whom music was a profession, House allowed them a measure of intimacy he denied to most of his young followers. It was not simply about the alcohol.

By 1973, House's various physical problems sometimes made performing difficult even in the more limited situations that Mooney and Williams provided. A newspaper article dated April 1, 1973 stated that he "could hardly get through a number when he performed for a class on the blues at the Rochester School Without Walls."[20] Yet, it might happen that two weeks later House could still deliver a cameo performance. But it was unpredictable, and it was necessary for musicians like Mooney and Williams to be on hand to pick up the slack if he faltered.

In 1974 Son and Evie moved out of their Greig Street apartment where they had lived for ten years to a newer apartment building, the Danforth Towers at 160 West Ave.[21] Their old neighborhood would soon vanish in "urban renewal," after House and Evie moved to the West Avenue apartment. But the stream of young blues devotees never faltered.

An aspiring young musician named Aleks Dysljenkovic began to visit him in the summer of 1974. Dysljenkovic called ahead. On his arrival,

19. *Son House Delta Blues and Spirituals*, Capitol Records, 1995.

20. John P. Morgan, *Upstate Magazine*, Sunday supplement to the *Democrat and Chronicle* (April 1, 1973), p. 22.

21. Possibly 1975, but more likely 1974. The 1973 City Directory still has him at the Greig Street address. But a single directory for the years 1974–75 has him at the new West Avenue address.

Dysljenkovic, who had never met House, found an older black man sitting in the lobby of the building waiting for him. He asked, "Are you Son House?" and House clapped his hands and began to sing, "Don't you mind people grinnin' in your face..."

Like all the other pilgrims, Dysljenkovic had brought the usual offering, alcohol. He played a bit for House and then gave the guitar to House who played "Levee Camp Moan." When House sang, he sang so loud that Evie shouted at him from the kitchen, "Keep it down! Keep it down!"

For the next two years Dysljenkovic visited House regularly, bringing House a quart of warm beer and usually some flowers to placate Evie. In all this time, however, Dysljenkovic was not certain that House ever learned his name—he certainly never greeted him, "Hi Aleks." To Dysljenkovic, House seemed often lost in his own private world, as he seemed that night at the Red Creek dancing by himself.

Once Dysljenkovic bought a guitar at a garage sale for five dollars and gave it to House. Dysljenkovic had been warned that House would pawn a guitar to buy alcohol, but figured that, after all, it only cost five dollars. When Dysljenkovic returned a couple of weeks later, he asked House, "Where's your guitar, Son?" House got up and began to walk around the living room lifting up a sofa pillow, "searching" for his lost guitar.

But a far better guitar could just as suddenly materialize. Dysljenkovic made arrangements with Larry Scahill the owner of the coffeehouse at the Genesee Co-op for Son House to play there, and a date was set about two weeks away. When Dysljenkovic came on the appointed day to pick up Son House, to his surprise, the old bluesman, who by this time often seemed to drift in and out of reality, was dressed in a suit and tie and ready to go, eager even it seemed. Even more surprising to Dysljenkovic, House had a National Steel guitar. How he got the guitar, Dysljenkovic never asked.

In this same period, in March of 1974, two young men began work on a documentary about House. Ron Mix had a degree from the School of the Photographic Arts and Sciences at the Rochester Institute of Technology. In the spring and early summer, he and Michael Rothman shot 16mm footage of House in Rochester, and in the second week of July, they followed him to Toronto where he played at the Toronto Island Blues Festival in what was his final public performance.

Mix's Toronto footage shows House at the festival in Toronto. House has even fewer teeth than he did in the 1969 Seattle footage, and his hair has finally gone gray. He wears a white shirt and fire engine red pants. The festival was on an island, and House and Evie ride out to the island in the

Son House, Toronto Island Blues Festival, 1974. Courtesy of Dick Waterman.

back of a motorboat. At the festival, he is squired around by Waterman. At one point he poses between two young women in bikini tops and cut-off jeans. (Undoubtedly, he used a line with them he often used, "I'm old, but I got young ideas!") Waterman leads him up onto the stage and hands him the National Steel. Additional footage, some of it clearly staged, shows him in Rochester. In one sequence, House emerges from the entrance of 61 Greig Street; in another, he plays the guitar on the steps of the Greig Street building. A wide shot reveals broken windows in the upper stories of the Greig Street apartment building they left. In yet another sequence, House ambles around in the spring sunshine on Genesee Street not far from his new address on West Avenue.

In May 1975, an article about the documentary called "Son House on film" appeared in an issue of a blues quarterly called *Whiskey, Women and....*[22] The article said that interviews had been done with "John Lee Hooker, Sonny Terry, Buddy Guy, Brownie McGhee, Junior Wells, Willie Dixon, and Dick Waterman."[23] More interviews were planned "with such blues notables as Muddy Waters, Howlin Wolf and Johnny Shines," and furthermore "Arrangements are also being made for B.B. King to do the

22. The article is described as an August 1974 press release of Reel Image Inc., Mix's production company.

23. *Whiskey, Women and...*, no. 7. The pages are unnumbered, but the article is on p. 20.

film's narration track." A photograph showed a young man sitting with Son and Evie on the steps of 61 Greig Street with the caption saying it was the "Director Louis Villalon." Mix had brought in Villalon in the intervening year.

Mix's documentary was suspended after the Toronto festival for lack of money. Mix gave some of his footage to another young Rochester resident named Mark Brady. Brady transferred some of the 16mm footage to the cheaper video format and added some sequences on Greig Street and Genesee Street. He subsequently made a 30-minute black and white video documentary about House that aired on the local public television affiliate in 1978, and then—rather like its subject—disappeared from view for almost twenty years.

House's 1974 Toronto performance marked the end of the journey begun one Saturday evening in Clarksdale almost five decades earlier. After that Waterman had little choice but to bring down the curtain on House's second career, once and for all. When the applause died down for the last time, the most difficult part of Waterman's work with House came to an end. What was more or less bookkeeping would continue. His relationship with House was the sort of unusual conjunction created in the sixties. Despite the difficulties House presented to him—or perhaps due to them in part—House would occupy a special place in Waterman's memories of the musicians he represented. This would be apparent even years later in the emotion in his voice when he would discuss Son House, and he would speak of "the majesty of the man."

As a result of Waterman's efforts, Son House earned money and recognition that he never expected before June 1964. In a way, for Waterman the trip on which he embarked on June 10 of 1964 never ended.

After 1974, with his mental and physical decline worsening, House began to inhabit, as Brian Williams put it, "some very strange spaces." Williams recalled visiting once and watching House shave before they took him out: "He took great delight and joy in shaving. He would put lather on his face and shave it. And he would lather up all over the place. And then he lathered up over his eyebrows and shaved his eyebrows! He was just like a little boy."

Williams began to suspect it was the early stages of dementia. By 1974, when he moved to West Avenue, House had begun suffering seizures and was taking medication for them. Possibly a sign of House's mental changes was evident in his conversations with Williams and Mooney, where he began to speak more often and more openly about sex. Previously, House, despite the evidence of his numerous lovers, had been reticent on the subject—his lyrics are modest by blues standards about the physical aspects of sex. His increasing volubility on this subject after 1970 may well have been symptomatic of mental deterioration—Williams spoke of the breaking down of certain walls and inhibitions in his mind. Recalling House's ruminations on the subject, Williams said:

> There was an implicit captivation with sexuality in his music as well, and I don't think I would have understood it quite as much if he hadn't talked about it in the privacy of the sessions that John and I had with him. He would talk about the devil, and when he would say that, he would point down, he would point at his genitals. And he would say, 'There's the devil.'" Almost as though to suggest that in his younger days when maybe he—I don't know that this is the case—but if he was unfaithful to his wife, or having affairs, or maybe just out womanizing, that that was part of the devil. It wasn't him doing that. It was the devil that was occupying him. And it was interesting that whenever he talked about it, he would point to his penis. And sometimes he would even touch himself there.

Of course, by his own admission House had been unfaithful to Evie. Clearly sex was another deep force, besides those of alcohol and blues, that drew him away from religion—seen in the fact that the very first time he strayed from the pulpit was when he ran off to Louisiana with a member of his congregation.

By 1976, probably due as much to his mental deterioration as to his physical condition, House had become too much of a burden for even the long-suffering Evie to carry by herself, and that year House and his wife left Rochester forever.

They moved to Detroit, to an apartment on the fifth floor of a high-rise on Second Avenue. Evie's three children, (Willie) Bea Powell, Sally Sledge, and Rufus Goff, who had moved with her mother to Detroit in the late 1940s, were still there. They helped Evie care for their stepfather the final twelve years of his life, during which time he his mental incapacity grew still worse. But there was to be one final reprise of the experience that had been so much a part of House's life in Rochester after June 23, 1964—the pilgrimage made by young white fans.

Encore

In 1981 a young man named Rich Gardner who hosted a blues show on WGMC 90.1 in Rochester decided to look for Son House. Gardner was recently divorced, and on the heels of that he had also lost his job. He saw a freelance article as a way of making some money as well as indulging his interest in music. But Gardner simply knew that House was gone and was unaware that he had moved to Detroit. Indeed, his fruitless first step was to go to the 61 Greig Street address, which had fallen victim to the "urban renewal" that was one of the long-term results of the 1964 riot and no longer existed. Gardner then went to a record store on Monroe Avenue, Play It Again Records, whose manager suggested he contact John Mooney. Gardner found Mooney playing in an old hotel in Naples, a little town forty miles south of Rochester nestled in a valley of the Finger Lakes region. Mooney gave Gardner a Detroit phone number.

When Gardner called the number Evie answered "in a tone that said she'd already seen and heard it all."[24]

She agreed that Gardner could come and interview House for an article for the *Democrat and Chronicle*.[25] Before he said goodbye, Evie yelled in the phone, "And they don't allow no geetar playin' here!"—treating Gardner to the well-known line from "Mr. Crump Don't Like It."

Gardner enlisted a recent acquaintance, Mark Sampson, who was a photographer, to go with him. On a Saturday morning in late April they set out from Rochester in Gardner's 1976 Plymouth Duster and drove the eight-hour drive through Canada to Detroit. House's apartment was in a rundown neighborhood immediately next to an industrial area of warehouses and factories. When they met Evie her mood was quite in harmony with that of the crumbling city to which she and her senile husband had come to spend the final years of their lives; a city whose main industry was being battered by Japanese competition and whose prosperous white residents had long since fled it for the suburbs.

When she opened the door of apartment 518, she skipped the niceties and asked them bluntly, "What's in it for him?"

"Recognition," Gardner replied.

24. Rich Gardner, "Seeking Son House." *City Newspaper*. Rochester (January 28, 2004) http://www.rochestercitynewspaper.com/archives/2004/01/Seeking-Son-House. All of the quotes are taken from this article.

25. The article in no. 23 about their visit only appeared until years later.

Behind Evie, Son House was sitting placidly in a La-Z-Boy. After considering Gardner's reply for a moment, Evie relented and let them enter.

The apartment was simply furnished. Crocheted coverlets and pillows in bold colors were placed on the sofa and chairs. There were a few photographs of Evie's children, but no memorabilia of House's musical career.

Evie began the conversation with Gardner and Sampson by informing them there were only two places in this world: you could be in the street with blues and whiskey and Satan or in the church with Jesus—a simplified version of the sermon House had always used to introduce "Preachin' the Blues," but not an auspicious beginning delivered now by Evie.

Evie and Son House, Detroit, MI, April 1981. Courtesy of Mark Sampson

Sampson took some photos, and then Gardner attempted to ask House some questions. But he found that House could barely speak: "I asked him which countries he had played in. He said, 'Uh, A...it starts with A...uh. Africa.' 'Austria,' his wife corrected."

Gardner and Sampson had brought along a National Steel for House to play, but this ended in miserable failure as House's fingers became caught between the strings and the fingerboard.

Though it hardly seemed possible, the mood soured even more. And after a few uncomfortable moments Evie intervened, extricating his fingers and removing the guitar.

At that point Gardner gave up trying to "interview" House, and he and Sampson simply talked to both Evie and House. Slowly the mood improved. It emerged that, despite her preamble about the blues and the Devil, Evie had apparently frequented some of the juke joints where House had performed. And her own recollections shook loose a few brief memories from her husband.

After about forty-five minutes, it was time to leave. And then, while the two young men were saying goodbye, House leaned forward and sang, "Don'cha mind people grinnin' in your face—"

And that was it. The somber finale of his musical career.

After seven more years in this weakened physical and mental state House died of cancer of the larynx in Harper Hospital on Wednesday, October 19, 1988—it was not his drinking but his smoking that claimed him. The funeral took place five days later on October 24, at the Mayflower Baptist Church. At the funeral were Evie, his stepson Rufus Goff, and stepdaughters Willie Bea Powell and Sally Sledge. He was buried in Mt. Hazel Cemetery on a raw fall afternoon, with a temperature in the forties, the wind blowing, and squalls of rain passing.

Son House, despite his habits, had outlived many younger friends from his musical world. Robert Johnson had died in 1938. Al Wilson had died in 1970. Howlin' Wolf had died in 1976, and Muddy Waters in 1983. He even outlived Nick Perls who passed in 1987.

Evie would say of Son, "I raised children, three of my own and one that was given to me, and he's more trouble than all of them put together."[26] She lived for another decade, finally following her husband to the grave on April 15, 1999.

Two years earlier, in 1997, the Detroit Blues Society had placed a new marker on her husband's grave. The top of the gravestone, cut at an angle,

---

26. Michael Rothman, "Son House Now," p. 5.

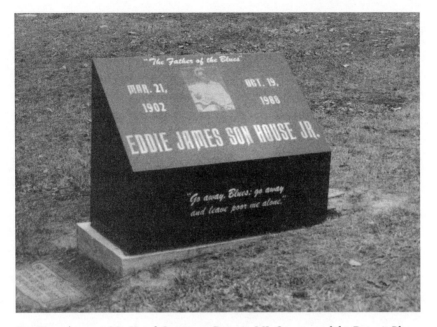

Son House's grave, Mt. Hazel Cemetery, Detroit, MI. Courtesy of the Detroit Blues Society.

has an etched image of Son taken from a photograph at the Philadelphia Folk Festival in 1964. It shows him cradling a National Steel and gazing intently into the lens.

Above the etching it reads "Father of the Blues." Beneath the image his name is given as "Eddie James Son House Jr." The verso side of the marker features a testimonial by Dick Waterman, part of which reads: "…the years seemed to roll away. He closed his eyes and the sweat broke out on his face. He started in a low voice which became louder and louder. It was as if he went into a trance and somehow willed himself to another time and another place."

Given his impoverished beginnings and the daunting combination of social barriers and personal weaknesses, anything but a dismal oblivion would have been unlikely for such a man as Son House. No one could have foreseen that the music he made in the backwater towns of Lula and Mattson and Robinsonville would one day be heard around the globe. As House himself said in another context, "Now a lot of people don't believe it, and they don't think it's possible—but it is." Now, this is the truth.

Rochester, New York, and Cairo, Egypt
2006–2010

Appendix 1

LYRICS TO SELECTED SONGS

"Preachin' the Blues," Part 1

Oh, I'm gonna get me religion, I'm gonna join the Baptist church
I'm gonna be a Baptist preacher, and I sure won't have to work
Oh, I'm gonna preach these blues now, and I want everybody to shout
I'm gonna do like a prisoner, I'm gonna roll my time on out
Oh, in my room, I bowed down to pray
Say the blues come along and drove my spirit away
Oh, I had religion, Lord, this very day
But the womens and whiskey, well they would not let me pray
Oh, I wish I had a little heaven of my own
(Spoken: "Great God Almighty..." Hey, heaven of my own)
Then I'd give all my women, a long, long, happy home
Yeah, I love my baby just like I love myself
Well, if she don't have me, she won't have nobody else

"My Black Mama," Part 1

Oh, black mama, what's the matter with you?
Said, it ain't satisfaction, don't care what I do
You say a brown-skin woman'll make a rabbit move to town
You say a jet black woman will make a mule kick his stable down
Say, t'ain't no heaven, say, there ain't no burnin' hell
Say, where I'm going when I die, can't nobody tell
Well, my black mama's face shine like the sun
Oh, lipstick and powder sure won't help her none
Well, you see my milk cow, tell her to hurry home
I ain't had no milk cow since that cow been gone
Well, I'm going to the race track to see my pony run

He ain't the best in the world, but he's a runnin' son-of-a-gun
Oh, Lord, have mercy on my wicked soul
Wouldn't mistreat you, baby, for my weight in gold

"Jinx Blues"

Well, I got up this morning jinx around (jinx around, around) my bed
You know I thought about you, honey, it liked to kill me dead
Look it here now, baby, what you want me to do
You know I done all I could just trying to get along with you
You know the blues ain't nothing but a low down aching chill
If you never had them, honey, lord, I hope you never will
The blues, the blues is a worried heart disease
Look like the woman you been loving, man, is so doggone hard to please
I'd rather be outdoors, walking up and down the road
Than to laying around here working just for my board and clothes
Look it here, little girl, don't you cry no more
When I leave this time, well, I'm gonna hang crepe on your door
I woke up this morning just at the break of day
You know I was hugging the pillow where my good gal used to lay
You know, ain't it terrible laying down by yourself
The blues got you, and your woman got somebody else
The sun going down behind the western hills...
It looked like you wanted me while I was loving and kind
Some day you're going to want me, and I'll be done changed my mind
I went in my room, sat down and cried
Well, I didn't have blues, just wasn't satisfied
The minutes seem like hours, the hours seem like days
It seems like my baby ought to stop her low down ways
I believe I'll go to the gypsy and have my fortune told
I got to believe somebody is trying to steal my jellyroll

"County Farm Blues"

Down South when you do anything that's wrong
They'll sure put your down on the county farm
Put you down in a ditch with a very long spade
Wish to God you hadn't ever been made
Put you down under a man called Captain Jack
He'll sure write his name up and down you back

"American Defense"

No use to shedding no tears, no use to having no cares
This war may last you for years
American defense will earn you some cents
Just how to take care of your boys
You must raise more produce, farmer...?
Just to save all your worries and toys
Chorus
The red, white and blue that ripples at you
You ought to do everything that you can
Buy war saving stamps, young men go to the camps
Be brave and take a stand
Chorus
Don't let trouble sometimes upset your mind
So you won't know just what to do
Keep pushing, keep shoving
Don't be angry, be loving
Be faithful and honest and true
Chorus
You can say yes or no, but we gotta win this war
Because General MacArthur's now afraid
There won't be enough chaps to shoot a little game of craps
Because the biggest of them all will be dead
Chorus
This war sure do bond our mother and father, our sisters and
brothers too
Dear friends and relations in this world's creation [?]
Don't let this worry you

Appendix 2

SOUTHOLD, NY, POLICE REPORT

Police Report, Southold, NY, October 8, 1955 (p. 1). Courtesy of Town of Southold, NY.

627

Saturday October 8, 1955. (Continued)

0231. Call from Lew Gratton, Southold (3115) going to Hospital
shortly with Bill Lindsay - will take statements, also will have
a D.A. stenographer with them.   Elmer

0233. Called Pat. King at Hospital, gave information.   Elmer

0237. Call from Henry Wolf, Cutchogue (6742) states a colored
man at his door who claims he killed a man. Contacted
Chief Conway via radio, gave information.   Elmer

Patterson, W. 4, York, S.C. - Dob. 5/10/36, Camden, S.C. Social
Security - 247-52-2609, Brought to Hospital by John Mack Brown-
Nathaniel Mills - Jimmie Williams - Aaron White, Crew Leader -
all of Cutchogue Labor Camp - 2 envelopes with bill folder,
cards and papers left at the Hospital office.   Pat. King

1340. Call from L.I. Press - stated they heard there was a
stabbing here. Wanted to know if it was fatal Told them
yes -   Elmer

0429. Call from L.I. Press for information on stabbing - Told them
no information at this time.   Elmer

0555. Call from World Telegram for information on stabbing of
Willie Patterson (col) of Cutchogue Labor Camp - stabbed by
Eddie Stone (col) of Cutchogue Labor Camp - Gave above information
                                                                  Elmer

0602. Call from L.I. Press, for information on above stabbing -
Gave same information as above.   Elmer

Police Report, Southold, NY, October 8, 1955 (p. 2). Courtesy of Town of Southold, NY.

628

Saturday October 8, 1955 (continued)

On call to Cutchogue Labor Camp, Willie Junior Patterson was stabbed by Eddie James Hoose. Patterson was taken to E.L.I Hospital by Nathaniel Miller, Jimmie Williams and John Mark Brown. Patterson was dead upon arrival at Hospital. Received a call from Elmer Grealy, that a colored man was at Mrs. Wolf's home and wanted him to call Police, saying that he had killed a man. Proceeded to Cutchogue, party had left Wolf's. Picked up Eddie James Hoose, at the Cutchogue Traffic Light. He had a large knife in his pocket, and said it was the knife, he stabbed Patterson with. At 6:30 A.M. arraigned Eddie James Hoose before Rafe W. Cuthill on charge of Manslaughter 1st degree, Sec. 1050. Hoose waived examination; committed to County Jail. Complainant Otto L. Aury. EDDIE JAMES HOOSE - B-M. DOB 3/21/02 - Place of Birth, Mississippi. Address 161 Atkinson St. Rochester, N.Y. 5'9". 167 lbs. Brown eyes - Black + grey hair - 5" scar upper left arm - Married - Slim build - S.S.# 425-38-7684. Chief Aury - Ptl. Fitzpatrick - Ptl. King - Sgt. Reilly + Tpr. Hoyn - Dea. Gratten + Wm. Lindsay.

Police Report, Southold, NY, October 8, 1955 (p. 3). Courtesy of Town of Southold, NY.

ACKNOWLEDGMENTS

I could not have written this book without the generosity and help of many people.

The first person I must thank is my friend, blues musician and Rochester resident Joe Beard. If I had not met Joe, I never would have conceived of writing this book. Joe, who was Son House's neighbor on Greig Street in 1964, was the first person I ever interviewed on any topic in my life, and it was his generosity with his time and his memories that set in motion the events that led first to my video documentary about him, *So Much Truth*, and that ultimately resulted in this book. Joe ranks with the very best people playing blues today, and he definitely deserves a wider audience. His recordings are not known widely enough.

Two close friends, Steve Grills and Jeff Harris, encouraged me to write this biography. Steve is a musician, and Jeff has done a blues radio show for many years; both are very knowledgeable about the history of blues, and they supplied me with many sources from out-of-date journals and the like. They also read drafts and made suggestions.

Armand Schaubroeck, proprietor with his brothers Blaine and Bruce, of the House of Guitars, was also generous with his time and recollections of his "adventures" with Son House. Armand read parts of the manuscript and corrected them. My evenings with Armand when I would drop off a chapter would usually turn into a long conversation that would end up on some topic far removed from Son House. Armand has his own remarkable story—one that I may yet write about at greater length.

Once I had a first draft of the manuscript, Emily Morry, a Ph.D. candidate in history at the University of Rochester read it. She made numerous valuable corrections and suggestions at all levels, substantive and stylistic. She also read subsequent drafts of several chapters where the revisions were extensive. Beyond those things, she was a constant source of encouragement, especially over Jacque Lacans at Hogan's Hideaway.

My daughter Lily Beaumont was my "lay reader." Lily read the manuscript before I submitted it to Oxford. Lily is already a fine writer herself, and the book benefited greatly from her stylistic suggestions. Someday, Lily will write a book herself, and it will be better than her father's efforts.

My friend Edward Komara, editor of *The Encyclopedia of the Blues*, offered very helpful comments and suggestions at every stage. He helped me think about some knotty issues of chronology, and beyond these things encouraged me in the face of various difficulties.

From the other side of the Atlantic came much advice and encouragement from three people. First of all, Alan Balfour supplied me with a number of documents, especially documents related to Son House's tours and recordings in England. When I was in Cairo in the summer of 2007 writing the first draft, Alan mailed me numerous documents. That process continued up to the last revisions.

His countryman John Cowley was especially helpful understanding and untangling the Lomax-Library of Congress material. As Alan Balfour wrote me, "John knows more about what Alan Lomax did than Alan Lomax knew." John read the chapter on the Fisk-Library of Congress project and provided me with very helpful criticism.

Finally, also from England came much assistance and information from Bob Groom—especially about Son's 1967 and 1970 tours of England.

The generosity and encouragement of Alan, John, and Bob has helped me through many rough patches. I hope this book has some of the dispassionate intelligence that has marked their writings over the years.

My lifelong friend Danny Ryan read the entire manuscript and offered invaluable comments, corrections, and suggestions.

Dick Waterman, one of the rediscoverers and the man who managed Son House's second career, was generous with his time, both via e-mails and phone interviews, and with permissions. Son House holds a special place in Dick's life, and this book could not have been written without his help and cooperation. A conversation we had one fall evening in Oxford, Mississippi was one of the crucial steps toward the decision to write this book. He was especially generous with his photographs of Son.

Phil Spiro, another rediscoverer, was also very generous—and patient—with his responses to my questions about events back in 1964.

The story of their search (with Nick Perls) for Son House would not be nearly as detailed and interesting were it not for his and Dick Waterman's generosity in responding to my questions.

Larry Cohn, who was present at the 1965 Columbia recording session, kindly answered my questions about that and other issues.

Ted Gioia offered some helpful advice at a critical point on how I might proceed with a couple of delicate issues.

The late Steve Calt read many drafts of chapters, corrected errors and offered welcome advice on numerous issues. It was also his tip that led to one of the major discoveries I made about House's life. More than that, the encouragement of someone so knowledgeable about blues was most welcome. After a point in our relationship, our conversations wandered far afield from the blues, into literature and politics. I feel fortunate to have gotten to know Steve in the last years of his life. He generously sent me material from his last book, *Barrelhouse Words: a Blues Dialect Dictionary*, before it was published.

The assistance of Todd Harvey and his staff at the Library of Congress made my visit there a very efficient one—and a happy memory.

Eric Likness, a friend who works in the Educational Technology Center at the University of Rochester, helped me with numerous technical issues relating to images and interviews. More than that, however, my conversations with Eric from the early stage of thinking about this as a documentary helped me to clarify how the narrative should be shaped. Fred Wagner and Tony DiPietro, also in the Educational Technology Center, also helped me with various technical issues, and with their humor. Marc Bollman in the Music and Art Library helped with an important last minute request.

My friend, Julia Rabkin, helped me with the photography and buoyed my spirits from time to time.

Richard Peek, Director of Rare Books, Special Collections & Preservation in Rush Rhees Library at the University of Rochester s told me of a particular event involving Son House and gave me a sound recording of that event. Nancy Martin, the University Archivist and Local History Librarian in Rare Books and Special Collections assisted me with many issues involving Rochester history and House's residence in Rochester. The chapter on his years between 1943 and 1964 is much richer due to her help. I must also mention Alan Unsworth among the librarians at Rush Rhees library for helping me with online searches and data bases.

Brian Williams in an extensive interview long before I thought of writing the book offered many sensitive insights into the sort of man Son House was in his later years. Likewise, the memories of his friend and musical colleague, John Mooney.

My friends and colleagues at the University of Rochester Anthea Butler, Dave Headlam, Ed Wierenga, Emil Homerin, and Victoria Wolcott offered me advice, encouragement and help in numerous and varied ways. Two other colleagues in my department, I must especially single out for helping me in a period of some personal turmoil: Anne Merideth who always listened to me and always encouraged me, and Douglas Brooks who gave me "shelter in the storm."

Our departmental administrative assistant Evie Hartleben assisted, especially in the last stage, reading chapters and beyond that just offered sympathy and encouragement.

I am grateful also for all the efforts and encouragement of June Avignone and Valerie Alhart in the Office of Communications at the University of Rochester.

I must also single out my friend Tanya Bakhmetyeva, a colleague in the history department at the University of Rochester, who read many chapters. But, more than that, her insights and contributions are evident in many of the analyses—to give only one example, the discussion of blues as a "secular homily" was the result of one of our conversations.

The Democrat and Chronicle, Rochester's daily newspaper, was very generous with their permissions, allowing me free use of articles and photographs. My thanks to Matt Dudek, there, especially.

City Newspaper, a Rochester weekly, also allowed me to quote liberally from their account of Rich Gardner and Mark Sampson's trip to Detroit in 1981.

Finally, I must thank my editor Suzanne Ryan (and her assistants Madelyn and Caelyn) at Oxford University Press. Suzanne's beneficial influence is apparent to me on every page of this book. Her patience and encouragement were especially appreciated.

While working on this book, one of the unforeseen consequences was the new friendships I formed. The book benefited greatly from the advice and help of all of these people—and likely some others I have forgotten to mention. Needless to say, the errors and shortcomings are my own.

Credits

SELECTED TEXT

Excerpts from Stephen Calt and Gayle Wardlow, *King of the Delta Blues: The Life and Music of Charley Patton*

© 1998 Rock Chapel Press.

Excerpts from Erick von Schmidt and Jim Rooney, *Baby Let Me Follow You Down: The Illustrated Story of the Cambridge Folk Years.*

© 1993 University of Massachusetts Press. Used by permission of the authors.

Excerpts from Betsy Bues, "Hunt For 'Blues' Singer Ends in City," *Times-Union*, July 6, 1964.

Used by permission of the *Democrat and Chronicle*.

Excerpts from "'Blues' Singer Making Try for Comeback," *Times-Union*, July 14, 1964.

Used by permission of the *Democrat and Chronicle*.

Interview with Son House, from Julius Lester, "I Can Make My Own Songs"

© 1965 *Sing Out!* Used by permission. All rights reserved.

Interview with Son House, May 8, 1971, Minneapolis, MN.

Printed courtesy of Jeff Todd Titon.

Interview with Phil Spiro, from conversations with the author

Printed courtesy of Phil Spiro.

LYRICS

All Son House song lyrics appear courtesy of Dick Waterman.

BIBLIOGRAPHY

Baggelaar, Kristin and Milton, Donald. *Folk Music: More Than a Song.* New York: Crowell Publishing, 1976.

Balfour, Alan. Liner notes for *Son House: John the Revelator.* UK: Sequel NEXCD 207, 1992.

Basiuk, Bo. "Eddie Son House-Delta Bluesman." *Blues Magazine* vol. 2 no. 5 (Oct 1976) 40–55.

Barlow, William. *"Looking Up at Down": The Emergence of Blues Culture.* Philadelphia: Temple University Press, 1989.

Beaumont, Daniel. "So Much Truth." *Living Blues* no. 169 (Sept.–Oct. 2003) 28–37.

———— "Son House." *Encyclopedia of the Blues,* ed. Edward Komara, 465–76. New York: Routledge, 2006.

Bertrand, Michael T. *Race, Rock, and Elvis.* Champagne-Urbana: University of Illinois Press, 2000.

Blues Life. "Son House: Sad Letter." 44 (1988) 18.

Briggs, Keith; Burke, Tony; Lomax, Alan: Cowley, John. "We Called It The Walking Blues: An Interview with Son House." *Blues & Rhythm* 37 (June 1988) 4–5.

Calt, Stephen. Liner notes for *Son House: The Real Delta Blues: 14 Songs From The Man Who Taught Robert Johnson.* USA: Blue Goose 2016, 1974.

————. Liner notes to *Charlie Patton: Founder of the Delta Blues.* Yazoo 2010.

———— *I'd Rather Be the Devil: Skip James and the Blues.* New York: Da Capo Press, 1994.

———— *Barrelhouse Words: A Blues Dialect Dictionary.* Champagne-Urbana: University of Illinois, 2010.

Calt, Stephen and Wardlow, Gayle. *The King of the Delta Blues: The Life and Music of Charlie Patton.* Newton, N.J.: Rock Chapel Press, 1988.

Catwell, Robert. *When We Were Good: The Folk Revival.* Cambridge, Mass.: Harvard University Press, 1996.

Charters, Samuel. *The Country Blues,* revised ed. New York: Rinehart, 1975.

Cohen, Ronald D. *Rainbow Quest: The Folk Music Revival and American Society 1940–1970.* Amherst: University of Massachusetts Press, 2002.

Cohn, Lawrence. "Son House: Delta Bluesman." *Saturday Review* vol. 51 no. 3 (Sept. 28, 1968) 68–69.

————. "Son Sessions." *Blues Unlimited* 148/149 (Winter 1987) 6.

————. Liner notes for *Son House: Father of the Delta Blues: The Complete 1965 Sessions.* USA: Columbia/Legacy C2K 48867, 1992.

Coombs, Norman. "History of African Americans in Rochester, NY" (unpublished paper), http://people.rit.edu/nrcgsh/arts/rochester.htm.

Cowley, John. "Walking Blues." *Blues Unlimited* no. 106 (Feb.–March 1974) 13.

————— "Really 'The Walking Blues': Son House, Muddy Waters, Robert Johnson and The Development of a Traditional Blues." *Popular Music* 1 (1981), 57–72. (Reprinted in *Juke Blues* no. 1 (July 1985) 8–14).

—————. "Son House: 1902–1988, an Historical Appreciation." *Blues & Rhythm* no. 41 (Dec. 1988) 8–10.

Daniels, Jonathan. *A Southerner Discovers the South*, New York: MacMillan, 1938.

Davis, Rebecca. "Child Is Father To Man: How Al Wilson Taught Son House To Play Son House." *Blues Access* no. 35 (Fall 1998) 40–43.

Down Beat. "Son House Records As Skip James Recovers" vol. 32 no.12 (June 3,1965) 9.

Du Bois, W. E. B. *The Souls of Black Folk*. Boulder, Co.: Paradigm Publishers, 2004.

Evans, David. "An Interview with H. C. Speir." *JEMF Quarterly* (Autumn 1972), 117–21.

—————. *Big Road Blues: Tradition and Creativity in the Folk Blues*. Berkeley: University of California, 1982.

Fahey, John; Hansen, Barret; Levine, Mark. "Son House Interview, May 7, 1965." Southern Folklife Collection at the University of North Carolina at Chapel Hill.

—————. *Charley Patton*. London: Studio Vista Press, 1970.

Feld, David. "Son House at Syracuse." *Blues Access* no. 16 (Winter 1993) 14–15.

Ferris, William. *Blues from the Delta*. Garden City, N.J.: Anchor Press Doubleday, 1978.

Filene, Benjamin. *Romancing the Folk: Public Memory & American Roots Music*. Chapel Hill: University of North Carolina Press, 2000.

Frith, Simon. "The Magic that can set you free." *Popular Music* 1 (1981) 159–68.

Gardner, Rich. "Seeking Son House." *City Newspaper*. Rochester, N.Y. (Jan. 28, 2004). http://www.rochestercitynewspaper.com/archives/2004/01/Seeking-Son-House/

Gioia, Ted. *Delta Blues: The Life and Times of the Mississippi Masters Who Revolutionized American Music*. New York: W. W. Norton, 2008.

—————. "The Red-rumor Blues." *Los Angeles Times*. (April 23, 2006).

Goodwin, Michael. "Son House: You Can't Fool God." *Rolling Stone* no. 49 (Dec. 27, 1969), 14, 16.

Gordon, Robert. *Can't Be Satisfied: The Life and Times of Muddy Waters*. New York and London: Little Brown & Company, 2002.

Groom, Bob. "An Interview with Son House." *Blues World*, no. 18 (Jan. 1968) 5–8.

—————. *The Blues Revival*. London: Studio Vista, 1971.

Groom, Bob and Cook, Les. "My Home is in the Delta." *Blues & Rhythm* no. 49 (Jan. 1990) 13.

Grubbs, Donald. *Cry from the Cotton*. Chapel Hill: University of North Carolina Press, 1971.

Guralnick, Peter. "Searching for Robert Johnson." *Living Blues* 53 (Summer-Autumn 1982) 27–41.

Harris, Sheldon. *Blues Who's Who. a Biographical Dictionary of Blues Singers*. New Rochelle, N.Y.: Arlington House, 1979.

Humphrey, Mark. "Prodigal Sons: Son House and Robert Wilkins." In *Saints and Sinners: Religion, Blues and (D)evil in African-American Music and Literature*, ed. Robert Sacré, 167–94. Liege, Belgium: Societe Liegeosie de Musicologie, 1996.

Hurt, R. Douglas. *African American Life in the Rural South, 1900–1950*. Columbia: University of Missouri Press, 2003.

Hutten, Rob. "This Old House…" *Blues & Rhythm* no. 111 (Aug. 1996) 10–11.

Jones, Yolanda. "Son House earns his place on Mississippi Blues Trail." *The Commercial Appeal*, June 18, 2007.

Kirby, Jack Temple. *Rural Worlds Lost: The American South 1920–1960*. Baton Rouge: Louisiana State University Press, 1987.

Klatzko, Bernard. "Finding Son House." In *Nothing but the Blues*, ed. Mike Leadbitter, 230–32. London, Hanover Books, 1971.

Komara, Edward. "Blues in the Round." *Black Music Research Journal* vol. 17 no. 1, (Spring 1997) 3–36.

—————. *The Encyclopedia of the Blues*. New York: Routledge, 2006.

—————. *The Road to Robert Johnson*. Milwaukee: Hal Leonard, 2007.

Leadbitter, Mike. *Nothing but the Blues*. London, Hanover Books, 1971.

Lester, Julius. "I Can Make My Own Songs: An Interview With Son House." *Sing Out!* vol. 15 no. 3 (July 1965) 38–47.

Levine, Lawrence. *Black Culture and Black Consciousness*. New York: Oxford University Press, 1977.

Library of Congress-Fisk University Mississippi Delta Collection, American Folklife Center. Washington D.C., 1967.

Library of Congress. The Alan Lomax Collection, American Folklife Center. Washington D.C., 2004.

Lincoln C. Eric and Mamiya, Lawrence H. *The Black Church in the African American Experience*. Durham N.C.: Duke University Press, 1990.

Lomax, Alan. *The Land Where the Blues Began*. New York: The New Press, 1993.

———. *Alan Lomax: selected writings1934–1997*, ed. Ronald D Cohen. New York: Routledge, 2003.

Lott, Eric. *Love and Theft: Blackface Minstrelsy and the American Working Class*. New York: Oxford University Press, 1993.

Mitchell, H. L., *Mean Things Happening in This Land*. Montclair, NJ: Allanheld, Osman, 1979.

———. *Roll the Union On*. Chicago: Charles H. Kerr, 1987.

Monge, Luigi. "Preachin' the Blues: An Analysis of Son House's 'Dry Spell Blues'." In *Ramblin' on my Mind*, ed. David Evans, 222–57. Champagne-Urbana: University of Illinois Press, 2008.

Newsweek. "Looking for the Blues," vol. 64 no. 2 (July 13, 1964) 82–83.

Norris, John. "Son House: New Gate of Cleve, Toronto, Ontario." *Downbeat*. Vol. 32 no. 24 (Nov. 1965) 38.

Obrecht, Jas. "Requiem for Son House." *Guitar Player* vol. 23 no. 1 (Jan. 1989) 15.

———. "Deep Down in the Delta: The Adventures Of Son House, Willie Brown & Friends" *Guitar Player* vol. 26 no. 8 (Aug. 1992) 66–81.

———. "Possessed by Song: The Deep Delta Blues of Son House." *Acoustic Guitar* no. 127 (July 2003) 68–70, 74–77.

———. "Mississippi John Hurt," http://www.mindspring.com/~dennist/mjhjas.htm.

Oliver, Paul. *Blues Fell This Morning*. New York: Cambridge University Press, 1960.

———. *Story of the Blues*. Boston: Northeastern University Press, 1997 (Reprint of 1969 Cresset edition).

———. *Screening the Blues*, Cambridge, Mass.: Da Capo Press,1989 (reprint of 1968 Cassell edition).

———. *Songsters and Saints*, Cambridge UK New York: Cambridge University Press, 1984.

———. "Middle Eight: Son House 1902–88." *Popular Music* vol. 8 no. 2 (May 1989) 195–96.

O'Neal, Jim and van Singer, Amy. *The Voice of the Blues* New York: Routledge, 2002.

Palmer, Robert. *Deep Blues*. New York: Penguin Books, 1981.

Pearson, Barry Lee and McCulloch, Bill. *Robert Johnson: Lost and Found*. Champaign-Urbana: University of Illinois Press, 2003.

Perls, Nick. "Notes on Son House and the Paramount Day." *Blues Unlimited* 18, January, 1965, 3–4.

———. "Son House Interview. Part One." *78 Quarterly* vol. 1 no. 1 (Autumn 1967) 59–61.

Randolph, Vance. *Roll Me in Your Arms: Unprintable Ozark Folksongs and Folklore*. Fayetteville: University of Arkansas 1992.

The Research Department of the Council of Social Agencies. *Rochester, New York: A Graphic Interpretation of Population Data by Census Tracts*. Rochester, N.Y., 1942.

Rothman, Michael F. "Son House Now: An Afternoon with The Father of Country Blues." *Talking Blues* no. 1 (April–May–June, 1976) 5–6.

Rooney, Jim. *Bossmen*. New York: Hayden Books, 1971.

Russell, Tony. "Son House in Person and in Retrospect." *Jazz Monthly* 188 (Oct. 1970) 23–24.

Sacré, Robert, ed. *The Voice of the Delta: Charley Patton*, Liege, Belgium: Presses Universitaires, 1987.

Santé, Luc. "The Genius of the Blues." *New York Review of Books* Vol. 41 no. 14 (Aug. 11, 1994) http://www.nybooks.com/articles/2165.

Santelli, Robert. *The Big Book of Blues*. New York: Penguin Books, 1993.

Segrest, James and Hoffman, Mark. *Moanin' at Midnight: the Life and Times of Howlin' Wolf*. New York: Pantheon Books, 2004.

Southold Police Department, Southold, NY. Police Report, Oct. 8. 1965.

Spiro, Phil. "How We Found Son House." *Broadside* vol. 3 no. 11 (June 24, 1964) 2, 4.

Titon, Jeff. "Living Blues Interview: Son House." *Living Blues* no. 31 (March-April 1977) 14–22.

———. *Early Downhome Blues: a Musical and Cultural Analysis*. Chapel Hill: University of North Carolina, 1994 (reprint of University of Illinois Press, 1977).

Tooze, Sandra B. *Muddy Waters: The Mojo Man*. Toronto: ECW 1997.

Van der Tuuk, Alex. *Paramount's Rise and Fall: A History of the Wisconsin Chair Company and its Recording Activities*. Denver: Mainspring Press, 2003.

Von Schmidt, Eric and Rooney, Jim. *Baby Let Me Follow You Down*. Amherst: University of Massachusetts, 1979, 1993.

U.S. Department of Commerce. *U.S. Census of Housing: 1940 Rochester, N.Y.* Washington D.C., 1942.

U.S. Department of Commerce. *U.S. Census of Housing: 1960 Rochester, N.Y.* Washington D.C., 1962.

Wald, Elijah. *Escaping the Delta: Robert Johnson and the Invention of the Blues*, New York: Amistad, 2004.

Wardlow, Gayle Dean. "Son House. Collectors Classics 14: Comments And Additions." *Blues Unlimited* no. 42, (March-April 1966) 7–8.

———. *Chasin'That Devil Music*. Milwaukee: Backbeat Books, 1998.

Waterman, Dick. "Finding Son House: Step By Step, They Followed A Trail That Led To Forgotten Blues Singer." *National Observer* (July 1964) 16.

———. "Son House" *Living Blues* no. 84 (Jan–Feb. 1989) 48–50.

———. *Between Midnight and Day*. Cambridge, Mass.: Da Capo Press, 2003.

West, Bob. "From the Vaults: Bob West Interview with Son House." Blues & Rhythm 207 (March 2006) a reprint of a 1968 interview.

Wilson, Al. "Son House, parts 1–8" *Broadside* 10 (March–July 1965). Reprinted in *Blues Unlimited*, Collectors Classics 14 (Reprints Vol. 3), October 1966.

Wirz, Stefan. Son House Discography. http://www.wirz.de/music/housefrm.htm.

Woodruff, Nan Elizabeth. *American Congo: The African American Freedom Struggle in the Delta*. Cambridge, Mass.: Harvard University Press, 2003.

Work, John W.; Jones, Lewis Wade; Adams, Samuel C. *Lost Delta Found: Rediscovering the Fisk University-Library of Congress Coahoma County Study 1941–1942*, ed. by Robert Gordon and Bruce Nemerov. Nashville: Vanderbilt University Press, 2005.

Wyman, Bill. *Rolling With the Stones*. London: DK Publishing, 2002.

INDEX